a+ CERTIFICATION COURSE

MINDWORKS STUDY MANUAL

VERSION 4.5

MINDWORKS
4141 N. GRANITE REEF ROAD, SUITE 101
SCOTTSDALE, AZ 85251
www.mindwork.com

Publisher: MINDWORKS
Executive Editor: Jim Gardner
Editors: Carol Hartwig
Technical Editor: Michelle Plumb, Dan Waldo
Page Layout/Design: Carol Hartwig
Layout & Graphics: Jim Knott
Cover Design: Tom Hagen, Jim Gardner
Author: Tom Hagen
Supported By: The Entire Staff at Mindworks

THIS BOOK IS DEDICATED TO ALL OF OUR VALUED STUDENTS AND
CUSTOMERS WITHOUT WHOSE SUPPORT THIS BOOK
WOULD NOT BE POSSIBLE.

THANK YOU!

Table of Contents

What is A+ Certification?

A+ Certification is a nationally recognized standard that certifies a benchmark level of competency in the microcomputer industry. This certification will be a valuable addition to your résumé. This certification sets a standard for those working in the personal computer industry as technicians, help desk and support staff.

Many computer resellers and service companies today are required by hardware vendors to have A+ Certified personnel on staff to ensure that these businesses are capable of providing high-quality, authorized service for their clients. Because of this requirement and because of the high standard set for attaining *A+ Certification*, employers often require that their personnel become A+ Certified. *A+ Certification* has become one of the most sought-after certifications in the computer industry.

Who Sponsors A+ Certification?

The *A+ Certification* program was established by the Computing Technology Industry Association (CompTIA, *www.comptia.org*) and is sponsored by many of the largest PC vendors in the industry, including IBM, Hewlett-Packard, and COMPAQ.

What are the Requirements for A+ Certification?

A candidate must pass two tests.

· The first required test is the **Core exam** which covers basic microcomputer hardware, configuration, installation, upgrading, diagnostics and repair.

· The second test (specialty exam) is the **DOS/Windows** exam, which covers DOS, Windows, and Windows 95.

Each test is approximately 70 questions. The pass rate is 66%.

To obtain more detailed information, or to register to take the exams in your area, call *Sylvan Prometric* at (800) 77 MICRO and ask for the A+ Registrar or your can check their website at *www.educate.com*.

A+ Certification Course

Introduction

The *MindWorks A+ Certification* Course is designed to provide an in-depth study of the various areas that are related to servicing microcomputers and peripheral PC devices. Because the expectations and knowledge level of customers are higher than ever before, a good customer service representative must have the skills necessary to meet the challenges of the market place.

This course will prepare you for the *A+ Certification* exam, and will also be a useful resource to anyone wanting to gain more knowledge about PCs and related hardware. The course is not intended to create hardware and software experts. Rather, the *MindWorks A+ Certification* Course will provide you with a solid base understanding of PC hardware, DOS, Windows 95, networking, printers and troubleshooting. Expertise in these areas will come from experience and continued study.

Objectives

When you've completed this course, you will have a thorough understanding of these subject areas:

· Safety when performing maintenance on computer equipment.
· Identification and knowledge of computer hardware.
· Assembly and disassembly of PCs.
· Installation and use of basic DOS commands.
· Configuration and optimization of the DOS environment.
· Configuration of computer equipment.
· Diagnosing and troubleshooting problems with peripherals.
· Installation and optimization of Windows 3.1 & Windows 95.
· Understanding the background and resources of the Internet.
· Proper use and troubleshooting of different printers.
· Familiarity with LANs and their basic components.
· Implementing a preventive maintenance program.
· Knowledge of basic hardware troubleshooting steps and potential causes for common problems, error codes and messages.
· Strategies for great customer service.

Section 1

Computer Safety

Section 1: Computer Safety

Introduction

During this course, you will work hands-on with various microcomputing components. You will disassemble and reassemble a personal computer (PC) and learn how to configure the various components that are integral to the system. It is important that we first discuss some basics for safety when working with personal computers.

There is serious potential for injury or worse if you do not observe basic safety rules when maintaining computer equipment. Components, such as the monitor, may hold electrical charges of up to 30,000 volts, even when turned off or unplugged. This is a very real and serious health hazard.

In this chapter we will discuss ways to identify hazards and how to prevent injuring yourself. We will also look at ways of preventing a less ominous but much more common occurrence: *the damaging of electronic components through very small electrostatic discharges (ESD).*

Objectives

When you've completed this section, you will understand and be able to discuss the following:

· Potential health hazards when working with computer equipment.

· Precautions to take to protect yourself from injury.

· Steps and techniques for preventing ESD damage to computer equipment.

· The proper grounding of computer equipment.

· Electromagnetic Interference (EMI).

Potential Health Hazards

Computers are relatively safe machines to work around. They are powered by electricity which does pose some physical hazards. Any electrical appliance has the potential to cause you harm, and PCs are no different. You should always take certain precautions when working on or around computers. There are two components you need to pay special attention to: the *monitor* and the *power supply*.

- Your ***monitor's screen*** (a.k.a. Cathode Ray Tube or CRT) is a big bulb filled with inert gasses. CRTs act like large capacitors and hold thousands of volts of electricity long after they are unplugged. Wearing a grounding wire around exposed CRTs is an open invitation for those trapped charges to use you as their ticket to freedom. The experience could literally kill you. Under the right circumstances this may hold true even if you are not wearing a ground wire, so be careful.

- The ***power supply*** displays a warning on its case to prevent you from trying to do maintenance on it. Power supplies are outfitted with internal capacitors and may hold large electrical charges even when they are turned off. These capacitors may pose a hazard similar to the CRT.

Aside from these dangers, there are no other major health hazards associated with PCs, unless you drop one on your toes.

Electrical Fires

While somewhat rare, a PC or one of its components could, for various reasons, catch on fire. For your safety, as well as the PC's well-being, it's important to know what type of fire extinguisher would be the best choice for an electrical fire.

Not all fires are the same and if you use the wrong type of fire extinguisher on the wrong type of fuel, you can make matters worse. It is very important to understand the four different classifications of fuel:

Class A Wood, paper, cloth, trash, plastics.
Solid combustible materials that are not metals.

Class B Flammable liquids: gasoline, oil, grease, acetone.
Any non-metal in a liquid state, on fire.

Class C **Electrical: Computers and printers.
As long as it's "plugged in," it would be
considered a Class C fire.**

Class D Metals: potassium, sodium, aluminum, magnesium.
Unless you work in a laboratory or in an industry
that uses these materiels, it is unlikely you'll have
to deal with a Class D fire.

Most fire extinguishers will have a pictograph label telling you which fuels the extinguisher is designed to fight. For example, a simple water extinguisher might have a label indicating that it should only be used on Class A fires.

Electrostatic Discharges (ESD): What Causes Them?

An electrostatic discharge is an energy flow between two objects with different electrostatic potential.

Imagine two containers filled with water to different levels. If you connect the two containers through a small hose at the bottom, water will flow from one to the other until the water level in both containers is the same.

An electrostatic discharge occurs in the same way; higher potential seeks to come into balance with lower potential. If no safe path is provided for this flow to occur, energy is released in the form of a spark (light and heat) as the objects come into close proximity.

Static potential is constantly generated by every move we make. Driving a car, walking across a carpeted room or simply taking off a jacket will increase your static potential.

Preventing ESD

The human body will notice discharges above 2000 volts, but charges as low as 20 volts may damage sensitive electronic equipment. Personal computer are comprised of many components which are ESD sensitive. All Integrated Circuits (ICs or "chips") are very susceptible to damage caused by electrostatic discharge. RAM and CMOS chips are especially vulnerable. Damage could occur even when you don't feel it.

How can you prevent damaging electronic components? You need to constantly remain in electrostatic potential balance with the equipment you are working on. The following recommendations will help you accomplish this:

1. When you are ready to disassemble the computer, turn it off, but leave the power supply cord attached to the AC outlet. The AC outlet provides the most reliable path to ground for any electrostatic potential to discharge.

Helpful Info

NEVER wear a wrist strap when servicing a monitor.

2. Stand on a anti-static mat. Wear an *anti-static wrist strap*. (The typical wrist grounding strap is composed of a strap and a wire that connects to a resistor and a metal clip. The strap uses the clip to attach to a known good ground. One good ground source is to attach this clip to the metal frame of the computer case itself.)

ANTI-STATIC WRIST STRAP

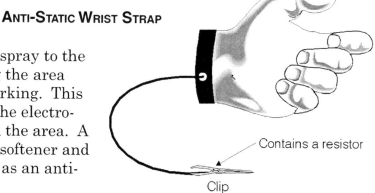

Contains a resistor

Clip

3. Apply anti-static spray to the floor surrounding the area where you are working. This will help reduce the electrostatic potential in the area. A solution of fabric softener and water works well as an anti-static spray.

Now let's say you are properly grounded: the power supply cord is plugged into the AC outlet; you are wearing a wrist-strap adequately secured to the computer case; you are standing on a rubber mat; you even applied some anti-static spray to the floor around you. Can anything go wrong? You bet!!! Depending on how carefully you handle your equipment, a kink or a fray in the grounding cable may prevent it from carrying electrostatic discharges. A periodic resistance check on your grounding wire will assure you it is working properly.

Components of a Good ESD Prevention Program

To prevent ESD damage to components as you work on personal computers, ensure that you always follow these steps:

- Maintain humidity levels between 70 and 90 percent. The greatest risk for static discharge is in low humidity.

- Always wear a wrist-strap before working with ESD-sensitive components.

- Never touch components by their electrical contacts.

- Anytime you are shipping ESD-sensitive components, make sure to enclose them in an anti-static shipping bag. This will prevent them from getting damaged during handling.

- Avoid nonconductors in areas around an open computer.

When is Grounding Necessary?

Grounding is necessary to prevent ESD damage to sensitive electronic equipment. This means that you need to be grounded any time you handle boards, chips or other electronic material. Sources for ground may include the center connector on the AC wall outlet or any known earth ground.

However, there are situations when wearing a anti-static wrist strap is not a good idea, such as if you are working near exposed monitors.

The Electronic Symbol for ground is: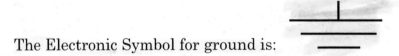

Electromagnetic Interference (EMI)

Electromagnetic interference is another potential problem for computer equipment. A common example of EMI would be running a network communication cable too close to an electric motor or across fluorescent lights in the ceiling. The motor or the lights will cause interference with the electronic signals passing through the network cable. This will cause the PC to malfunction when attempting to communicate with other parts of the network.

Similar problems can occur when a monitor is placed too close to another powerful electrical device. The interference from the device will disrupt the monitor's performance.

The major difference between EMI and an ESD event is that EMI is recoverable. In the above examples, the cables or monitor merely need to be moved away from the interfering device. However, static damage is permanent and sometimes fatal to components.

EMI is recoverable

ESD is not recoverable

Summary

In this section we discussed two key areas of safety. The first and most important is your personal safety when working with personal computers. For the most part, servicing PCs poses little risk of physical danger. The exceptions to this rule are monitors and open power supplies. Servicing these two devices is best left to those individuals with specialized training.

The second area of safety is the protection of sensitive electronic components from damage by electrostatic discharge (ESD). A static charge can affect not only the useful life of a component, but, under the right circumstances, may destroy it. Remember to take precautions to prevent ESD from damaging PC components. Always transport ICs, adapter cards, and components in static-shielding bags.

Review Questions

1. The following symbol represents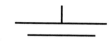

   A. Diode

   ✗ B. Ground

   C. Capacitor

   D. A wrist strap

2. An ESD (static) event is recoverable.

   A. True

   ✗ B. False

3. An EMI event is non-recoverable.

   A. True

   ✗ B. False

4. When servicing a monitor, you should always wear a wrist strap.

   A. True

   ✗ B. False

5. A typical computer monitor can hold a potentially harmful charge, even after being unplugged.

   ✗ A. True

   B. False

6. What class of fire extinguishers would you use for an electrical fire involving computer equipment?

   ✗ A. Class C

   B. Class D

   C. Class A

   D. Class E

Section 2

PC Hardware, Components and Tools

Section 2: PC Hardware, Components & Tools

Introduction

To understand something as complex as a computer, it helps to first understand the various parts that form the whole. In this section we will discuss the various components that make up today's PC.

To successfully repair, assemble or disassemble a computer, a technician must be able to identify the different PC components and understand the relationships between them.

Objectives

When you've completed this section, you will be able to explain and identify the following:

- Basic PC computer terms
- Basic PC tool kit
- Connectors and buses
- Microprocessors (CPUs)
- Memory
- Power supplies
- Disk drives
- Input/output devices
- Portable systems

Repair Tools

There are two types of tools that you need when working with personal computers: hardware tools and software tools.

Hardware Tools

- **Screwdrivers** - Most minor maintenance work will require only a pair of screwdrivers. A size 1 Phillips will fit most screws. A much more involved repair job may require that you have various sizes of both Phillips, straight-slot and Torx screwdrivers. Apple computers and Compaq utilize Torx screws on their machines.

- **Anti-Static Wrist Strap/Grounding Wrist Strap** - This is a very important tool for your tool kit. There are several types. One of them plugs in directly to the ground port of the AC outlet. A different type has an alligator clip that should be attached to any non-painted metal surface on the computer case. There is also another type of grounding wrist-strap that plugs directly to a port on the power supply box.

- **Anti-Static Mat** - Anything that helps you eliminate the possibility of static discharge is a good addition to your tool set. It is important to make sure that any mat you use is full rubber and not a rubberized carpet.

- **Flashlight** - Flashlights are always useful in locations that are poorly lit. Consider also carrying a spare set of batteries.

- **Mirror and Magnifying Glass** - A small mirror (the best type is a dentist mirror) and a magnifying glass makes it much easier to work with hard-to-see components.

- **Extractors** - Extractors are used to remove chips from their sockets. This tool can sometimes be relatively expensive, but not having one could cost you a lot more in the long run. Chips will damage easily if you don't use the proper tools.

- **Tweezers** - A set of tweezers may be used to remove small parts that have fallen in places that your fingers can't reach. Any tool with a magnet is not recommended since you could erase the magnetic data contained in the hard drive or floppy diskette.

- **Compressed Air Cans** -Compressed air cans are very useful for flowing dust or small debris from any surface. They are especially useful on keyboards and power supplies.

Software Tools

- **Diagnostics Disk** - Diagnostics disks are great tools for troubleshooting purposes. Some of the best diagnostics software on the market are *Norton Utilities* or *PC Tools*.

- **Operating System Emergency Diskette** - This diskette comes in handy when the computer locks up and does not allow you access to the data on the hard drive. Additionally, you should create bootable DOS diskettes for every version of DOS you work with. The emergency diskette could include utilities like **FORMAT, FDISK, SYS**, and other key utilities from that particular DOS version.

- **Anti-Virus Software** - Anti-virus software is useful for detecting and cleaning viral infections. Some of the best known programs are *Norton Anti-Virus, McAfee's Anti-Virus and Cheyenne's InocuLAN*. Anti-virus software must be continuously updated to keep up with newly created viruses. It is important to maintain the most current versions of this software.

HARDWARE / TOOLS

Specialty Tools

Most of the tools discussed so far have been fairly straightforward in their usage, however the **multimeter (Volt/OHM Meter)** requires more discussion.

A multimeter is a hand-held instrument that is typically used to measure voltages, both AC (Alternating Current) and DC (Direct Current). It is important to remember, when using the multimeter to measure DC voltages, the proper polarity must be maintained. Usually this means that the black test probe will go to ground and the red test probe to the positive side of the circuit. When using the meter to measure AC voltages, it is not necessary to maintain polarity.

Multimeters usually come in two types: analog (with a needle on a scale) or digital. The digital meters tend to be more precise and require less expertise by the user. Another common use of the multimeter is to measure for resistance or continuity. This is very helpful when checking the value of a resistor or checking for a potential break in a wire or cable.

The following checklist should be helpful when using a multimeter:

· When checking unknown voltages, always start with your meter on the highest setting.

· When checking a resistor, set your meter for the OHMs scale.

· Capacitors are measured in Farads.

· Be careful. Since the multimeter contains a battery, use caution when testing sensitive components. The very current from the meter itself could damage some integrated circuits.

NOTE: THE READINGS ON INDIVIDUAL METERS WILL VARY, HOWEVER, A GOOD FUSE SHOULD READ 0.0 OHMS AND THE BAD FUSE WILL TYPICALLY READ 0.L. GENERALLY, THE 0.L IS DISPLAYED IF THE INPUT SIGNAL STAYS EITHER HIGH OR LOW. (SOME METERS MAY JUST FLASH.)

Basics

A computer is a collection of electronic parts (hardware) that gathers, processes and relays information. Some of the parts can be separated into two categories: **input** and **output** devices.

- **Input devices**, such as the keyboard, mouse, light pen, etc., collect information provided by the user and convert it into electronic signals for further processing.

- **Output devices**, such as the monitor, a speaker, or a printer, convert electronic information into some kind of format that the user understands. Outputs take the form of images on the screen or paper, or sounds.

Inputs are converted into electronic signals which are sent to the CPU or Central Processing Unit (CPU) for processing. The CPU processes **all** communication among the various components of the PC. Once the task is completed, the CPU relays information to the user by means of an output device and waits for more input. This cycle is repeated continuously.

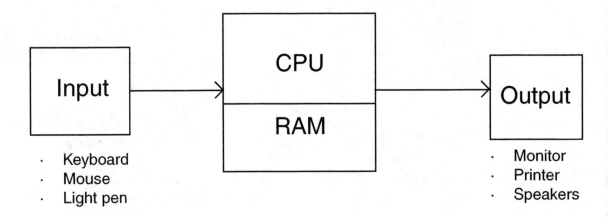

Input	CPU	Output
· Keyboard · Mouse · Light pen	RAM	· Monitor · Printer · Speakers

The CPU and many other electronic components are considered **integrated circuits**. They contain thousands of microscopic digital switches (transistors) which continually produce two voltage states, high and low.

A computer uses a binary system to count. This means that the computer understands only two numbers: one and zero. These 0s and 1s are called bits or binary digits. A grouping of eight bits form a byte. As a general rule, it takes one byte or eight bits to represent a character, symbol or a number.

ASCII Codes

The above method of combining 1s and 0s to form character sets has become the industry standard and is referred to as ASCII (American Standard Code for Information Exchange).

The code original used only seven of the eight bits, which allowed for 128 different combinations of characters. The remaining eighth bit was used for error checking.

Later, the IBM Corporation developed a character code that used all eight bits, which created additional characters (256 total). This was referred to as EBCDIC.

Binary Representation	ASCII Character
01000001	A
11000001	a
10000010	B
11000010	b

HARDWARE / TOOLS

System Board

From the beginning, most PCs have had, as a central component, the **system board.** The system board is also commonly referred to as the **motherboard** or **planar board.**

The system board is a printed circuit board that provides a common platform for attaching the chips and other devices that make the PC functional. The system board also provides output and input connections to the computer.

The key function of the system board is to provide a central "home" for the CPU and the input/output cards. Math functions, sometimes referred to as floating point functions, are built into the CPU. CPUs have had math capabilities built into the chip since the advent of the Intel 486 chip. Prior to the 486, a separate math co-processor chip handled the math functions of the PC.

All of these components are connected to the system board and rely on their connection here to communicate with each other. Communication takes place on the system board through its Bus connectors.

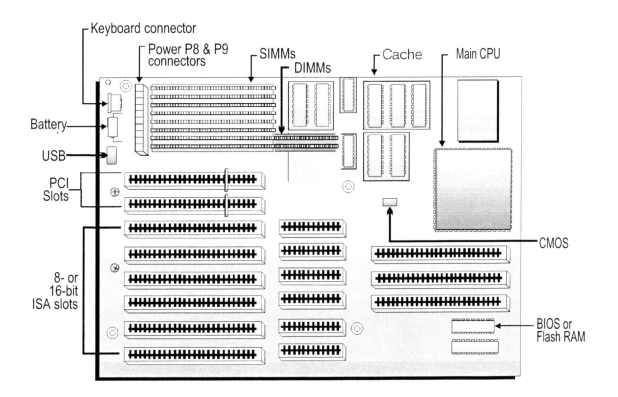

TYPICAL SYSTEM BOARD

Bus Design

Before we discuss the different types of Bus designs, it is first necessary to understand the meaning of a "Bus."

The CPU (Central Processing Unit) is the heart and soul of the computer, and as such, needs the ability to talk to the other components of the computer system. These other components are devices like the keyboard, expansion boards and memory modules. All of these pieces need to be connected to the CPU. This connection is accomplished through what is referred to as **Bus connectors**, or adapter slots.

The adapter slots are wired to the CPU via a series of small traces (those shiny thin metal strips that are on the system board). These adapter slots allow for an access point to the system. Following is a list and description of the most popular type of Bus designs:

- **PC or XT Bus** - IBM developed the XT Bus around the 8088 processor. The 8088 processor had an 8-bit data path, so it comes as no surprise that the adapter slots were called 8-bit slots. Actually, there were 62 separate lines feeding into the connectors, but only eight of these were used for the actual data transfer.

- **AT (ISA) Bus** - When development on the AT computer started, IBM decided to create a new Bus architecture to exploit the new 80286 processor which supported a 16-bit data path, twice that of the XT system. AT system boards also contained at least two of the older 8-bit slots to ensure backwards compatibility.

  While the ISA design gave the computer a wider highway to move data, the speed at which the data could move was still the same as before: 8MHz. The implication here was that even if the CPU could perform internal instructions at 25MHz, the data could only move across the Bus at the 8MHz speed. Attempts to boost the speed limit beyond 8MHz on the AT-type Bus created noise and tended to be unworkable. This was a drawback on the ISA Bus that would be addressed in future Bus designs.

The MCA Bus Architecture - Early in 1987, IBM announced its PS/2 line of computers. To facilitate a faster data transfer rate and to clean up the noise levels that plagued the ISA Bus at higher speeds, IBM developed a new Bus design. The new architecture was call MCA (Micro Channel Architecture). The design was completely new and did not offer any backwards compatibility with older designs like the XT or ISA expansion boards. IBM introduced the MCA architecture in both 16-bit and 32-bit versions.

The MCA design also included a new feature: POS (Programmable Option Select). This feature allowed expansion boards to be smarter and more interactive in attaching to and communicating with the rest of the computer. This feature also simplified the configuration of the boards and lessened the dependencies on switches and jumper settings.

EISA Bus - The industry response to IBM's very proprietary MCA design was the EISA Bus (Extended Industry Standard Architecture). The industry in this case was actually a group of companies known as the "Gang of Nine." Included in the group were Compaq, Tandy, AST, Zenith, AT&T, Olivetti and a few others. This joint effort took the best features of the MCA design without giving up the backwards compatibility with the older AT (ISA) Bus.

The EISA architecture features a full 32-bit data path and supported speeds up to about 20MHz. EISA also incorporated the POS type features found in the MCA system. While the EISA and MCA Bus designs increased Bus speeds, they still could not match the speed of the CPUs.

HARDWARE / TOOLS

VESA Local Bus - In 1992, the VESA Local Bus was introduced. This design is sometimes referred to as VL Bus. The designers of the VL Bus created a special type of high speed slot on the system board which could operate at speeds equal to the speed of the CPU. As would be expected, this slot only accommodates cards designed specially for it. These special slots are called "Local" Bus slots. Local Bus slots currently support disk controllers, video and memory boards.

Note: Beware! There are no standards for this design. Compatibility is a problem.

PCI Local Bus (Intel) - The VESA Bus technology was an important step forward, but did not fully exploit the advantages of the newer CPUs. The VESA solution was essentially a beefed-up version of the old ISA technology. It did not allow for Bus mastering or software setup of boards like the MCA and EISA designs did.

The Intel Corporation was keenly aware of these shortcomings and developed an even faster and more flexible Bus slot called the PCI Bus. The PCI design used a 64-bit Bus that was more in line with the new Pentium processors. PCI still supported a 32-bit data path, making it a viable solution for high-end 486 systems.

Peripheral Component Interconnect

The PCI Bus supports speeds up to 133MHz and also provides backward compatibility with ISA and EISA slots all on the same board. Like MCA and EISA, the PCI design supports Bus mastering and software configurable boards. The PCI architecture also conforms to the new "Plug-and-Play" standards defined by hardware vendors.

PCMCIA - The PCMCIA (Personal Computer Memory Card Industry Association) released in 1990 was designed to meet the special needs of laptop computers. The standard itself came from a group of Japanese vendors of memory-related products. While originally intended for memory products, the standard was also extended to support modems and hard disks. Because the design constraints are different for memory cards than they are for modems or hard disks, there are many different types of PCMCIA cards. There are three types of PCMCIA cards, each a different thickness:

> **Type 1** - 3.3 millimeters
>
> **Type 2** - 5.0 millimeters
>
> **Type 3** - 10.5 millimeters

The current PCMCIA cards support a 16-bit data path, although a 32-bit version is in the making. The speed of the Bus is limited to a 33MHz clock rate.

HARDWARE / TOOLS

· **Universal Serial Bus (USB)** - This is a new connection interface for all types of peripheral devices. USB replaces all the different kinds of serial and parallel connectors with one standard plug and port combination. The USB was developed by Intel for communication between a PC and external peripherals over an inexpensive cable using biserial transmission. The USB transfers data at 12MBps *bits* and supports up to 127 devices with both isochronous and asynchronous data transfers.

Because of its relatively low speed, USB is intended to replace existing serial ports, parallel ports, keyboard and monitor connectors and be used with keyboards, mice, monitors, printers, and possibly some low-speed scanners and removable hard drives. For faster devices, existing IDE or SCSI interfaces can be used. Another nice feature of USB is "hot swapping" which allows you to attach a device and have the PC detect it without restarting your machine.

IEEE (1394)

Fire Wire — digital video —
— speed 12.5, 25, 50 mbps fast transfer of data

Central Processing Unit (CPU)

The Central Processing Unit, which is often referred to as "the processor," is the heart and soul of the computer. Without this chip, no other function of the PC is possible. It is the CPU that understands commands, executes program instructions and does all the basic processing in the computer. The capabilities of the CPU will basically define the design of the computer.

The lead manufacturer and designer of processors for the personal computer is the Intel Corporation. Most of the material presented in this course is based on the Intel chip design. Other companies that manufacture processors are AMD, IBM and Cyrix.

The PCs of today are built around the family of Intel processors, starting with the 8088. Every couple of years, a new chip is released. The 8088 was succeeded by the 8086, which was followed by the 80286 and then the 80386 chip. The new major leap came with the 486. Today, the Pentium MMX processor is the latest of the Intel line of chips. Each of these chips is more powerful than its predecessor, capable of performing more commands and dealing with data more quickly. Emphasis is also placed on backward compatibility. It is important that each chip has the ability to run software that was originally designed for the previous generation(s) of chips. There is some question as to whether this trend will continue in future design generations.

The CPU on the newer style system boards will usually be mounted into a ZIF (zero insertion force required) socket. This type of socket makes removal and replacement of chips much easier than the older soldered types of mounting.

HARDWARE / TOOLS

CPU Performance Factors

Clock Speed

Computers, like musicians, run or play to a beat. In music, the drummer must synchronize with the rest of the band in order for the music to sound right. In the computer world, the beat is controlled by a CPU clock. If the clock rate is too fast, malfunctions will occur. This would not result in actual damage to the chip. It would mean, however, that the PC would not function correctly.

The computer's speed or clock rate is integral to its overall design. The computer's clock rate is the frequency at which it can execute a set of instructions. Computer clock rates are measured in Megahertz (millions of clock ticks per second).

There are two types of speeds that should be considered when evaluating system performance:

- **internal clock speed** - The internal clock speed is the speed at which the processor can obtain information within the CPU itself. An example of internal clock speed would be the speed at which the chip communicates with its internal cache of memory or its registers.

- **external clock speed**. The external clock speed is the speed at which the CPU communicates with components outside itself, like the external memory (system RAM or external cache memory).

HARDWARE / TOOLS

Cache Memory

Internal to the design of some processors is something referred to as "cache memory." This is a very high speed memory that is actually built right into the chip itself. It supplies the processor with the instructions and data which can be accessed faster than instructions and data located in main memory. The more data the processor can access directly from cache memory, the faster the computer runs.

There are two levels of cache memory:

more cache is better

- **Internal Cache** (Primary or level 1 cache)
  Located inside the CPU chip. The function of the internal cache is to hold a copy of frequently used instructions that enhance CPU performance.

- **External Cache** -(Secondary or level 2 cache)
  Located on the system board.

CPU performance is certainly instrumental in determining overall computer performance. It should be noted that other factors, such as speed, amount of system RAM, and types of Bus architecture, also influence the ultimate computer performance as well.

Intel Processors: Now and Then

There might come a time when you will have to replace or up-grade a processor in order to fix a problem. Listed below are details and characteristics of some of the most popular chips from Intel and other manufacturers.

8088

This is the chip found in most of the IBM XT-class machines. The 8088 came in a 40-pin DIP package. Translated, this means the 8088 is a small, rectangular chip with two rows of 20 pins each. The original speed of this chip was 5MHz. Later versions reached a top speed of about 8MHz.

80286

Introduced in 1981 by Intel, this chip became the mainstay of the AT-class computers. The chip itself was packaged in a square called a Pin Grid Array (PGA) instead of a rectangle. The chip contained about 130,000 transistors -- about 100,000 more than the 8088.

80386

The 80386 was introduced to the market in 1985 and came in two different types: DX and SX. This chip was also packaged in the PGA configuration. The 80386 contained 250,000 transistors and also provided features like multitasking of DOS programs and a 32-bit data path. The 32-bit data path was available only in the DX version, while the SX version had a 16-bit data path. This made the SX more compatible with the 80286 computer and hardware.

HARDWARE / TOOLS

80486

The 80486 chip was actually a "beefed-up" version of the 80386. The 486 processor was a composite of three other chips. The 80486 consisted of a 386 chip, a 385 cache controller and a 387 math co-processor. The 486 contained about 1.25 million transistors and 8k of internal cache memory. It provided a 32-bit data path and a built-in math co-processor. Like the 80386, the 80486 came in two types: the DX and SX. The 80486 SX had all the features of the DX version minus the math co-processor. Actually, the math co-processor was still on-board but disabled in the SX version.

80486DX2

To understand the 80486DX2, it is important to understand another Intel creation designed to increase system speed: the "Overdrive" chip. The Overdrive chip could run at two clock speeds simultaneously. If the chip was placed on a 486SX/25MHz system board, it was placed in the socket for the co-processor chip and took over for the 486SX chip.

When data was passed through the Bus or memory, it was done at the speed of the processor; in this case 25MHz. This is referred to as the external clock speed. All the internal calculations were done at twice the 25MHz speed, at 50MHz. The 80486DX2 is very similar to the Overdrive chip in that it runs at a certain external speed "X MHz" but performs all internal calculations at "two times X."

80486DX4

The plot thickens. DX4 chips used a technology developed by IBM called Clock Tripler (nicknamed "Blue Lightning"). Under an agreement with Intel, IBM manufactured 486 chips using the Intel mask. Using their own Clock Tripler technology, IBM took an Intel 486DX 25MHz chip and increased its speed to approximately 75MHz.

Intel followed suit and announced the 80486DX/99MHz chip. This chip would run external speeds of 33MHz and perform internal calculations at 99MHz.

Pentium

In 1993 Intel introduced the Pentium processor. The initial market response was not overwhelming, but the Pentium has now become the standard for personal computers sold today. The Pentium processor contains over 3 million transistor and provides a 64-bit data path. Pentium speeds range from 60MHz to about 450MHz at the time of this writing.

The first generation of Pentium chips were subject to heat problems. Computers not designed to deal with high temperatures tended to experience high failure rates. Newer versions of the Pentium chip were designed to run cooler. System boards and internal components were also designed to cope with the higher temperatures.

The Pentium chips will run both internal calculations and external processing at the same speed. Another unique feature of the Pentium chip is the cache. The Pentium has two 8KB caches: one that is used for program code and another used for data cache. The Pentium chip was also designed to be fault tolerant, something Intel refers to as "superscalar." This feature is only functional when the Pentium chip is installed on a system board that will support multiple processors. Fault tolerance simply means that when two processors are present on the system board, the second chip takes over if the first chip fails.

MMX Technology

The MMX technology is based on a new set of instructions that are built into Intel's Pentium microprocessors. This new instruction set enables the chip to efficiently process video and audio data. Prior to the MMX technology, multimedia operations, in video and sound, had to be handled by separate components like sound cards and enhanced video boards. These same functions can now be managed by the processor.

MMX chips' internal memory (cache memory) has doubled in size (32KB). This is the area in memory that holds recently accessed data. It is designed to speed up subsequent requests to this data. This means that more instructions and data can be stored internally in the chip, reducing the number of times the processor has to access slower external memory. Most multimedia applications run dramatically faster and smoother. To really get the most out of the new MMX chip, you must run the enhanced MMX applications that have been written to exploit the true power of the technology. As of this writing, these applications are still somewhat rare.

Pentium II

The Pentium II processor is available in speeds from 233MHz to 450MHz. It utilizes the innovative 0.25 micron manufacturing process that enables these CPUs to include over 7.5 million transistors. This results in more power in less space. The processor core is packaged in the Single Edge Contact (SEC) cartridge enabling ease of design and flexible motherboard architecture. The processor also includes MMX technology. The Dual Independent Bus (DIB) architecture increases bandwidth and performance over single-bus processors.

came before Pent. III

Pentium III

The new Intel Pentium III processor is groundbreaking in terms of graphics capabilities. The chip has been built to exploit many of the new and expanding 3-D graphic images and their manipulation. The following are some of the highlights of the Pentium III.

· Added 70 new instruction sets for enhanced graphics, video and sound.

· An embedded serial number...to help companies with an inventory of computers. This feature will also enhance on-line security transactions. Although it also raises some very serious privacy concerns.

· A clock speed of 500 Mhz with a 550 already set for release in the near future.

Pentium Pro

The Pentium Pro processor has a different look and design than the other chips. It is the first Intel processor to combine Level 1(L1) and Level 2 (L2) cache in the same package as the CPU. The Pentium Pro processor is a dual-chip configuration that houses the Pentium Pro CPU on one side of the dual-cavity package and the L2 cache memory on the other. According to Intel, this simplifies system design and saves space. The Pentium Pro processor has about 21 million transistors in total. The CPU core has 5.5 million transistors and the L2 cache has 15.5 million. The Pentium Pro was designed to support multiple Pentium Pro processors connected in parallel. The Pentium Pro is a true 32-bit processor. It operates at speeds of 200MHz.

Motorola Chip Family

The Motorola chip set is not quite as well known in the PC market as Intel. For the most part, it is associated with the Apple computer line.

68000

Introduced in 1979, the 68000 chip is closely associated with the Apple computer. The 68000 chip employed a 32-bit design and used a 16-bit data Bus. The 68000 was far ahead of Intel's efforts at the time.

68010

In 1982, Motorola introduced the 68010 chip. The major difference between the 68000 and the 68010 was the addition of virtual memory support. This chip also incorporated internal cache which made the processing of sub-routines much faster. This chip did not find widespread use in the computer world but was used extensively in Motorola's component division.

68020

This chip was introduced in 1984 as the first full 32-bit chip in the Motorola line. The 68020 had the ability to access 4 GB of RAM and utilized floating point processing capabilities. It was used in the Macintosh II and found widespread use in mini-computers as well.

68030

Introduced to the market in 1987, the 68030 had all the features of the 68020 plus demand page memory management. Other enhancements to the chip also increased the speed of the chip. It was used most widely used in the Macintosh II series of computers.

68040

In 1989, Motorola's answer to Intel's 486 was the 68040. However, the 68040 did not gain the market share that Intel's 486 enjoyed.

Power PC

Apple, IBM and Motorola all joined together to develop the PowerPC family of chips. *PowerPC* stands for Performa2 Optimization with Enhanced RISC. Currently Apple incorporates the chip in its PowerMac series of computers. This chip can also be used in everything from laptops to computers functioning as servers. IBM also plans on using it in its RS6000 line of computers.

HARDWARE / TOOLS

Processor Sockets and Slots

Motherboard sockets were originally designed to provide a place to insert the processor into the motherboard. Recently, Intel has defined standardized socket and slot specifications for use with various Intel processors. Intel is the primary manufacturer of PC processors, however, two of Intel's main competitors (AMD and Cyrix) have been able to use these same standards.

These standardized sockets allow motherboards to accommodate future processors that are designed to fit these sockets.

PROCESSOR SOCKETS AND SLOTS				
Designation	Number of Pins	Pin Rows	Voltage	Motherboard Class
Socket 1	169	3	5 volts	486
Socket 2	238	4	5 volts	486 & Pentium Overdrive
Socket 3	237	4	5 volts/3.3 volts	486 & Pentium Overdrive
Socket 4	273	4	5 volts	Pentium 60-66, Pentium Overdrive
Socket 5	320	5 (staggered)	3.3 volts	Pentium
Socket 6	235	4	3.3 volts	486
Socket 7	321	5 (staggered)	2.4-3.3 volts	Pentium
Socket 8	387	5 (dual pattern)	3.1-3.3 volts	Pentium Pro
Slot 1	242	2	2.8-3.3	Pentium Pro/Pentium II

System Memory

RAM (Random Access Memory)

The most common type of memory installed in a computer is called RAM (Random Access Memory). This type of memory is also considered volatile. Volatile simply means it is not permanent and can be changed. This is an important characteristic of RAM. Anything that is written to RAM will be lost if the machine loses power or if the machine is turned off.

RAM can be broken down into two types: DRAM (Dynamic Random Access Memory) and Static RAM. DRAM memory chips need to have an electrical current supplied to maintain their electrical state. Static RAM chips do not need an electrical current for refresh purposes. Static RAM is much more expensive than DRAM.

Another key point to remember about RAM is that data stored in RAM in accessed much more quickly than data retrieved from a hard disk. Theoretically, data retrieved from RAM is accessed 100 to 300 times faster than the same information from a hard disk, optical drive, or floppy drive.

RAM is physically installed by adding chips to the motherboard. The most common configurations of these chips today is called:

- **SIMM (Single Inline Memory Modules)**. One of these modules actually contains either eight or nine separate RAM chips. The ninth chip is actually called the parity chip or parity bit. For each byte stored, the system adds the bits together. The parity bit determines whether the result is odd or even and is used for error checking. SIMM memory is configured with 30 and 72 pins.

- **DIMM (Dual Inline Memory Module)** Typically DIMM is configured with 168 pins.

HARDWARE / TOOLS

Besides SIMMs, other types of RAM are detailed below:

MEMORY	DESCRIPTION
EDO RAM (Extended Data Output RAM)	A faster type of pin-compatible RAM. If system can accommodate this type of RAM,speed can be increased up to 25% without the need for static cache.
VRAM (Video RAM)	Special type of memory found on faster video boards.
WRAM (Windows RAM)	Windows RAM allows blocks of memory (in "windows") to be addressed in just a few commands. More expensive, but a good value in video boards.
DIMM (Dual In-Line Memory Module)	Small circuit boards carrying memory integrated circuits, with signal and power pins on both sides of the board. In SIMMS memory, the pins are on both sides of the chips but are connected to the same memory chip. On DIMM, the connections on each side of the module connect to different chips

Specialized Memory

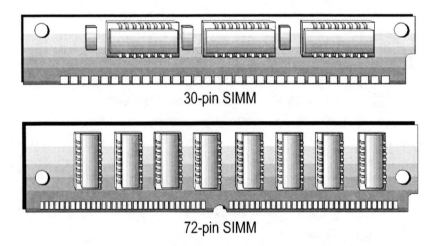

30-pin SIMM

72-pin SIMM

SINGLE INLINE MEMORY MODULES (SIMM)

Power Supplies

In this section, we'll take a look at computer power supplies. The computer needs electrical power to operate. It is plugged into a wall outlet which is a 110 volt socket and uses AC (Alternating Current). Computers utilize 5 and 12 volt DC currents. Therefore, a device is required to convert the AC current from the wall outlet to the DC current required by the computer. This is the function of the computer power supply.

Computer power supplies come in all different sizes and shapes and are rated in different ways. The most common rating is in watts. A watt is a unit of measure for electrically powered devices and is determined by the amount of electricity that is passed through it. Because computer components are becoming increasingly more efficient and require less power, a 200-watt power supply is typically large enough for most systems.

The power supply itself is typically located in the rear corner inside the computer case. It will usually have several colored wires extending from it. These colored wires are called power connectors and are used to connect peripheral devices such as floppies, hard drives and tape backups. Another component of the power supply is the fan. The job of the fan is to maintain an internal temperature acceptable to the design of the particular power supply circuitry.

HARDWARE / TOOLS

On a more technical note, the power supply takes the AC current from the wall and converts this to a DC or direct current. This DC output is split into four different voltages: +5 volts, -5 volts, +12 volts and -12 volts. **A positive 5 volts is the voltage used by PC board digital circuitry.** The power supply not only converts the AC voltage into these DC voltages, but also performs somewhat of a filtering function, ensuring that the flow of electricity into the computer circuitry takes place evenly.

Because PC power supplies are fairly complex and because of the different voltages, attempting to repair them is not recommended. The power supply is generally considered an FRU, a Field Replaceable Unit, and such replacement is the best option.

There are several important factors in choosing a power supply replacement. You must determine what voltage, ampere rating and wattage you need. You should also take into consideration the size and shape of the power supply as well as on/off switch placement. This will ensure that the new power supply will fit in the computer case.

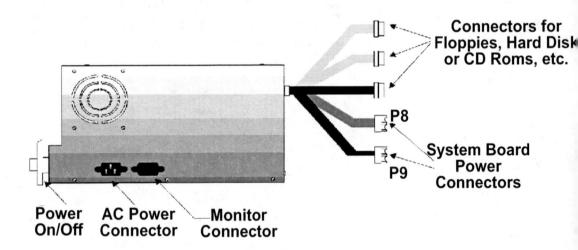

POWER SUPPLY CONFIGURATION

Hard Disk Drive

The hard disk, or hard drive, stores large amounts of information for long term usage. The Random Access Memory (RAM) discussed in the last section is good for intermediate, temporary high speed storage. But RAM loses its information when you turn the machine off and provides a limited amount of storage space.

The advantage of the hard disk drive is that it stores information magnetically on a metallic platter. As a result, information is retained even after the machine is turned off or loses power.

Hard disks are capable of storing large amounts of information, often hundreds of megabytes. In most cases, a typical user will keep all the programs and all the data they need on the hard disk. The major components of the hard drive are

- The platter
- Read/write heads
- Head actuator
- Spindle

The **platter** is an aluminum disk that has been coated so it can accept magnetically recorded data. Multiple platters are then connected to a **spindle** which, in turn, is connected to an electrical motor that spins the platters. The rotation of the platters is somewhat like a record spinning on a turntable. Most modern hard disks are capable of 3,600-5,000 rotations per minute.

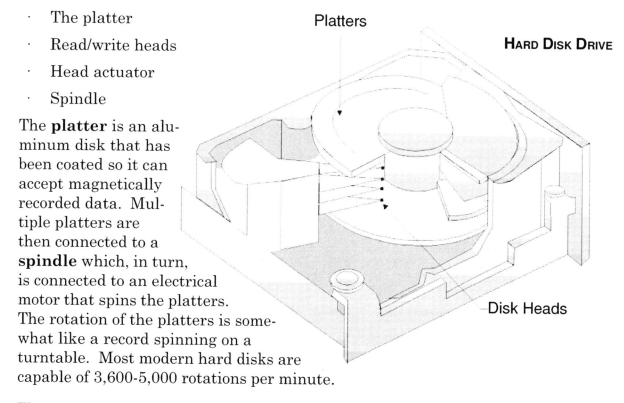

Platters

HARD DISK DRIVE

Disk Heads

The mechanisms that allow data to be written to or read from the platters are called the **read/write heads**. The read/write heads have the ability to access both sides of the platter and to retrieve or write information to either side of the platter. The mechanism that allows the read/write heads to move back and forth across the platters is the **head actuator**.

HARDWARE / TOOLS

Hard Disk Layout

The information on the hard disk platter is recorded in a circular fashion in **tracks**. (The tracks are like tracks on a record.) Tracks are then subdivided into pie-like slices that are referred to as **sectors**. A **cylinder** is a vertical stack of these sectors. Finally, the minimum unit that DOS uses to store information is called a **cluster**. Clusters are formed from several sectors on the same track.

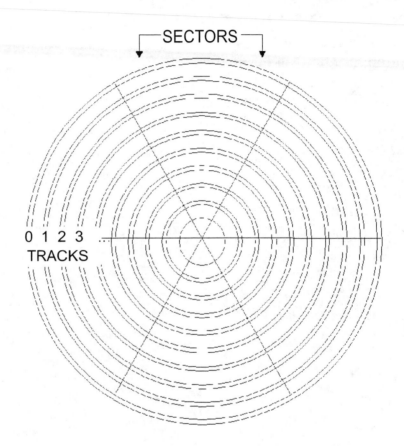

LAYOUT OF A HARD DRIVE

File Allocation Table

The File Allocation Table (FAT), is usually created at sector zero for DOS-based systems. The information recorded in the FAT keeps track of the location of each file on the hard disk. The File Allocation Table is automatically created when the hard disk is high-level formatted.

Encoding

There are many different methods that may be used to store data magnetically on the drives. These methods are called encoding techniques. The different encoding schemes determine how much data can be placed on a disk or how fast that data can be accessed. There are three major types of encoding schemes used for hard disks: MFM (Modified Frequency Modulation), RLL (Run Length Limited), and ARLL (Advanced RLL). A common characteristic to each of these encoding schemes is that they use **state changes** on the magnetic surface of the platter to indicate a binary 1, or binary 0.

HARDWARE / TOOLS

Hard Drive Interfaces

The hard disk in and of itself cannot directly communicate with the CPU. For the hard disk to communicate with the computer, it depends on two more components: the **controller**, which links the drive to the computer and **Host Bus Adapter**, which converts the signals used by the hard drive to those used and understood by the computer.

Originally in older systems, all three of these were separate devices. As computers and computer components evolved, the controller and the Host Bus Adapter were combined on the same physical board. In some cases, this single board was actually built into the same housing as the hard disk itself. The hard disk interfaces determine how all of the individual devices work together.

There are four major interfaces: the ST-506, ESDI (Enhanced Standard Device Interface), IDE (Integrated Drive Electronics), and SCSI (Small Computer System Interface).

Seagate Technology

ST-506

The ST-506 was the original IBM PC interface. Two cables were used to connect the drive to a separate controller: a 20-pin data cable and a 34-pin control cable. The data was transferred on the cable via a serial format one bit at a time. This interface supported the following three encoding methods: MFM, RLL and ARLL.

ESDI

The ESDI interface was actually a hybrid ST-506 but was more efficient in translating and transferring the data. The ESDI interface used the RLL encoding scheme. The ESDI interface also supported much larger drive capacities than that of the old ST-506 interface. Many of these drives were capable of storing more than one Gigabit of data. The interface used the same type of 20-pin data cable and the 34-pin control cable as the ST-506.

IDE

The IDE (also referred to as the AT attachment) was the first interface to actually embed the controller within the housing of the hard drive itself. Because of the integration of the hard drive and controller in one unit, the cost of the drives also came down. This, along with its improved performance, has made the IDE drive a very popular selection for most personal computers sold today. Unlike the ST-506 interface and the ESDI interface, the IDE interface only requires a single 40-pin control and data cable which connects the hard drive to the actual system board.

When installing an IDE drive into a PC, the CMOS setting is usually set for type 47 or user-defined. The drive type setting is critical for proper functioning of the IDE drives. Some of the older BIOS versions may not work. If the PC has one of these older versions of the BIOS, it must be replaced with a compatible or new version. DOS relies on BIOS to issue commands to the hardware. BIOS is not loaded from the operating system. It is stored in ROM.

Older PCs (manufactured before 1982) must have upgraded BIOS software to support an EGA board, a hard disk, a LAN card or any other expansion board that contains ROM. An upgraded BIOS disk is available from the memory manufacturer. To upgrade BIOSs, remove the current BIOS from your motherboard and replace it with the new one. Two BIOS chips are usually needed for 80286 to 80486 systems. Only one BIOS chip is needed for XT clones.

HARDWARE / TOOLS

You may also need to upgrade BIOS on other machines if you've added a drive or peripheral that is not supported by the current BIOS. For example, if you added a 2.88MB floppy drive to replace a 1.44MB floppy drive, the BIOS will need to be upgraded to support the new drive.

Most Pentiums and some laptops store BIOS on a memory chip called a **flash RAM**. To upgrade flash RAM BIOS, just run a BIOS upgrade program (provided by the laptop manufacturer). Newer plug-and-play computers all have flash RAM BIOS.

An EIDE host adapter is usually a combination of an EIDE host adapter channel, which can support two drives, and an older IDE host adapter channel, which can support two additional drives. The IDE interface supports two drives physically attached to the same cable, but one drive must be configured as the master and the other as a slave. This is done by setting the **master-slave** jumper on the second hard drive to slave. The master drive then performs the single decoding for both drives. A failure to the master drive renders the slave useless or inaccessible as well.

SCSI

As the PC world started to blossom, there were an ever-growing number of peripheral devices that could be connected to a computer, and an ever-growing number of vendors who were trying to interface these devices to the individual PCs. This created somewhat of a problem in that there were no standards to specify how the interface was to take place.

One way to solve this problem would be to agree on a kind of computer Bus that would be used by all types of small computers. This Bus would need to provide an interface for a hard disk, but would also need to support other peripherals like CD-ROMs, WORM (Write Once, Read Many Times), optical disks, and other types of removable disk storage devices and optical scanners.

The standard that evolved from this mandate was called the **SCSI** interface (pronounced "scuzzy" from Small Computer Systems Interface). The SCSI is a system interface that is actually a complete expansion Bus. It allows up to seven intelligent devices to connect to it in a parallel format.

The length of a SCSI cable is critical for proper operation. A SCSI cable should not exceed 6 meters or approximately 20 feet. As you approach the length limit, errors will increase.

Every SCSI device that connects to the cable must have a unique address. This is what makes it possible for multiple SCSI devices to work together. There are several types of SCSI devices:

Regular	8-bit parallel interface between a SCSI device and SCSI controller. Transfer rate is 5MBps
Fast	8-bit interface that transfers data at twice the rate of the regular SCSI interface. Transfer rate is 10MBps.
Wide	8-bit interface that uses extra cable increasing the data path to 16 or 32 bits.
Ultra-Wide	Uses a wider cable for a greater transfer rate, up to 40MBps.

[handwritten margin note: Zip / CD-ROM / Tape Backup / Scanner]

[vertical text in right margin: HARDWARE / TOOLS]

Host Adapter = ID#7

When configuring SCSI devices, remember that SCSI drives have address jumpers. Drive C: must be set to be SCSI ID 0 on most PCs. Set a second SCSI drive to ID 1. A third or fourth SCSI device can be set to any of the remaining address (2-7), but DOS will not recognize those drives without a special device driver. The host adapter or SCSI controller is always set for address seven, which has the highest priority. The rest of the devices can use addresses zero through six. The hard disk that will be the bootable device should be addressed as zero. All of the SCSI devices are daisy-chained together using a straight ribbon cable with a 50-pin connector. Macintosh systems are the exception to this rule. They may use a 50- or 25-pin D-Shell connector.

Another important configuration issue when using SCSI devices is termination. The host adapter or controller, as well as the last SCSI device in the chain, must be terminated. For both hard disk and host adapters, this termination is accomplished through a device called a *resistor pack*. Usually hard drives are shipped with this resistor pack already installed. But the resistor pack can be removed if termination is not necessary or required. In the case of an external SCSI device, switches, or perhaps a dummy SCSI connector, provide the necessary termination. It is imperative for SCSI configuration that there would never be more than two terminators in a SCSI chain.

The SCSI interface provides the fastest transfer rate of all hard drives, ranging anywhere from 5MBps to over 100MBps allowing up to seven intelligent devices to connect to it in a parallel format.

Hard Disk Characteristics

Capacity

The basic unit of storage on the hard drive is a sector. Each sector holds 512 bytes of data. By multiplying the number of tracks the drive contains by the amount of data each track can hold, you will have the approximate capacity of the hard disk.

The amount of data capacity is not the only factor to consider when evaluating a hard disk. Performance is also a very important issue. A hard disk may be able to store vast amounts of information, but if you are unable to access the data efficiently, the increased amount of data will cause performance to suffer.

Access Time

An important performance criteria for hard drives is the Drive Access Time. This access time is the actual time it takes to find data on the hard disk. Access time is usually measured in milliseconds -- the lower the better. Hard drives manufactured just a few years ago were considered fast at access times around 85 milliseconds. A typical hard drive manufactured today will have an access time of less than 10 milliseconds.

Data Transfer Rate

Another performance benchmark is the Data Transfer Rate. Access speed measures how fast data can be located on the disk. The data transfer rate measures how fast that data can then move between the hard disk and the CPU itself. The data transfer rate of a hard disk is usually expressed in megahertz or megabytes per second.

HARDWARE / TOOLS

Sector Interleaves

The hard drives of modern PCs no longer use sector interleaves, although they're still used by CD-ROMs. There was a time when the speed of the microprocessor was actually slower than the speed of the hard disk. This meant that the data transfer speed of the drive needed to be slowed to match the data handling ability of the CPU. Sector interleaves allowed the CPU to process data in pieces, allowing the CPU to finish with a piece of data before reading further. This was accomplished by forcing the disk drive to skip a given number of sectors. The time lapse created by skipping sectors would give the CPU a chance to catch up with the disk. Interleaves were measured in terms of ratios. For example, a one-to-one ratio meant that no sectors were skipped. A one-to-four ratio meant that four sectors were skipped before any more data was read from the drive.

Caching

Hard drive performance will always be limited by the sheer mechanical operation of the disk itself. There will always be limits to how fast a hard drive can spin due to centrifugal force. One method used to overcome this limitation of mechanical hard drives is something called *caching*. A cache is an area of Random Access Memory (RAM) where the most frequently used files are stored. Access to the data and files located in cache is theoretically one hundred times faster than access to that same information on the hard disk.

Preparing the Hard Disk

The three basic steps to prepare a hard disk to accept data are:

- Low-level formatting
- Partitioning
- High-level formatting

Low-Level Formatting

A hard drive is a lot like a new file cabinet. When you first buy it, it is essentially empty. Just like an empty file cabinet, the hard drive must be organized. Organization, as it pertains to the hard drive, is the process of defining the hard drive's tracks and sectors. This process of creating tracks and sectors on the new hard disk is called low-level formatting.

The process of low-level formatting will also detect areas on the hard disk that may be defective and prevents data from being stored there. Low-level formatting software comes in a variety of flavors. Some low-level software routines are included with the purchase of a new hard disk. Some computer systems also include in their CMOS and BIOS settings a low-level software routine. For the most part, this low-level software formatting routine is for older models of hard disks. Most newer drives, especially IDE drives, rarely use low-level software formatting.

Partitioning

Partitioning is the first step in configuring the hard drive on your system. In order to accommodate multiple operating systems on a hard disk, DOS allows you to create multiple partitions with a program called **FDISK** found in the DOS directory. Another reason to create partitions on a hard disk is that, prior to DOS Version 4.0, DOS only recognized a 32MB partition or smaller. The newer versions of DOS allow for partitions as large as 512 megabytes.

up to 4 primary

or

3 primary + 1 extended partition

HARDWARE / TOOLS

MBR *master boot record*

When creating multiple partitions on a hard disk, one partition will be set aside to contain the information necessary to "boot" or start-up the system. The partition that contains the boot information is called the bootable partition. The DOS **FDISK** program is the software that tells the computer which partition will be bootable. The **FDISK** program will ask which partition to make active. The primary or bootable DOS partition should be partition number one. After selection number one from the **FDISK** menu, you can escape once to get back to the main menu and then exit the **FDISK** program. The computer will now reboot to the partition set as active.

When you partition your hard drives it is important to understand that each logical disk in the system will be identified with a different letter of the alphabet. A and B are reserved for the system's floppy drives. The C drive is designated for the first primary partition, and the D drive is reserved for the first extended partition etc. If a disk is present in either the A or B drives when you start up the system, it will check there first for the information necessary to boot up your system. If the disk present is not a system disk, you will get a "non-system disk" error. Simply remove the disk and continue with the boot process. Your system will automatically search the C drive for boot up information if the A and B drives are empty.

High-Level Formatting

Finally, the last step for DOS-based systems is to run the DOS **FORMAT** program. The **FORMAT** command creates a DOS boot record, a file allocation table (sometimes called FAT) and DOS root directory. The **FORMAT** program allows a hard disk to be formatted with or without system files.

Hard Disk Maintenance

Hard disk preventive maintenance is performed to protect the data on the drive. The hard disk itself is fairly fragile, so careful handling procedures can minimize the chances of damage. One of the best methods to reduce harm or loss of data is to park the heads outside the data area and power down. This process of moving the heads to an area on the hard drive that does not contain data is called "parking and locking." On some of the very early hard disks this required a separate software program. Newer equipment now include automatic head parking.

Disk Fragmentation

Normally new files are all contiguous, meaning that they are written to sequential sectors. As files are deleted they create holes in the usable disk space. When DOS is requested to write a new file and find new sectors, it responds by taking the first sector available. This can easily lead to a new file being spread out over several separate areas or sectors. These files are then called "noncontiguous files" and are inefficient for a number of reasons.

The disadvantage of noncontiguous files is that they take longer to read. The drive must search all over the disk platter to read the information, slowing down the disk access time.

Another disadvantage of noncontiguous files is that they are more difficult to recover if erased. In the event a file is erased and then needs to be accessed again, certain steps can be taken to recover the file. If you have kept your disk de-fragmented, you increase your odds for successful recovery of the erased file.

HARDWARE / TOOLS

There are many programs that will rearrange the data on your disk so that all files are contiguous. DOS itself is bundled with programs like **CHKDSK** and **SCANDISK**. There is also a wide variety of third party programs that will defragment a disk, such as Disk Optimizer from *Soft Logic Solutions* and *Norton*'s Speed Disk program.

BEFORE DEFRAG   AFTER DEFRAG

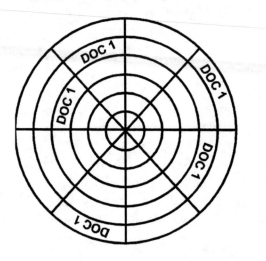 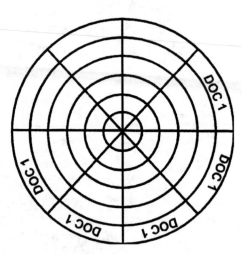

BEFORE AND AFTER DISK FRAGMENTATION

Floppy Disks

Before the creation of the hard disk, the floppy disk was the primary method of storage. It is still used widely today as a convenient method of transporting and moving data between PCs. Virtually all PCs purchased today come with at least one floppy disk drive as standard equipment. Floppy disk drives come in different sizes and capacities, but all work essentially the same way.

The two most common types of floppy diskettes are the 5¼" diskette, introduced in 1976 by IBM for use in the original IBM PC, and 3½" floppy. The most common type of floppy diskette used today in personal computers is the 3.5-inch 1.44MB, however newer technologies that facilitate higher capacity drives are emerging everyday. A simple way to determine approximate capacity is to multiply the number of tracks times the number of sectors per track. (80 tracks x 18 sectors would yield about 1.44MB - a high density diskette). A low density, 3.5-inch disk that has 80 tracks and only 9 sectors per track, would yield about 720KB. The shell surrounding the 3½" floppy is more rigid than the shell for the 5¼," with a metal shield covering the head access area. This makes for a safer storage medium than the older 5¼" floppies.

Floppy disk drives work in a similar fashion to hard drives by using heads that read and write to the disk. Drives use a spindle motor to rotate the disk and stepper motor to move the read/write heads to appropriate position.

DISK TYPE	CAPACITY	SECTORS	TRACKS
369K (DSDD) (5.25 inch)	360/320K	8 or 9	40
1.2MB (5.25 inch)	1.2MB	15	80
3.5 inch	720K	9	80
3.5 inch HD	1440K	18	80
3.5 inch Super HD	2880K	36	80

Floppy disks are connected to the system board via the floppy disk controller. The floppy disk controller not only acts as a pathway or means of connecting the disk drive to the system board, but it also translates the logical signals of the computer into electrical pulses the disk drive can understand.

A ribbon cable with connectors for two floppy drives is used to connect the floppy disk controller and drives. This cable is usually a 34-pin cable with a twist at one end. The floppy cable will determine whether a drive will be identified as the 'A' drive or 'B' drive. Drive A uses the connector with a twist, while Drive B uses the connector without it.

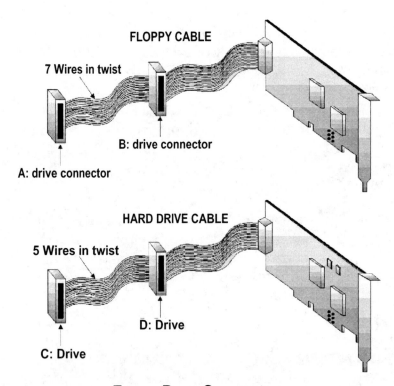

FLOPPY DRIVE CONNECTORS

Complementary Metal Oxide Semiconductor (CMOS)

The CMOS holds system information, like time, date, installed memory and type drives installed in the machine. The CMOS is a special type of chip that combines a Real Time Clock (RTC) with at least 64KB of Non-Volatile RAM (NVRAM).

The clock's function is to provide date and time information to all the software applications that need it. The NVRAM's function is to store system configuration information. Every time the computer is turned on it needs to be told what type of hardware it contains so that it can control it. The NVRAM provides that information.

A battery provides the CMOS with the power it requires to preserve stored information and run the clock while the computer is turned off or unplugged. Due to very low power consumption, the CMOS can run on a battery for several years.

Information or software programs stored on a non-volatile chip (such as CMOS) is called **firmware**. The non-volatile nature of the chip insures that the information stored within the chip will not be lost after power is removed.

A word of caution: If you are performing maintenance that requires the removal of the battery, make sure to record all setup information prior to disconnecting the battery. Once power is removed, all the information contained on the chip is lost.

HARDWARE / TOOLS

Communication Ports and Devices

Computers communicate with devices through communication ports. Each computer is outfitted with two basic types of ports: serial and parallel.

Serial Ports

Generally used by devices that require bidirectional communication with the computer, serial ports are also known as Asynchronous Serial Interfaces and are used by devices such as mice, scanners and digitizers. Asynchronous means that no synchronization or clocking is taking place. This allows data to be entered at irregular time intervals. (For example, data coming from the keyboard is fed to the computer in irregular patters by the computer user. Serial ports channel data one bit at a time.

25-PIN MALE CONNECTOR

9-PIN MALE CONNECTOR

Parallel Ports

Parallel ports operate normally as one-way ports but they may also be used for bidirectional communications. They are also known as Centronics Interfaces and their most common use is to support printers. PCs can support three parallel ports. They are referred to as LPT1, LPT2 and LPT3 (Line PrinTer one, etc.). Parallel ports are much faster than serial ports. They move data in 8-bit clumps along parallel lines.

25-PIN FEMALE CONNECTOR

NOTE: GENERALLY, THE ABOVE CONENCTORS ARE ALSO CALLED D-SHELL CONNECTORS.

Boards and Connectors

Circuit boards are used to handle the communications between the computer and the peripherals they support. Each one of them has a built-in connector that is used by the peripheral to attach to the computer. A good way to identify individual boards is by the type of connector they have. This section outlines the different types of connectors available and their various applications.

BNC Connector

Named after its inventor (Naur), the Bayonet Naur Connector, is used mostly for network applications.

ETHERNET LAN BOARD
BNC & AUI PORTS

The Centronics Connector

Not to be confused with the Centronics interface, this connector takes its name from the company that made it popular. This type of connector is used on SCSI interfaces and also on printers.

DIN Connector

DIN is a German name that stands for "German Industry Standard." The DIN Connector is about one inch across and is round in shape. This type of connector is commonly used to fasten the keyboard to the motherboard and may have anywhere from three to seven pins.

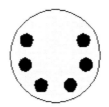

DIN CONNECTOR

Miniature DIN Connector

This smaller version of the DIN connector is used for some Bus mouse interfaces, some keyboard interfaces, and serial port applications.

RJ45 or RJ11 Connector

Registered Jack type 45 or 11 connectors are modular jacks. The RJ45 has eight wires and is used for Ethernet and LocalTalk (Macintosh Network) connections. The RJ11 is a regular phone line jack and is used on fax/modem boards. The RJ45 is a somewhat larger version of the RJ11 telephone connector, except the RJ11 only uses two pair of wires.

A 10BASE T ETHERNET CARD WITH RJ45 CONNECTOR AND A FEW LEDS

Mini-plug

Mini-plugs are found in the back of sound cards or CD-ROM players. They are used to connect a set of speakers, a microphone or headsets to the computer.

RCA Plug

RCA plugs are used on video capture boards for video inputs or on sound cards for sound inputs and outputs.

Portable Systems

As the world of computers grows beyond the traditional office setting, more users are relying on portable computing systems such as laptops to conduct business away from the office. Whether working from home, on an airplane, in a foreign country, or at a remote job site, portable systems are a vital link in the communication highway.

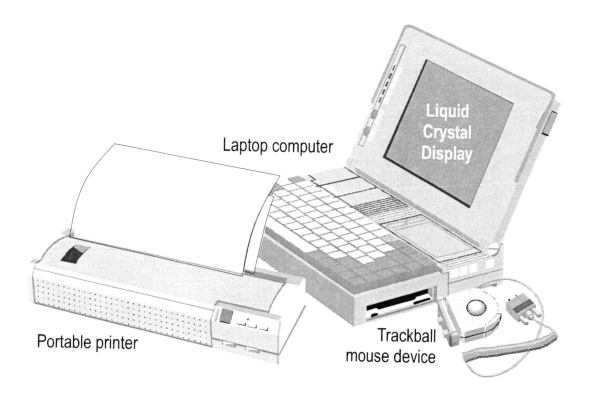

Laptop computer

Liquid Crystal Display

Portable printer

Trackball mouse device

Components

Most laptop computers contain the following components:

Battery Power Supply

Three different types of batteries can power laptop systems. Whichever type is used, a good rule of thumb is to always carry an extra battery for your laptop so that you won't risk losing valuable data when your laptop runs out of juice.

The most common type is the *nickel cadmium* battery, also used in camcorders, portable shavers and mobile phones. The nickel cadmium battery must be completely discharged before it can be recharged.

Another type is the *nickel metal hybrid (NiMH)* battery which was designed to hold 80% more charge than the nickel cadmium battery. However, the NiMH battery must also be completely drained before recharging and it takes longer to charge than the nickel cadmium.

The newest battery type is the *nickel ion* which holds three times the charge of a nickel cadmium and it does not need to be completely discharged before being recharged.

To conserve battery life:

Lower the LCD screen's light output.

· Use a Disk Cache to make the hard and floppy drives work less. Use **SmartDrive** if you're running *Windows* on your laptop, or *PC Tools* **Cache** utility if you're running *DOS*.

When you're selecting a laptop, buy one that allows you to replace a low battery in the middle of a session without losing data, ending your current session or blowing a fuse.

HARDWARE / TOOLS

LCD

A portable computer uses a Liquid Crystal Display (LCD), a flat-screen display using several hundred "tanks" of liquid crystal, each connected to its own capacitor. Earlier laptops used a monochrome LCD but most of today's laptops have color displays. To prolong the life of the LCD (and prolong the laptop's battery life), it's a good idea to lower the screen's light output. To adjust the settings for your LCD screen, click on the **Color** icon within **Control Panel** and select colors that give off less light but are still readable. Don't sacrifice readability, however, just to conserve battery power.

AC Power Supply

Most laptop manufacturers provide a grounded AC adapter to use when a power outlet is available. Check your laptop's transformer (converts AC to DC) if you plan to use your laptop overseas where foreign voltages and currents vary greatly. Consult a computer retailer to see if your adapter will function properly in the country you will be visiting.

PCMCIA Card (Types I, II and III)

Personal Computer Memory and International Association card. Most laptops have at least one, if not two, PC card slots to link to devices like modems and printers. Usually the size of a credit card, these peripheral cards for memory, network interfaces and modems plug into the laptop's slots. There are three types of PCMCIA card slots: I, II and III which can be identified by their thickness. Type I PC cards can also fit in Type II slots.

- **Type I slot (3.3MM thick)**
  Either normal RAM or flash memory card interface.

- **Type II slot (5MM thick)**
  Internal modem

- **Type III slot (10.5MM thick)**
  Removable hard disks

memorize

Network Cards

If you have the need to connect your laptop to a network, purchase a Network Interface Card (NIC) -- either an Ethernet or ARCNet card -- and the necessary device drivers and networking software to make your laptop compatible with the network.

Memory

Most laptops support up to 128MB RAM at this writing. Today's laptops are comparable to a desktop PC in RAM. There is normally an expansion slot, but you might want to save the expansion slot for a peripheral such as a fax-modem, network interface card, etc.

Summary

In this section, we discussed the various components integral to a personal computer.

· The **CPU** or processor, is the heart and soul of the computer and processes all communication among the various components of the PC.

· The **system board**, with its Bus design and expansion slots, provides the connections and means for communicating among the components; the processor, RAM, hard and floppy drives and input/output devices are all connected together through their attachment to the system board.

· **Memory**, or RAM, temporarily stores information for quick access by the processor.

· The **power supply** converts the standard 110V AC electricity from a wall outlet to the 5 and 12 volt DC currents required by the computer.

· **Hard and floppy drives** provide more static, permanent memory storage. Most programs are installed on the hard drives and this is also where files are most frequency stored. Floppy drives are used most often for transporting files from one computer to another and installing new programs.

· **Input/output devices,** such as the keyboard, monitor and printers, make it possible for the computer user to communicate with the computer and vice-versa.

· **Portable systems**, such as laptops, give users the flexibility to conduct business away from the office.

HARDWARE / TOOLS

Review Questions

1. A system board is sometimes called a planar board.

   ✶ A. True
      B. False

2. The AT computer is usually equated with what type of Intel processor?

      A. The 80486
      B. The 80386
      C. The 8088
   ✶ D. The 80286

3. The EISA took the most popular features from the other Buses and enhanced them.

   ✶ A. True
      B. False

4. The MCA Bus architecture was developed by:

      A. Intel
   ✶ B. IBM
      C. Compaq
      D. Olivetti

5. What are the three steps in preparing a hard disk?

   low level format
   partition
   high level

6. When connecting two floppy disk drives, Drive A should be attached to the connector with a ___*twist*___ .

7. The MCA architecture comes in both _____ data paths.

    A. 8- and 16-bit

✶ B. 16- and 32-bit

    C. 32- and 64-bit

    D. 8- and 24-bit

8. A 25-pin female connector located on the back of the PC would be typical of what type of port?

✶ A. Parallel

    B. Serial

    C. Bus

    D. SCSI

9. What are the typical output voltages on a PC power supply?

    A. 120 V AC

    B. 120 V DC

✶ C. 5 V and 12 V DC

    D. 5 V and 12 V AC

10. A computer's digital logic circuit uses which of the following voltages?

    A. 12 V DS

✶ B. 5 V DC

    C. 5 AC

    D. 15 DC

Section 3

PC Configuration

Section 3: PC Configuration

Introduction

Installing new hardware involves more than just attaching the pieces together. New components need to be told how to communicate with other hardware. This is what configuration is all about. A manufacturer ships new equipment with a preset configuration, but it doesn't always match the configuration of your system.

In order for a personal computer to function, each of its components must be configured properly. Much like communication by mail, the communication between the different PC components relies on addresses. Input and output devices are assigned addresses and given unique settings so that information is sent to and from the appropriate component, and so conflicts do not arise. If components share the same settings, they will not be able to communicate. This kind of conflict is similar to what happens when two people try to talk at the same time: they cancel each other out and neither can communicate.

In this section we will discuss the various addresses and settings that a PC uses to communicate with itself and we will learn how to resolve conflicts between components.

Objectives

When you've competed this section, you will be able to:

· Understand and know how to work with I/O addresses, DMA, and IRQ settings.

· Configure new circuit boards for an installation.

· Resolve device conflicts.

Understanding I/O Addresses, DMA Channels and IRQ Lines

Part of the hardware configuration process requires you to select the paths or channels the CPU utilizes to communicate with the devices it serves. The CPU recognizes a device by the path it uses to communicate. When a path is assigned to more than one device, the CPU cannot talk to the devices and they will likely fail. Most computer manufacturers reserve addresses for specific uses. There are only a few channels that remain available for additional peripheral installations. Manufacturers provide their boards with a preset address, but since they do not know what channels may already be taken, it is up to you to determine the correct settings. In order to solve device conflicts, you must understand how devices communicate. The descriptions and tables in this section outline the rules that govern communication between devices.

Input / Output (I/O) Addresses

These addresses are the paths that a circuit board uses to communicate with the CPU. Each peripheral must have an exclusive I/O address. These addresses are actually locations set aside in the PC's RAM (Random Access Memory). Think of these locations as a mail drop or box. When the circuit board wants to communicate with the CPU, it drops off a request in this "box." The CPU then retrieves the information and replies with a message in this same "box." The CPU and circuit board use this address as a pipeline for communication between the two of them. The following chart gives you a list of commonly used I/O addresses in PCs.

No two devices can share the same I/O address.

When installing a network interface card, what I/O address could you use?

COM 1 uses eight (8) I/O address
- One address holds received data
- One address holds outgoing data

DEVICE	I/O ADDRESS
COM1	3F8 - 3FF
COM2	2F8 - 2FF
LPT1	378 - 37F
LPT2	278 - 27F
XT CONTROLLER	32Ø - 32F
FLOPPY CONTROLLER	3FØ - 3F7
EGA/VGA	3CØ - 3CF
CGA	3DØ - 3DF
MONOCHROME	3BØ - 3BF
HERCULES ADAPTER	3B4 - 3BF

do not memorize I/o Addresses

COMMON I/O ADDRESS LISTINGS

PC CONFIGURATION

DMA (Direct Memory Access) Channels

When a peripheral device needs to access or write to a location in memory, it will normally have to go through the CPU for the request. This process can at times be very slow. DMA (Direct Memory Access) attempts to speed up this process. When a device uses a DMA channel, the CPU is bypassed. One way to understand DMA channels is to think of them as a trust relationship between the CPU and device. The CPU trusts that the device will use only the memory allocated to it and thusdoes not have to intervene with each request to use memory.

There are eight DMA channels on today's PC which are numbered 0-7. The following table lists the DMA channels and their availability.

DMA CHANNEL	USE
0	(Available by most machines) used by XT class machines
1	Used by XT class for hard disk. Controller available for others
2	Used by Floppy controller
3	Available
4-7	Available

DMA CHANNELS

IRQ (Interrupt Request) Levels

IRQs make a physical connection between a device and the interrupt controllers inside a computer. When a device requires service from the CPU, an IRQ line is used to get the CPU's attention. When the interrupt signal arrives, the CPU puts its current task on hold and executes an "interrupt service routine." Then it goes back to the original task. Motherboards have up to 16 different interrupt levels built in, numbered from 0 through 15. Lower interrupt numbers get higher service priority.

Just as with DMA channels, it is very important that no two devices use the same interrupt. Avoiding these conflicts is one of the major challenges when installing new equipment.

The following table lists the 16 different interrupt levels and their typical assignments:

IRQ	DEVICE
0	TIMER
1	KEYBOARD
2	CASCADE
3	COM2
4	COM1
5	LPT2
6	FLOPPY
7	LPT1
8	CLOCK
9	IRQ2 REDIRECTED
10 - 12	USUALLY AVAILABLE
13	COPROCESSOR
14	HARD DISK
15	USUALLY AVAILABLE

Interrupt Levels & Their Addresses

Installing Circuit Boards

When you buy a new peripheral for your system, such as a new sound card, most likely it will come configured with default settings. This is no guarantee that the card will work with your system. Configuring the board is not a difficult task, but complications may arise if you lack proper board documentation or information about the computer you are installing the board into. A successful board installation involves three steps: **configuration**, **installation**, and **testing**.

Configuration

Configuration consists of identifying and resolving any device conflicts and providing software support for the board in the form of BIOS or device drivers. In essence, the configuration tells the board how to communicate with the rest of the system. Configuration may also involve selecting specific combinations of jumper or DIP switch settings that tell the board which services to provide. Information about jumper or DIP switch settings should be included in the board's installation documents.

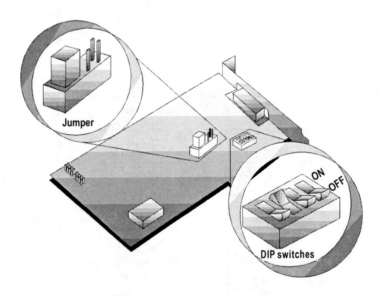

JUMPER AND DIP SWITCH CONFIGURATIONS

Installation

The board needs to be installed to an open expansion slot in the computer and all required cables need to be appropriately connected. Again, the board should come with documentation to demonstrate correct installation.

Testing

After configuration and installation, test the board to see if it actually works. Testing is a necessary step and will tell you if the board is functioning. However, configuration problems are varied and may or may not directly affect the new board's operation. Here are some examples of problems that may arise before and after testing a new board:

1. You just installed a new sound card and it seems to be working properly, but your system crashes every time you try to print from Windows.

2. A newly installed internal modem refuses to work. In addition, the computer's mouse also refuses to respond.

3. You installed a new network card on a system and it did not work, so you replaced it a second and even a third time with an identical card. None of the cards function.

These types of problems can be directly attributed to device conflicts. In the case of the sound card, it is likely that both the printer and the card are using the same interrupt address. In the second example, the modem is most likely using the same COM port as the mouse. In the third example, the network card is probably trying to utilize a memory address reserved to another device. (This is a software-related problem.)

A Typical Configuration

A typical configuration requires:

- Telling a serial port whether it is COM1 or COM2.
- Telling a printer port whether it is LPT1, LPT2, or LPT3.
- Selecting DMA channels on a board.
- Selecting IRQ lines on a board.
- Selecting I/O addresses on a board.

There are many software programs that will aid in avoiding potential address and IRQ conflicts. **MSD**, Microsoft Diagnostics Program, ships with DOS version 6.0. **MSD** will list devices, the address and interrupts used by that device. However, these programs are not perfect. They will sometimes provide misinformation. As a last resort, you may have to physically examine each device, modem, printer port, etc. in order to determine what I/O address and IRQ it uses.

Exercise 3.1: Avoiding Conflicts

Objective

Configuring a network interface card for nonconflicting IRQ and I/O address.

Preparation

You are installing a 3COM 509 network board in your PC which has the following equipment:

- Standard disk controller

- Serial ports COM1 and COM2

- Parallel port LPT1

- Standard VGA monitor

Using the charts from the previous pages, determine what IRQs and I/O Addresses are currently in use.

	IRQ	I/O Address
Standard Disk Controller		
COM1		
COM2		
Parallel Port LPT1		
Standard VGA Monitor		

Available IRQs_____

Available I/O addresses_____

Exercise 3.2: Installing and Configuring Peripheral Cards

Objective

Configure and install one of the following: modem, network interface card or sound card into your PC.

Preparation

Obtain a peripheral device as listed above with the required software and documentation necessary to complete the exercise.

Step 1 - **Determine what IRQs and I/O addresses are currently in use and which ones are available.**

- Boot your PC to DOS.
- Change to the MS DOS directory by typing **cd\dos**
- Locate and run the **MSD** program (Microsoft Diagnostic Program.)
- Determine what IRQs and memory I/O addresses are currently available.

Step 2 - **Using the board and documentation provided, configure the board with nonconflicting settings.**

Step 3 - **Install the board into any open Bus slot.**

Step 4 - **Test the board by using the diagnostics that came with it.**

Step 5 (Optional) - Set the board for a conflict.

(*For example*, you might configure the board for IRQ 7, which is the printer port.) Run the diagnostics again and review the resulting message.

Summary

The various components that comprise a personal computer need to communicate with each other. In order for this to happen, these components are designed with unique addresses and settings.

- **Input/Output addresses** are locations in RAM that act as "mailboxes" for input and output devices to trade messages with the CPU.

- **Interrupt levels (IRQs)** make a physical connection with the interrupt controllers that demand the immediate attention of the CPU with an interrupt service routine. This action causes the CPU to pause its current operation and perform the process that the interrupting device requests.

- **DMA channels** allow a device to circumvent the CPU and communicate directly with RAM.

Through these configuration addresses and settings, the PC components are able to communicate with the CPU and each other. **The key to configuring a PC is to make sure that each device has its own unique address and settings.** If multiple devices share an I/O address or are configured to the same DMA or IRQ settings, conflicts will arise and the computer will not function properly.

Review Questions

1. The floppy drive uses which IRQ?

    A.   1
  ✷ B.   6
    C.   7
    D.   5

2. Two devices can share a common IRQ.

    A.   True
  ✗ B.   False

3. IRQ 4 is used by what device?

    A.   Floppy
  ✷ B.   Com1
    C.   Com2
    D.   Hard Disk

4. DMA stands for _____.

    A.   Direct Memory Address
    B.   Diverted Memory Access
  ✷ C.   Direct Memory Access
    D.   DRAM Memory Address

5. What MS-DOS version 6.0 program aids in troubleshooting potential IRQ conflicts?

    A.   **FDISK**
    B.   **MEM**
  ✷ C.   **MSD**
    D.   **SCANDISK**

6. How many DMA channels are available on today's PC?

  ✷ A.   8
    B.   4
    C.   2
    D.   6

Section 4

Peripheral Hardware Devices

Section 4: Peripheral Hardware Devices

Introduction

In Section 2, we discussed internal PC components such as the system board, Buses, microprocessors, memory, disk drives, and power supplies. In this section, we'll discuss external hardware components such as the keyboard, monitors and the various peripheral devices that can be attached to the PC.

Objectives

When you've completed this section, you will be able to:

·   Describe the different types of monitors used with micro-computers.

·   Discuss the different types of PC input devices such as keyboards, scanners and digitizers.

·   Discuss a modem and its functions.

PERIPHERAL DEVICES

Monitors

The monitor, or video display unit, is the television-like screen the computer uses to display information to the user. Some of the earliest PCs could only display text and certain fixed graphic items that took up the full space of a single character. Most modern PCs, however, display high resolution and full graphics in a full color environment.

Monitors today still use a rather old technology invented around the turn of the century, called cathode ray technology. The monitor, or CRT (Cathode Ray Tube), is a vacuum tube that houses a flat phosphor-covered screen at one end and an electron gun at the other end. The video image on your monitor is created by projecting a narrow beam of electrons onto the phosphor-covered screen. The area where the beam hits the phosphor will glow for a brief period of time and then fade out.

Because the glow created by the electron beam fades very quickly (actually in hundredths of a second), it must retrace its path constantly to keep the image on the screen. The electron beam in the video monitor must repaint the screen at least 60 times per second or your eye will perceive flicker. This retracing is referred to as the monitor's refresh rate. The higher the refresh rate the less flicker and eye strain. Monitors that utilize a very low refresh rate are termed "interlaced monitors." Non-interlaced monitors use a higher refresh rate and thus reduce or eliminate the effects of flicker altogether. Most monitors today are non-interlaced.

high refresh rate reduces eye strain.

Video Resolution

A monitor's resolution is determined by how dots (sometimes called pixels) can be displayed both across and down the screen. For example, a resolution of 800 by 600 means that 800 dots can be displayed horizontally and 600 dots vertically. The more dots, the higher the resolution and the sharper the image.

For performance reasons, sometimes a lower resolution might be the preferred choice. When displaying full-color graphics, especially with today's multimedia systems, lower resolution settings will increase the speed of the system.

The following table lists the different types of monitors used with PCs and their corresponding maximum resolutions. Most monitors sold today are SVGA monitors.

Helpful Info

The VGA board provides the best performance...

but the SVGA provides the highest resolution.

Standard	Maximum Resolution	Colors Supported
Mono	720 x 350	Mono
CGA (Color Graphics Adapter)	640 x 200	2
EGA (Enhanced Graphics)	640 x 350	64
HGC (Hercules)	720 x 350	3
MCGA (Multi Color Graphics Array)	640 x 480	2
VGA (Video Graphics Array)	640 x 480	256
SVGA Super VGA	800 x 600	256

pay attention

COMMON TYPES OF MONITORS

PERIPHERAL DEVICES

Keyboard

While the monitor is probably the most common type of **output** device for the PC, the keyboard is probably the most frequently used **input** device. To the user, the keyboard may seem a simple device on the exterior. Inside the keyboard, however, there are many complex operations taking place both mechanically and electronically.

The original PC keyboard had a full typewriter key set plus a numeric keypad. The keyboard also incorporated ten function keys that programs use for their own special purposes. The most common keyboard today is the 101 Enhanced keyboard. This keyboard has all of the original keys plus two more function keys, a group of cursor keys, and nine additional keys dedicated to special functions. Recently, special compact and ergonomic keyboards have been developed, as well as a special keyboard designed for use with the Microsoft Windows 95 software.

These different designs all function in the same way. Every key on the keyboard is linked to a switch on the circuit board inside the keyboard. A chip on this board constantly scans every circuit and, if the switch opens or closes, the chip passes that information along to the computer. The keyboard sends a message every time a key is pressed and another one when you take your finger off the key and it springs back up. The PC can tell when you are holding a key down.

There are two types of technologies used in today's keyboards: **capacitive** and **mechanical** switches. Capacitive technology is generally used in more expensive keyboards, while mechanical switches are found in less expensive keyboards. There are far fewer moving parts in a capacitive keyboard. This makes them less prone to failure.

Keyboard Interface

The first interface between the keyboard cable and the PC is the DIN plug, which has five pins. The voltages between the pins 1, 2, and 3, or between pins 5 and 4 should be in the range of 2 - 5.5 volts DC. When troubleshooting a keyboard, check these voltages. If the voltages do not fall within the acceptable range, the problem probably lies in the computer itself, most likely in the system board. If all the voltages are present and within the required ranges, the problem is probably in the keyboard.

Perhaps one of the major problems with keyboards is not caused by system board malfunctions or cables, but rather from spills. Disassembling a keyboard for repair or cleaning is not hard in-and-of itself, but reassembling the keyboard is not recommended for the faint-hearted. As with other PC components, you might want to view the keyboard as a disposable unit.

Multimedia

It's hard to believe, but not too long ago only a select few PCs came equipped with multimedia devices. Multimedia consist of three major hardware devices; a CD-ROM drive, a sound card, and a set of speakers. These items can be purchased as a package or purchased and installed separately. The multimedia kit package tends to be more expensive than buying the components separately.

In past years CD-ROM drives were a luxury, but in today's PC world it has become a necessity. Most of the large software vendors ship their software packages on CD-ROMs. It's much more cost effective for the vendors and a blessing for anyone installing the software.

CD-ROM technology uses laser light to store and read the data on compact disc. The most obvious advantage of this type of storage, as compared to floppies, is the amount of data that can be stored on a disc. Most compact discs can store greater than 650MB per disc depending on the format used to encode the data. The type of CD-ROM drive installed in most computers today are read-only devices— the data is written to the disc one time and cannot be changed.

There are many types of CD-ROM drives, but lucky for the consumer, the companies that produce CD-ROMs formed a group to develop a set of standards. The fruits of their labors is called the **High Sierra Standard.** Like many manufacture standards, the International Standard Organization **(ISO)** modified it and came up with the **ISO 9660 standard.**

CD-ROMs can be internal or external to the PC. Usually the internal CD-ROM drives use a standard IDE interface while the external drives lend themselves to a SCSI interface. There are many speeds available, starting from older and obsolete 1X up to 32X as of this writing. This implies that a 32X CD-ROM drive spins 32 times as fast as a 1X drive, but that is not the case.

Sound Boards

From the very first PC, sound was possible although very limited by the small speaker embedded in the PC's case. There were even early programs that attempted to make our computers speak, but for the most part, they just beeped. Thanks to the new sound boards, a whole new world of sounds and music are available to us. A sound card is a board that will allow us to record and play back bits of sound. The sounds are saved to files, usually with a **WAV** (Windows sound files) or a **MIDI** (Music Instrument Digital Interface) extension.

Speakers

While the sound card generates the sounds, it's the speaker that allows us to hear the sound. The types of speakers available for today's PCs are unlimited. Most PC speakers will be stereo, some powered by the sound card itself, while other speakers require an external power supply. Whatever your choice, it's important the speaker is properly shielded to avoid interfering with other components such as your monitor.

PERIPHERAL DEVICES

Pointing Devices

Mouse

The mouse is a device used to position the cursor or pointer on screen. Using a mouse is relatively easy. When you slide the mouse left across the table or mousepad, the pointer moves to the left hand side of the screen. Slide it to the right, and the mouse moves to the right. Pushing the mouse forward or back causes the pointer to move up and down.

Seeing the cursor move in the same direction as the mouse makes the mouse much more instinctive and precise than the cursor keys. When using the cursor keys, you tell the computer what direction to move with the cursor. When using a mouse, you are not giving the computer a direction, you're giving it an exact position to place the cursor or pointer.

Depending on the type of mouse, it will also have a number of buttons on the top which are used in different ways. For example, in the Paint Program, the left button might be for drawing and the right button would be for erasing.

There are generally two different types of mice. The mechanical mouse has a ball on the bottom. When you slide the mouse, the ball rolls against a set of rollers inside the mouse. One roller will pick up the side-to-side movement. The other will sense the up-and-down movement. The rollers are both connected to axles. Each axle is then connected to an encoder wheel. By telling how fast and how far those wheels are turning, the system can then determine how fast and far you have moved the mouse.

The second type of mouse is the optical mouse. It does not have a ball on the bottom. Instead, an optical mouse shoots a beam of infrared light. This type of mouse requires a special reflective pad with a grid painted on it.

Joy Stick

A joy stick is a simple, limited controller used mainly for playing games. The basic joy stick design is a moveable rod sticking out of a pad, with a couple of buttons attached to it.

not exam related

Light Pens

Light pens are pointing devices that look like a pen. They are attached to the computer via a long cord. Light pens allow you to touch and interact directly with the screen. These pointing devices take advantage of the fact that the computer always knows precisely where the scanning electron beam is on the screen.

The pen itself has a photo detector in the tip. This photo detector is designed to be fast enough to detect when the electron beam sweeps past it. The computer can then calculate the X and the Y position of the light pen. When the light pen is pressed against the screen, it activates a switch in the very tip of the pen. This switch is roughly analogous to the function of a mouse button. Depending on the type of pen, it may have at least one or two additional switches that can be programmed like the mouse button and utilized for different purposes depending on the program or software.

PERIPHERAL DEVICES

Scanners

A scanner is a device which will transfer paper images and text into the computer. The scanner does this by converting the images and text into digital information. Scanners are rated by two factors: the size of the grid they break the image into and how many different shades those dots can be. The actual grid size is measured in dots per inch. Usually, a single number refers to both the horizontal and the vertical measurements. The number of shades on a non-color scanner is referred to as the "gray scale." In the case of a color scanner, color resolution is referred to by the number of bits or the total number of colors those bits can represent. For example, an 8-bit color scanner is the same as a 256-color scanner.

There are generally three types of scanners: hand held, flatbed, and drum scanners.

Hand-held Scanners

By far the most affordable scanners are hand-held scanners. These are simple, hand-held devices which are dragged across the page you wish to scan.

Flatbed Scanners

Flatbed scanners are very similar to office photocopiers, having a large glass surface on which the original can be placed face down. The document is not moved. Instead, the scanning head is moved past the document at a precise speed. This ensures a smoother scan. The cost of a flatbed scanner is considerably more than that of the hand-held scanner. Flatbed scanners were designed for more than casual scanning needs and are generally worth the additional cost.

Drum Scanners

Drum scanners are similar to a laser printer running in reverse order. Drum scanners keep the scanning head stationery and use a transport mechanism to move the document past the scanning head.

Modems

A modem is the most common type of hardware to interface with a serial port. It enables computers to communicate over standard telephone lines. Modems take the incoming analog data signals from the telephone lines and convert it to a digital format that the computer understands.

It allows you to access other computers attached to modems at remote locations. Anywhere you can reach by a phone, your computer may now also be able to reach. The modem gives you the ability to transfer files between distant computers. It also allows you to have access to a wide range and variety of computer networks, bulletin boards, and other specially-designed services.

The word "modem" is actually derived from two words. The first, "**Mo**dulate," means to adapt and to vary the pitch of a sound. A modem adapts data from the cable to a telephone line by creating a tone of varying pitch. "**Dem**odulate," the second word, means to interpret this tone back into data. A modem does both, modulating data going out and interpreting the modulated data that comes in.

Just like all other peripheral PC devices, modems have evolved over the years, getting faster, cheaper and sometimes smaller. However, they still serve the same basic purpose: connecting computers over long distances as if they were hooked up locally via their serial ports.

PERIPHERAL DEVICES

Helpful Info

Windows 95 uses TAPI (Telephony Application Programming Interface) as an interface to devices that need telephony access. This standard interface makes it easy for third party developers to create programs that are modem-ready. You can view the TAPI settings by clicking on the **Dial Properties** button for your modem in **Control Panel**.

PC Modems

PC modems are divided into three basic types: external, internal, and acoustic. Most PC modems, regardless of whether they are internal or external, are usually serial devices. External modems can be attached to any serial port, however, you must configure your software for that port. For example, COM1 or COM2. Serial ports are often referred to as RS 232 ports.

- **External Modems** - As the name implies, external modems are peripheral devices that are attached to the serial port of the computer. These are very popular because they can be hooked up to any type of computer with a serial port. They also have a series of LEDs that display status information, such as the modem speed or whether the modem is set to answer the phone or the state of incoming signals.

- **Internal modems** - Internal modems contain the same circuitry as external modems. The difference is that while an external modem is housed in its own casing and attached to the system's serial port, an internal modem is a board that fits into any open expansion slot on the motherboard. Internal modems are generally cheaper than external modems and don't tie up any serial ports.

- **Acoustic Modems** - Acoustic modems are all but obsolete. Unlike today's modems, acoustic modems did not plug directly into a phone jack but were built with a "cradle" for the phone headset. The computer user would dial the phone number manually, as if placing a normal call, then place the headset in the modem's cradle. The modem would then communicate with tones through the headset.

Modem Speed

Today's modems are rated for performance according to their **baud rate**. The term baud rate is a bit confusing. Early modems could only send out one bit per second, so the baud rate and bits per second measurement were the same. Baud rate became the general term for referring to modem speed. This is misleading because today's baud rates actually refer to the number of bits per second a modem can transmit.

Since the modem was introduced in early 80s, the speed of the data transmission has constantly been improved. Gone are the days of the 300, 1200 and 2400 baud modems. These have all become, for the most part, obsolete. Today's modems run at baud rates greater than 14.4, which translates to greater than 14,000 bits per second. Modem speed can also be improved beyond the rated speeds through the use of data compression techniques.

Another important factor that affects the speed of modems is the version of the UART chip that is installed on the serial card. UART is short for Universal Asynchronous Receiver/Transmitter. There are three main UART chips: **8250**, **16450** and **16550**.

If you find yourself troubleshooting a modem that is not transferring data at the full rated speed, check the version of the UART chip and replace it with the newest and fastest. In most cases, this would be the 16550 chip.

There are also two other chips that you will find installed on most serial cards, the 1488 and 1489. Both the 1488 and 1489 chips are very sensitive to power surges caused by electric spikes and lightning storms. These chips are very inexpensive, about a dollar a piece, but they are usually soldered in and not easily replaced.

PERIPHERAL DEVICES

AT Command Set

When modems were first introduced for PCs in the early 80s, they were programmed with a set of commands written to control the various functions and settings of the modem. Originally this set of commands was developed by the Hayes Company and became known as the AT Command Set.

As other companies started manufacturing PC modems, they used the same AT command set and soon the AT command set became the *de facto* industry standard. However, the AT command set can vary between different manufacturers and is specific to each modem type. The AT in the AT command set actually stands for Attention Code. Listed below are two of the more common AT commands:

AT Z sets a modem back to its default.

AT D tells the modem to dial a specified number.

The standard Hayes compatible code to dial is **ATDxxxxxxx.** A **T** is sometimes added to signify tone dial. The following is a list of the more common AT commands.

AT Commands	
A	Answer the phone immediately.
D	Dial a phone number and then wait for connection.
E	Set command echoing (0=off, 1=on)
H	Hang up phone line = (HO), Pick up phone line = (H1)
L	Set speaker volume (both 0 and 1 = low, 2 = medium, 3 = high)
M	Speaker control (0 = off, 1 = on while connecting, 2 = always on, 3 = on until a carrier is detected).
V	Set type of return codes (0 = numeric, 1 = verbose/words)
Z	Reset parameters and register settings.
&C	Data Carrier Detect Control (0 = always on, 1 = only when a carrier is detected.)
&F	Reset parameters and settings to factory defaults.
&W	Write current parameter values and settings.
+++	Break signal, change from data mode to command mode.

Summary

In the previous section, we discussed those components that are internal to the basic PC, including the system board, hard disk and memory. We also discussed some of the most common peripheral devices, monitors, keyboards, modems, and multi-media hardware.

We mentioned that today's monitors are still built around old technology called cathode ray technology (CRT). Most of the monitors in the marketplace today are non-interlaced, meaning that they incorporate a very high refresh rate to eliminate flicker.

Modems are devices that act as an interface between your computer and standard telephone lines. They convert digital data from your computer into analog data suitable for transmission over telephone lines.

Some of the newest peripheral hardware today falls under the broad category of multimedia, which includes CD-ROM drives, sound boards, and external speakers.

PERIPHERAL DEVICES

Review Questions

1. What is the resolution of the typical VGA monitor?

    A.　800x600

    B.　720x480

    ✳ C.　640x480

    D.　640x200

2. Which type of display will yield the best performance?

    A.　XGA

    B.　SVGA

    ✳ C.　VGA

    D.　CGA

3. What is another term for monitor?

    A.　TV

    B.　CBT

    C.　Tube

    ✳ D.　CRT

4. What modem AT command will set a modem to default settings?

    A.　AT D

    ✳ B.　AT Z

    C.　AT DD

    D.　AT S

5. Which of the following is the newest version of the UART chip?

   A. 16450

   ✗ B. 16550

   C. 16850

   D. 14850

6. What are the two types of switches used on most keyboards?

   A. Mechanical and infrared

   ✗ B. Mechanical and capacitive

   C. Click and non-click

   D. Magnet and wireless

7. A 14.4 modem should transmit ________ bits per second.

   ✗ A. 14,000-15,000

   B. 140-150

   C. 1400-1500

   D. 140,000-150,000

Section 5

Disassembly and Reassembly

Section 5: Disassembly and Reassembly

Introduction

Proper computer disassembly requires organization and attention to detail. It is not difficult to take apart a computer, but, if you do not take careful steps as you disassemble, you may damage components and reassembly will be complicated. No matter how many times you have disassembled a computer, you are liable to create problems for yourself if your work is not organized. Simple steps will help you to properly organize your work as you disassemble. These steps will make the reassembly process much easier.

Objectives

When you've completed this section, you will be able to:

· List procedures that will optimize PC disassembly and reassembly.

· Properly disassemble a personal computer.

· Properly reassemble a personal computer.

· Test for proper operation.

DISASSEMBLY / REASSEMBLY

Before You Begin

Attention to detail is crucial as you prepare for disassembly of a PC. There are several steps you need to take before you begin to prevent you from making some common mistakes;

· First, always have a **complete back-up** of your system software and files before you remove the first screw from the case.

· Secure the **proper tools** for disassembly. Using the right tools not only saves time, but also prevents damage to the equipment.

· **Record all information for your system's CMOS program.** This may be one of the most important steps you take before disassembly. If the CMOS loses its memory, you'll need that information to reconfigure it.

· Write down information about any peripheral boards, noting the location and positions of any switches and jumper settings. It may be helpful to draw diagrams and pictures.

Disassembly

Now that you have taken the proper steps to prepare for disassembly, you may begin:

· Turn the computer and all peripherals off. Do not disconnect the power supply until you are ready to remove it from the case. The power supply connection is a good, reliable connection to ground.

· Wear your anti-static wrist strap. If you do not have an anti-static wrist strap, touch the power supply metal case. If it is still plugged into an outlet, it will help reduce your electrostatic potential.

· If you need to remove the monitor, do it carefully and place it in a safe spot.

· Locate, remove, and store the screws that hold the cover in place. On most units you will find some retaining screws in the back. Be careful not to confuse them with the screws that secure the power supply.

· Remove the cover gently. Most covers may be removed by applying a gentle lifting action at the back of the PC. Be careful not to damage any of the components inside.

· Start taking notes. Draw diagrams and label wires.

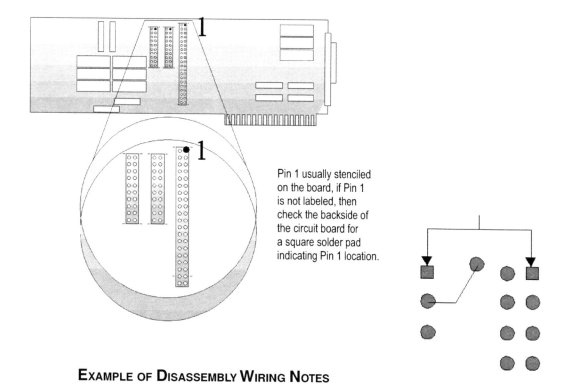

Pin 1 usually stenciled on the board, if Pin 1 is not labeled, then check the backside of the circuit board for a square solder pad indicating Pin 1 location.

EXAMPLE OF DISASSEMBLY WIRING NOTES

Remove Boards

Removing the expansion boards is a simple and straight-forward procedure as long as you follow these steps:

· Gently remove all cables attached to the boards. Make a note about the orientation of the colored stripe.

· Remove the retaining screw.

· Grasp the top edge of the board, front and back with both hands, then pull the board gently UPWARDS with a rocking motion. Do NOT rock the board from side to side.

Disconnect Cables

Before you start disconnecting cables, remember to diagram carefully how they are laid out. An improperly connected power cable may cause a short.

There are two different types of cables connected to a drive:

· A *power* cable, which brings energy to the drive from the power supply.

· A *data* cable (the flat ribbon type) connected to a controller.

None of these cables require a great deal of force to pull out, but some of the connectors may have a plastic latch that secures them in place. If your connector has a latch, gently pick the latch with a small screw driver and pull it out with a gentle rocking action.

Remove Drives

There are four different types of drives that may be installed in your PC:

- Floppy drives
- Hard drive
- Tape back up
- CD-ROM

All drives will be connected to the computer in much the same way. Locate and remove the screws that secure each drive to the chassis. Generally there are four of them: two on either side of the drive. Gently pull the drive out of the metal frame.

Remove the Power Supply

In addition to the power cables that you already removed from the drives, the power supply has two other cables that connect to the motherboard. These cables need to be removed next. Be very careful to label them properly since improper reassembly will damage the motherboard. These two cables may already be labeled P8 and P9. Tower-type cases may have an additional cable going to the back of the computer's power switch. Once the cables are disconnected, locate and remove the screws which secure the power supply to the frame, and remove it from the case.

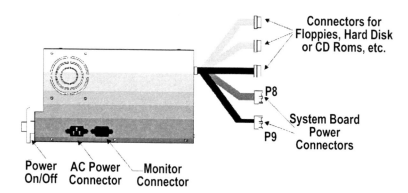

Connectors for
Floppies, Hard Disk
or CD Roms, etc.

P8

System Board
Power
Connectors

P9

Power
On/Off

AC Power
Connector

Monitor
Connector

DISASSEMBLY / REASSEMBLY

Remove the Motherboard

There may be several small, colored cables still attached to the motherboard. These are used to power the LED lights in the front of the case, the speaker, and the keylock, for example. Not all motherboards have batteries, but if it does and you have to remove it, remember that you will need to rewrite the CMOS data when you restart the computer. There may be a combination of screws and plastic spacers securing the motherboard. Once you remove the screws it should slide over with ease. If no spacers are visible, the board should lift out of the case as soon as all screws are removed.

Reassembly

Reassembly may seem like an uncomplicated process: simply put the pieces back together in the reverse order that you disassembled them. But as easy and straightforward as it may seem, it is during reassembly that mistakes are most often made. If you are replacing components, switches and jumpers may need to be configured before installation. This increases the odds that you will make mistakes. One very good piece of advice is to take your time. If you rush, you are more likely to make mistakes. The following is a list of common oversights:

Improper Cable Connections

Computer components are very unforgiving when it comes to mistakes in attaching cables between them. Make sure that you link the right objects and the cable itself is attached correctly and seated properly. Data cables carry a different color lead in one of the extreme edges. This lead attaches to pin # 1 on the connector ONLY. Most board connectors have numbers stenciled on them for easy identification.

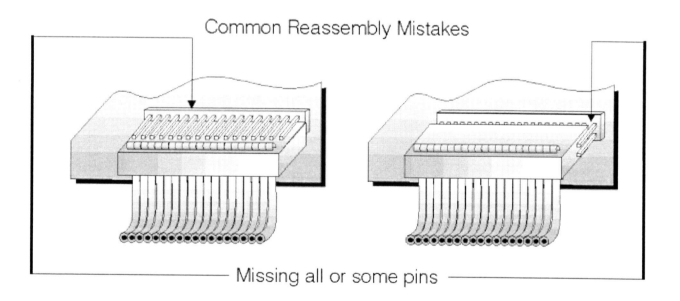

Common Reassembly Mistakes

— Missing all or some pins —

COMMON REASSEMBLY MISTAKES

DISASSEMBLY / REASSEMBLY

Power Supply Not Connected to Motherboard

This could potentially be a dangerous mistake. There are two small cables labeled P8 and P9 that carry power to the motherboard. If these two cables are not connected when the power is turned on, the power supply could explode.

Power Supply Not Connected to Hard Drive

The screen will display a Disk Boot failure message. This is an easily corrected error.

Improper Motherboard Seating

Anytime that you insert the motherboard back into the case, make sure that it is not touching the frame. This could cause it to short circuit. Also, check to be sure the motherboard is properly positioned on the spacers.

Forgot to Connect the Battery

This oversight will prevent you from saving the configuration of the system.

Proper Seating of ICs (chips) *Note the graphic below.

When replacing one chip with an identical chip, the most important thing to remember is the orientation of the chip as it applies to the socket. Most CPUs have a notched corner that must be aligned with a corresponding notch in the socket.

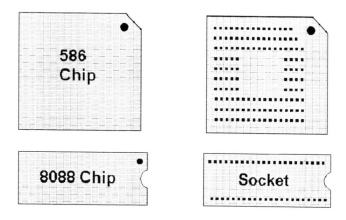

PROPER SEATING OF ICS (CHIPS)

*   The notch of the IC must match the corresponding notch on the socket.

Final Check List

The following is a list of commonly overlooked check points:

- Connect the ribbon cable to the floppy drive(s).Remember, the floppy cable will determine whether a drive will be identified as the 'A' drive or 'B' drive.
- Connect the ribbon cable to the controller card.
- Connect the power cable to the floppy drive.
- Connect all cables and power to the hard drive.
- Replace all slot covers. Computer manufacturers spend large amounts of time and money engineering case design to create optimal air flow. If empty slots are not covered, the air flow may change enough to cause heat related problems.
- Check all connections for the reset button, power LEDs, etc.
- Plug in the keyboard.
- Plug in the monitor.

These steps may seem basic, but because they are basic, they are very often overlooked. Remember to always take a systematic, step-by-step approach to reassembly and you will not forget to take each necessary step

Testing the System

Once you have completed reassembly and reviewed the final check list to make sure all of the system components are properly connected, you may power on the system. Allow the system to boot up and begin the operating system. Test the different system components to make sure they are functioning correctly. Is the keyboard working? Is the system responding to the mouse? Are you able to open software programs and files?

If each system component is functioning properly, you have successfully disassembled and reassembled a personal computer!

DISASSEMBLY / REASSEMBLY

Summary

In this section we discussed the procedures you should follow before, during and after the disassembly and reassembly of a personal computer. Always ensure that you have a complete system back-up before disassembling a PC.

Record the system CMOS settings. Choose proper tools and create a clean and static-free work environment. Document and note configuration settings of boards before removing. Follow careful steps as you disassemble and reassemble the PC.

By taking a systematic approach, you will make the process much easier and reduce the possibility for error. After reassembly, test your system to ensure that all components are functioning properly.

Review Questions

1. What two connectors attach to the system board in most internal PC power supplies?

    A. P1 and P2
    B. F5 and F8
    ✱ C. P8 and P9
    D. Positive and Negative

2. How is Pin number 1 on a peripheral circuit board usually designated?

    A. Round solder joint
    B. Red arrow
    ✱ C. Square solder pad
    D. Triangle

3. It is very important to record all the information from your system _____ before disassembly?

    A. Floppy disk
    ✱ B. CMOS
    C. RAM
    D. DRAM

4. When inserting a chip (IC) into a socket, the notch may go in either direction.

    A. True
    ✱ B. False

5. The colored strip on a ribbon cable indicates which of the following?

    A. Pin 0
    ✱ B. Pin 1   page 5-9
    C. Negative
    D. Positive

DISASSEMBLY / REASSEMBLY

6. When removing a battery from the system board, what must be done first?

    A. Secure a new battery.

   ✶ B. Record CMOS settings.

    C. Short the battery in the case.

    D. Remove the ground wire.

7. Recording jumper settings is not crucial because they are usually set for defaults.

    A. True

   ✶ B. False

8. After assembling a PC, you are asked to enter system configuration each time you boot. What could be the problem?

    A. No serial port.

    B. Reversed hard disk cable.

   ✶ C. Forgot to connect battery.

    D. Forgot to connect P8 and P9.

Section 6

DOS

Section 6: DOS

Introduction

Since its introduction in the early 1980s, DOS (Disk Operating System) has fast become the most widely-used operating system in the world. Literally hundreds of thousands of programs have been written for the DOS environment. With millions of users worldwide, DOS affects more people than any other software product ever developed. There have been volumes and volumes written about DOS. The following section will focus on the key concepts and functions of DOS to prepare you for *A+ Certification*.

DOS allows the user to organize the hard drive for storing and retrieving files. It does this through a file system that uses directories, subdirectories and files. This file system is hierarchical. DOS follows certain rules for naming and identifying files. These rules are called "naming conventions" and set limitations on the length of file names and the characters that can be used.

Before DOS can run on a system, the hard drive or disk that will be used must be formatted. Formatting prepares a disk to accept data by creating sectors, tracks, and clusters on the disk. In addition, certain files must be present within DOS that tell the system how DOS will be configured. The two most important files for DOS configuration are the **CONFIG.SYS** and the **AUTOEXEC.BAT** files.

Objectives

When you've completed this section, you will be able to:

- Understand DOS file and directory naming conventions.

- Use basic DOS commands.

- Discuss the use and contents of the **CONFIG.SYS** and **AUTOEXEC.BAT** configuration files.

- Understand and create DOS batch file programs.

DOS

What is an Operating System?

We've reviewed all the different hardware components that make up a computer. Once assembled, these components are ready to start processing requests by the software that you have installed on your system, such as word processors, spreadsheet programs, games, etc. The operating system's function is to organize the way in which information is processed by the hardware. It manages and prioritizes the application's demands for hardware resources.

Starting DOS

When you turn the power on, the computer runs a series of self-diagnostic tests that check for hardware configuration problems. Once the tests are completed, the computer is ready for use. This process is commonly known as *booting*.

The first step involves the activation of the **Power On Self-Test** or **POST**. **POST** is a program recorded on a ROM chip (BIOS), which instructs the computer to diagnose the hardware. **POST** needs RAM to work, so one of the first things **POST** will check is the lower contiguous portion of RAM. The numeric count that you see on screen at the beginning of the boot process is the computer testing the installed memory (RAM) chips.

Next, **POST** analyzes the computer's setup information, which is stored in a special kind of chip called the CMOS (Complementary Metal Oxide Semiconductor). The CMOS contains information about the configuration of the hard disk and other hardware, and also about the system's date and time settings. Information or software programs stored on a non-volatile chip (such as CMOS) is called **firmware**. The non-volatile nature of the chip insures that the information stored within the chip will not be lost after power is removed. The information contained in CMOS can be stored for several years as long as a minimal source of power such as a battery is available. Any time the battery is removed, the CMOS information is lost.

DOS

BIOS

The BIOS tests your system whenever you power-up the PC. The BIOS start-up procedure consists of these steps.

Step 1	*Low Memory Test*	If this test fails, it means the lowest bank of RAM has failed.
Step 2	*Scan for other BIOS*	Some installed boards may contain their own ROM BIOS. The system BIOS searches for any additional BIOS.
Step 3	*Yield to other BIOS*	The system BIOS yields to other BIOS it may find before it checks the main system.
Step 4	*Inventory the system*	Reads the CMOS and checks all hardware (drives, memory, etc) that it will control. This may take several minutes, so be patient.
Step 5	*Test the system*	This is the diagnostic part of the BIOS. Any failed device will generate an error message at this point.
Step 6	*Load DOS*	Before the BIOS loads the operating system, it first loads DOS. The system looks for a drive that's ready. (It looks in the boot-up sequence you've chosen in CMOS...first Drive A, then Drive C, for example.)
Step 7	*DOS loads Master Boot Record (MBR), then DOS Boot Record (DBR)*	The DBR contains the hidden files IO.SYS and #1 MSDOS.SYS. #2 #3
Step 8	*IO.SYS loads MS DOS.SYS, CONFIG.SYS, then COMMAND.COM*	CONFIG.SYS loads device drivers which can shut down a system if they have a bug. If the COMMAND.COM has #4 been corrupted somehow (wrong version, contaminated by a virus for example), you'll get a Bad or Missing Command.Com error message and your system will not boot.
Step 9	*COMMAND.COM loads AUTOEXEC.BAT*	TSRs such as anti-virus programs, network shells, protocol stacks, disk cache programs and disk #5 compression programs are loaded by the AUTOEXEC. BAT. Problems with any of these programs will cause your system not to boot.

Once the system checks are successfully completed, another program called the bootstrap loader looks for the operating system (in this case DOS) and loads into memory the necessary files to make it run.

#1

· The first file loaded is **IO.SYS**. It controls the basic input/output services DOS provides.

#3

#2 **MSDOS.SYS** is loaded next, which looks for the **CONFIG.SYS** file and loads it into memory.

#4

· The last file is **COMMAND.COM**. This file is the user interface to DOS and evaluates the validity of keyboard and batch file commands. Internal DOS commands are those commands that are built into the **COMMAND.COM** program. Examples of these commands are **DIR, COPY, CD, CLS**. As the name implies, these commands are available as soon as the **COMMAND.COM** program is loaded. External DOS commands are those that must be physically present on the hard disk. The DOS **FORMAT** and **FDISK** programs are both examples of external DOS programs.

If the presented commands are illegal, **COMMAND.COM** issues an error message on screen. **COMMAND.COM** also checks to see if the batch file **AUTOEXEC.BAT** is present in the boot directory.

#5

DOS

Booting the Computer

The PC boot process starts when a small program within the BIOS chip looks for an active partition and loads the operating system. There are two methods for booting a computer: *cold* and *warm* booting.

Cold Boot

Cold booting occurs when the computer's power switch is turned on. The effect of a cold boot is that it brings the system to the very beginning of the boot process, beginning with the **POST**. This may become necessary when the computer stops responding to any commands, including warm boots.

Warm Boot

A warm boot bypasses the first two system tests and goes directly to the bootstrap loader (the point where DOS loads). A warm boot is triggered by pressing the *Ctrl, Alt*, and *Del* keys at the same time.

CTRL + ALT + DEL

Rebooting the computer should be used only as a last resort. Any information in open application files could be lost when rebooting takes place.

POST Audio Signal	Probable Cause
No beep, nothing happens	Bad power supply or power supply not plugged in.
Continuous beep	Bad power supply or keyboard stuck.
Repeating short beep	Bad power supply.
1 long beep, 1 short beep	System board has failed.
1 long beep, 2 short beeps	Display adapter or cable is missing or has failed.
1 short beep, no boot	Floppy drive adapter has failed.
2 short beeps (PS/2)	Configuration error.

Creating Boot Disks

Every once in a blue moon your system may refuse to boot. There are numerous reasons that could cause this. If you are prepared with an emergency boot disk for such an occasion, you will save yourself a lot of anxious moments

The steps for preparing a boot disk are as follows:

- Format a floppy disk using the **/S** switch. Put a blank diskette into your floppy drive.

- Type **format A: /S**

- Copy the **AUTOEXEC.BAT** and **CONFIG.SYS** files to the newly **/S**-formatted disk.

- Copy any files and drivers that are essential to the boot process such as **IO.SYS, COMMAND.COM** and other files necessary for your particular system.

- Label the disk appropriately and write-protect it by flipping the black switch on the bottom of the diskette.

- Store the disk in a safe and readily accessible spot.

By default, every time the computer is started, it searches in drive A for a bootable floppy disk. In the event that the hard drive does not boot, you are able to access the system from drive A. This allows you the opportunity to look for the problem.

Understanding DOS Files and Directories

The two primary roles of DOS (Disk Operating System) are the storing and the retrieving of data. In order to do this, DOS must provide a common platform for file storage and retrieval. This common platform allows software programs to access information easily and quickly.

DOS File System

A computer running the DOS file system is roughly analogous to a file cabinet system. The hard disk and floppy disk are used to store data electronically and use many of the same conventions used in the file cabinet system. Every file on the disk has a unique name, just like a letter in a file cabinet. The files are placed in directories on the hard disk, which makes them easier to find, much the same as a file cabinet might use a group of file folders to store individual letters.

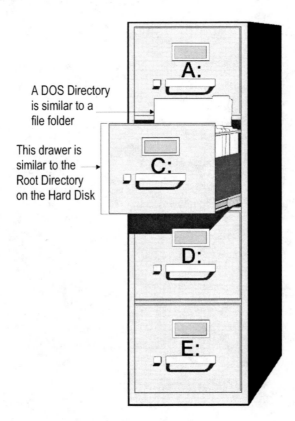

A DOS Directory is similar to a file folder

This drawer is similar to the Root Directory on the Hard Disk

A DOS File

A DOS file is a collection of related information that is referenced by a name. The electronic file can contain various pieces of related information which is grouped in an electronic file folder referenced by the file's name. These files can serve many purposes. For example, a word processor file might hold all the sentences in a letter or a database file might contain the names, addresses and phone numbers of the customers for a business. Much like an office person would use color-coded labels to indicate the type of information contained in a folder, DOS uses file names that also indicate what kind of information that particular file holds.

DOS File Name Conventions

The DOS operating system applies rules or conventions to the way the file is named. A DOS file name consists of 1-8 characters followed by a period and an optional 3 character extension.

Examples: **install.exe; readme.txt, work.doc.**

The period and the extension are optional, but are normally used. The 8-character name portion of a file usually provides an association or description of the contents of the file. The 3-character extension after the period will traditionally describe the type of file and its format.

By default, the DOS operating system ensures that every file on your hard disk has a name. Whenever a file is created, the File Allocation Table (FAT) stores information about the file and the physical location where it can be found This is similar to a book's table of contents. The DOS operating system will also place each file in a special structure called a directory.

DOS

File Name Rules

As mentioned earlier, DOS applies certain rules for creating files. Listed below are the rules for creating legal DOS file names

· A file name can consist of the following items: a name from 1-8 characters, an optional extension of 1-3 characters, and a period between the name and the extension.

· The following characters are allowed in a file name: the letters A-Z (lower case letters are transformed into upper case automatically), the numbers 0-9, and the special characters: $ # & @ ! ( ) - { } _ .

· DOS reserves certain ASCII character codes for other uses and does not let them be part of a file name. These are called illegal characters. The following are illegal characters: any control character, the space character, and + = / [ ] " : ; ? * \ > < | .

Reserved Names

It is important to understand that certain names are used by the operating system and these names cannot be used for other purposes like a file name. Listed below are the DOS reserved file names:

com1, com2, com3, com4, con, aux, clock$, lpt1, lpt2, lpt3, lpt4, nul, prn.

Commonly Used DOS File Extensions

· A file containing executable commands will usually have an extension of **.com, exe** or **.bat.**

· A file that the actual operating system uses will usually have an extension of **.sys**.

· A text file or a user-generated document will usually have an extension of **.txt** or **.doc.**

· A file that is a backup of another file will generally have a **.bak** extension.

DOS Commands

DOS commands that are typed into the computer from the keyboard allow the user to instruct the operating system to perform an operation. Some of these commands can be a bit overwhelming to the new user. However, with a little practice the commands can be an effective tool in managing the DOS environment.

NOTE: From a DOS command prompt you can press the **F3** function key to recall the last command typed. Later versions of DOS expanded this functionality with the **DOSKEY** program. **DOSKEY** is a TSR program that allows you to scroll through previous commands by using the up and down arrows.

Terminate - Stay - Resident

DIR Command - Viewing DOS Files

The DOS **dir** command allows you to view files that have been stored on the hard disk or a floppy disk. By simply typing **dir** followed by a carriage return all of the files in the current directory will be displayed. The **dir** command can also be used to sort output based on a given search criteria, such as; extensions, file names, the size of the files, or any of the file's special attributes. To view information about the use of the DOS **dir** command, type **dir/?**. This will bring up the **dir** help screen.

TYPE Command

After locating a file using the DOS **dir** command, the **type** command can be used to read the file's contents. The proper syntax for the use of the **type** command is: **type**, space, the drive letter, followed by the path and the file name.

> *Example*: To display the contents of a file called **readme.txt** located in the **C:\procomm** subdirectory of the hard disk (C:\), type the following: **C:\procomm\readme.txt**

The **type** command should only be used with standard ASCII files. Using this command with **.com** or **.exe** files will yield erroneous results and should be avoided.

REN Command - Renaming Files

The DOS **ren** command allows you to change the name of a file that has already been created on the disk. The rename command can be very useful when a file needs to be updated and the original version needs to be saved for backup purposes. This is often done in the case of configuration files, such as **.INI** files, the **AUTOEXEC.BAT**, and the **CONFIG.SYS**. The syntax for the rename command is: **ren**, space, the drive letter, path, old file name, space and then the new file name.

> *Example*: To rename the **AUTOEXEC.BAT** file found in the root directory of C to **AUTOEXEC.BAT** you would type **ren c:\autoexec.bat autoexec.bak**

DEL Command

The DOS **del** command allows you to remove or erase a file from a floppy or hard disk. The syntax for the delete command is **del**, space, drive letter, path, file name.

> *Example*: To delete a file in your current directory called **helpme.txt,** you would type **del helpme.txt.**

Wild cards can also be used in conjunction with the delete command allowing for the deletion of many files with one command. Another handy option is the **/p** which can be placed at the end of the command to give the user a final chance to abort the process.

Another file which is closely related to the **del** command is the **undelete** command. As the name implies, the **undelete** command will restore any previously deleted files.

ATTRIB Command

The **attrib** command allows you to view or change a file's attributes.

> *Example*: To use the **attrib** command to set a file called **cbt.exe**
> as a "read only" file you would type **attrib +r cbt.exe**

DOS "ATTRIB" Command + extensions	Operation
ATTRIB *.*	Displays the attributes of all files in a directory.
ATTRIB +R test.dat	Assigns the *read-only* attribute to the file **test.dat**
ATTRIB +A test.dat	Assigns the *archive* attribute to the file **test.dat**
ATTRIB -R *.*	Turns off the *read-only* mode for all files in a particular directory.
ATTRIB +R A:\USERS /S	Assigns the *read-only* attribute to all files and subdirectories in **A:\USERS**
ATTRIB +H Secret.BAT	Sets the file **Secret.BAT** as a hidden file. (File will not appear in a directory listing.)

COPY Command

Occasionally the user needs the ability to copy files. The DOS **copy** command is used to copy files from one disk to another disk or from one subdirectory to another subdirectory. The format for the DOS copy command is: **copy**, space, the source drive letter, path, file name to be copied, space, destination drive letter, path.

> *Example*: The following command will copy a file named **AUTOEXEC.BAT** on the root of the C drive to the SAVE directory on the A drive: **copy c:\autoexec.bat a:\save\autoexec.bat**

Much like the other commands, wild cards can also be used with file names and the extensions. If the actual location of the source is not entered, DOS will assume that the action is to be performed in the current directory.

MOVE Command

Sometimes a file can be placed in the wrong directory or subdirectory on the hard disk. There are many ways to remedy this situation. The file could be copied to the new location, but the net result would be two copies of the same file on the hard disk. A better option is to use the **move** command. The syntax for the **move** command is: **move**, space, drive letter, path, file name, space, new drive letter, path.

> *Example*: To move a file called **report.txt** located in the **DATA** directory of the root drive C to the **ACCOUNT** directory on the same drive, you would type: **move c:\data\report.txt c:\account**.

This command would actually take the file **report.txt** and move it to the directory **c:\account**.

DOS

VER Command

Occasionally a user needs to verify the version of DOS currently in use. Usually this occurs when adding new software or confirming which commands are available. To view the version number of DOS running on a computer, from the command line, type **ver**, then press **Enter**.

CLS Command

The display of your CRT will show all previously typed commands and associated output. This clutter can be very distracting. To solve this, you can clear the screen by typing **cls**. This will clear the screen of any old information and will move the command prompt to the top of the screen.

PROMPT Command

The standard and most common command prompt shows the current drive letter followed by :\, the actual path, and >. For example, if you were working in the DOS WINDOWS directory the command prompt would read as follows: **C:\WINDOWS>**

This standard prompt can be changed by the user with the use of the **prompt** command. This command can be executed either from the command line or included as part of the **AUTOEXEC.BAT** configuration file located in the root directory. The syntax for the default prompt is created by typing: **prompt=pg**

The **$p** is a DOS variable that displays the current drive letter and path. The **$g** is a variable that will display >. The following table shows additional variables that can be used with the prompt command:

Variable	Value
$Q	Equal sign (=)
$$	Dollar sign ($)
$T	Current time
$D	Current date
$P	Current drive letter & path
$V	DOS version number
$N	Current drive only
$G	Greater than sign (>)
$E	ASCII escape code (27)
$H	Backspace (erases last character of prompt)
$L	Less than sign (<)
$B	Pipe sign (	)
$_	Enter or linefeed

PROMPT COMMAND VARIABLES

MEM Command - Viewing Memory

Another very useful command is the DOS **mem** command. The **mem** command will display information about your memory usage. It will tell you the amount of free memory and which programs are currently loaded in memory. This information is very useful when trying to diagnose problems or when attempting to optimize available memory on your system. To execute the **mem** command, simply type **mem** at the DOS prompt and then press **Enter**.

DATE and TIME Command

A system clock is built into every PC. The system clock is responsible for recording date and time information about files and directories. Every time a file is created, saved, or modified, a date and time stamp is applied to that file. There are two commands that allow the system clock to be changed: the **date** command and the **time** command. The **date** command displays the current system date and also allows it to be changed. The **time** command displays the current time and also allows it to be changed. To execute these commands, type **time** or **date** at the DOS prompt and then press **Enter**.

Directory Commands

MD Command - Making a New Directory

The **md** command, also known as the **mkdir**, is used to make a directory or a subdirectory on a hard or floppy disk. The syntax for the **md** command is: **md**, space, directory or subdirectory name. To create a subdirectory named **programs** in your current location, you would type **md programs**

CD Command - Changing From One Directory To Another

To move into the newly created directory, you type in the DOS **cd** (change directory) command. The syntax would be **cd programs**

RD Command - Removing a Directory

The DOS **rd** command allows you to remove a directory or subdirectory from the PC's hard disk (if the directory contains NO files). The syntax for removing a subdirectory in your current location would be **rd programs**

CHKDSK Command

The DOS **chkdsk** command reports the status of a disk. It will tell you how many files are on it and how much of the disk is in use and by which files. It can also check for a lost cluster.

TREE Command

The **tree** command will display a visual representation of your hard drive directory and subdirectory structure.

VOL Command

The **vol** command will display a disk volume label.

FORMAT Command

The DOS **format** command prepares a hard disk or floppy disk to accept data. The **format** command will create sectors, tracks, and clusters on the diskette. The file allocation table, or FAT, is also created on the diskette. This table will reference the location of files and directories stored on the diskette or hard disk.

There are several options available when using the **format** command. One of the most commonly used commands is the forward slash s (**/s**), or the system option. This option places the necessary operating system files on the disk.

Example: To format the C drive, type: **format c: /s**

There are three files necessary to make a bootable diskette: **COMMAND.COM, MSDOS.SYS,** and **IO.SYS**. The **MSDOS.SYS** file and the **IO.SYS** file are both hidden files so they cannot be viewed using the basic **dir** command. However, these files can be viewed by using the forward slash A (**/a**) **option** with the **dir** command. To view these files type: **dir /a**

LABEL Command - Creating a Volume Label

At the completion of the formatting process, the DOS operating system will ask for the volume label or name to be associated with the disk. This makes for easy identification at a later date. The volume label name can be changed in the future by using the **label** command.

UNFORMAT Command

The **format** command will erase all data from the diskette. If, however, the **format** command was used inadvertently, there are several methods that can be used to restore the data.

The DOS **unformat** command will reverse the effects of a format. The **unformat** command will work as long as no changes have been made to the disk after the format. The syntax for the unformat is: **unformat**, drive letter. For example, if you wanted to unformat drive C, type **unformat C:**.

UNDELETE Command

It is also possible to recover just an individual file with the use of the **undelete** command. However, much like the **unformat**, the **undelete** should be used as soon as possible. If the space on the disk is written over by a new file, the old file cannot be recovered. The syntax for the **undelete** command is: **undelete**, drive letter, path, file name. For example, if you wanted to undelete a file named **program.txt** on drive C, type **undelete C:\program.txt**

DOS

CHKDSK & SCANDISK Command - Checking for Corrupted Disks

As a hard disk or floppy disk is used over and over again, it will eventually show signs of wear. This means that some files and directories may become corrupted. There are several DOS commands that will attempt to repair these files and directories. The two most common DOS commands for repairing corrupted files are **chkdsk** and the **scandisk**.

The **chkdsk** command will check the drive for any defective areas and display the results on the screen. The **chkdsk** command can be run a second time using the forward slash f (/f) option. Using the **chkdsk** program with the /f option will attempt to repair any defective areas on the disk.

The **scandisk** program, introduced with DOS 6.21, is a more powerful version of the **chkdsk** command. To execute either of these commands, simply type **chkdsk** or **scandisk** followed by the letter of the disk you want to check or repair. For example, if you wanted to repair a floppy disk in drive A using the **scandisk** command, type **scandisk A:**.

The **scandisk** program will display a menu allowing you to fix any errors that may have been found.

Exercise 6.1: Formatting Diskettes

Objectives

When you've completed this exercise, you will be able to:

- Format a blank diskette.
- Create a boot disk using the format system option.
- Unformat a diskette.
- Create a volume label on the diskette.

Preparation

Obtain a blank, high-density diskette.

Part One: *Formatting a diskette using the* **FORMAT** *command.*

Step 1 - **Change to the root directory.**

- Type **cd**

- Verify your location by typing **dir**

  You should see the **AUTOEXEC.BAT** and **CONFIG.SYS** files.

Step 2 - **Format the diskette in drive A.**

- Insert the blank diskette in drive A.

- Type **format A:**

- Press **Enter.**

- When completed, you will be asked to supply a volume name. Type in your first name. (It cannot exceed 11 characters.)

- Answer **No** to *not* format another diskette.

Step 3 - **View the volume label on the newly-formatted diskette.**

· Type **dir a:** at the DOS prompt

· Press **Enter**.

Step 4 - **Copy the DOSKEY.COM file from your hard disk to the floppy diskette in drive A.**

· Change to the DOS directory by typing **cd\dos**

· Press **Enter**.

· Locate the Doskey program by typing **dir doskey.com**

· Press **Enter**.

· Copy the file to a floppy diskette in drive A by typing **copy doskey.com a:**

· Verify that the file is on the diskette by typing **dir a:** Is the file listed?

Part Two: *Formatting a diskette using the quick formatting option.*

Step 1 - **Change to the DOS directory.**

· Type **cd\dos**

· Type **format a: /q**

· Press **Enter**.

· When prompted for a label, type **quick**

· Press **Enter**.

· Answer **No** to *not* format another diskette.

Note: The quick format should have been much faster than the previous format.

· Type **dir a:**

· Examine the directory. The file that you copied to the diskette will no longer be there. Formatting a diskette erases all files on the disk.

MindWorks © 2000

Part Three: *Using the* **UNFORMAT** *command to recover data erased by the* **FORMAT** *command.*

> **Step 1 -** **Verify your location in the DOS directory.**
>
> · Type **cd\dos**
>
> · Press **Enter**.
>
> · Type **unformat a:**
>
> · Press **Enter**.
>
> · Answer **Yes** to update the system area.
>
> · After the disk is unformatted, type **dir a:** The **doskey.com** file should be restored.

Part Four: *Creating a DOS bootable diskette.*

Step 1 - **Format the diskette in drive A using the /s system option.**

- Type **format a: /s**

- Press **Enter.**

- When prompted for a volume label, type **bootable**

- Press **Enter.**

Step 2 - **Boot the system using the newly formatted bootable diskette.**

- Restart your PC with the diskette in drive A.

- Press the **Enter** key when prompted for the date and time.

Step 3 - **Verify the system files on the diskette.**

- Type **dir a: /a**

- Press **Enter.**

- Examine the directory. What files did the **format /s** put on the disk?

  Note: You now have a bootable diskette that could be used to boot your PC in case something caused the boot files on your hard drive to become corrupted.

Part Five: *Formatting a diskette using the unconditional* **FORMAT**.

    Step 1 -   **Remove the diskette from Drive A and reboot.**

    Step 2 -   **Format the diskette using the /u option.**

- Type **format a: /u**

- Press **Enter**.

- When prompted for the volume label type **format**.

- Press **Enter**.

- Answer **No** to *not* format another diskette.

    Step 3 -   **Attempt to unformat the disk.**

- Type **unformat a:**

- Press **Enter**.

- View the resulting message. Was the unformat successful?

Note: The unconditional format command does not allow for unformatting later.

Creating DOS Directories

The DOS operating system is capable of dividing the disk into separate storage and work areas called directories. Directories and subdirectories are roughly analogous to the folders found in a file cabinet. A directory would be like a file folder that contains several smaller related folders. These related folders would be similar to subdirectories in DOS. This allows the DOS user a system of organization on the disk that groups related data. Every disk has one main directory, called the *root directory*. The root directory is identified by a single back slash (\ ). All other directories on the disk are then subdirectories under the root directory.

The directories and subdirectories on the disk are structured much like the organization chart of a business. At the very top of the disk structure is the root directory. All successive layers of directories and subdirectories start below the root. The only limitation to the number of directories and subdirectories is the amount of disk space in your system.

The root directory and all of its subdirectories are sometimes referred to as the DOS TREE. It is this tree structure that enables the user to find a particular file on the hard disk. When trying to find a file in the DOS file system, it is not only important to know the name of the file but where the file is physically located. This location is known as the DOS PATH.

The DOS PATH starts from the root directory working down, one directory at a time, until the file is located. This path is represented by the name of the root and subdirectories that hold the actual file and then the file name itself. Each directory (and file) is separated by a backward slash.

For example, the path to the PACMAN directory below would be written as: C:\GAMES\PACMAN

Exercise 6.2: Creating a Directory Structure

Objectives

When you've completed this exercise, you will be able to:

- Use the DOS **md** command to create directories and subdirectories.
- Use the **rd** (remove directory) command to delete directories.
- Use the **tree** command to view DOS directories and subdirectories.
- Use the **cd** (change directory) command to move into a directory.
- Copy files to a DOS directory.

Preparation

Change into the root directory of your hard drive by typing:

cd

Step 1 - **View the current directories on the hard disk.**

- Type **dir** to view the current directories.

- Press **Enter.**

Step 2 - **Create a directory using your first name as the directory name.**

- Type **md joe** *(type in your name)*

- Press **Enter.**

- Type **dir** and confirm that the new directory is listed.

Step 3 - **Move into the newly created directory.**

· Type **cd joe** *(type in your name)*

· Press **Enter.** What does your prompt display?

Step 4 - **Create two subdirectories under your directory.**
Name them DATA **and** GAMES.

· Type **md data** to create a new directory named DATA.

· Press **Enter.**

· Type **md games** to create a new directory named
GAMES.

· Press **Enter.**

· Type **dir** to view the list of directories.

· Press **Enter** to verify that the new directories are
listed.

Step 5 - **Use the DOS** cd **command to move one level up the**
directory tree.

· Type **cd..** to move one step up the directory tree; in
this case, all the way up to the **root** directory.

· Press **Enter.**

Step 6 - **Use the** cd **command to move into the newly created** DATA **directory.**

·   Type **tree**

·   Press **Enter** to find the data directory.

·   Type **cd\yourname\data**

·   Press **Enter.** What does your prompt display? It should show that you are now in the **data** directory.

Step 7 - **Use the** rd **(remove directory) command to delete the** GAMES **directory.**

·   Type **rd games** to remove the **GAMES** directory.

·   Press **Enter.** What happened? You should get an error message telling you this is an invalid path. This is because you need to be in the directory which contains the subdirectory you want to remove in order to use the **rd** command.

·   Type **cd..**

·   Press **Enter.**

·   Type **rd games** again.

·   Press **Enter.**

·   Type **dir**

·   Press **Enter** to view the directory's contents. The **games** directory should no longer be listed.

Step 8- **Make a directory named** backup **and copy the** AUTOEXEC.BAT **file from the root to this directory.**

· Type **md backup** to create a new directory named **Backup.**

· Press **Enter.**

· Type **cd backup** to change to the **backup** directory.

· Press **Enter.**

· Type **copy c:\autoexec.bat** to copy the file to the **backup** directory.

· Press **Enter.**

· Type **dir** and verify that the **AUTOEXEC.BAT** file was copied to the **backup** directory.

DOS Configuration Files

When the computer is turned on and the DOS operating system starts to load, it looks for two very important configuration files, the **CONFIG.SYS** file and the **AUTOEXEC.BAT** file. These are both text files that can be created and edited with any DOS text editing program. Both files must be located in the root directory of the bootable drive to ensure that the operating system will locate them. These files are executed in a particular order.

- **CONFIG.SYS** - The first of the files to be executed is the **CONFIG.SYS** file. This file contains special commands relating to the hardware devices found in the computer, such as the mouse, the printer, the keyboard and disk drive present in the computer.

- **AUTOEXEC.BAT** -The second file to execute is the **AUTOEXEC.BAT** file. The **AUTOEXEC.BAT** file is used to customize your DOS environment. It can be used to automatically start any application, to present the user with a menu, and to set DOS environmental variables such as the **PROMPT** command.

Bypassing the Start-Up File

It is possible that something could be placed in the **AUTOEXEC.BAT** file or the **CONFIG.SYS** file that may cause the computer not to function correctly or, in some cases, not to boot at all. In this case, the DOS operating system gives you the ability to bypass both files during the booting process. Follow these steps to accomplish this:

- Boot the computer
- Press the **F5** function key immediately after the starting DOS message appears on the screen.

The above procedure allows the user to boot the computer without any of the special commands that may have been specified in the **CONFIG.SYS** or the **AUTOEXEC.BAT**. At this point, the user can try to determine what command or commands in the configuration files are causing the problem.

The **F8** key serves a similar function to the **F5** key. The main difference between the two function keys is that while the **F5** key bypasses the configuration files altogether, the **F8** key allows you to selectively bypass commands either in the **CONFIG.SYS** or the **AUTOEXEC.BAT** The user is prompted with a message asking if each step is to be performed. If the user tells DOS to bypass the command it will then proceed to the next step.

CONFIG.SYS File

The contents of the **CONFIG.SYS** file can be roughly broken down into two categories: commands and device drivers. Some of the more common **CONFIG.SYS** commands are **files** and **buffers**. The **buffer statement** tells DOS the amount of memory to reserve for information transfers to or from the hard disk. This parameter can be set between 1 and 99, with each buffer taking up approximately 530 bytes. The **Files** command specifies the number of files that can be open concurrently. The range is 8 to 255.

CONFIG.SYS Commands	
BREAK	Turns on or off extended Ctrl-Break checking.
BUFFERS	Sets the number of disk buffers used by DOS.
COUNTRY	Sets country information.
DEVICE	Loads an installable device driver.
DEVICEHIGH	Loads an installable device driver into high (UMB) memory.
DOS	Determines whether DOS will use the HMA or UMB.
DRIVPARM	Redefines the physical characteristics of an existing disk drive.
FCBS	Sets the maximum number of open File Control Blocks.
FILES	Sets the maximum number of open files that DOS will allow.
INCLUDE	Includes the commands from one CONFIG.SYS block within another.
INSTALL	Loads TSR programs into memory from CONFIG.SYS.
LASTDRIVE	Sets the maximum number of letters available to DOS.
MENUCOLOR	Sets the color of the screen for the CONFIG.SYS start up menu.
MENUDEFAULT	Sets the default menu choice in a CONFIG.SYS menu block.
MENUITEM	Sets the text and configuration block associated with menu items in CONFIG.SYS.
NUMLOCK	Sets the state of the NumLock key when the computer starts.
REM	Inserts a remark into CONFIG.SYS.
SET	Sets environment variables.
SHELL	Sets the name of the program used as a command-line shell by MS-DOS.
STACKS	Sets the number of stacks set aside for hardware interrupts.
SUBMENU	Defines a submenu in CONFIG.SYS.
SWITCHES	Sets miscellaneous control options for MS-DOS.

In addition to the **CONFIG.SYS** command, there are also a number of device driver options that can be used. For example, the **ANSI.SYS** device driver expands the ability of a system to respond to advanced video command sets. The **ANSI.SYS** driver must be loaded in the **CONFIG.SYS** file.

A device driver simply tells DOS how to control each hardware device attached to the computer. Some of the more common device drivers and their associated functions are listed in the following table.

Device Driver	Associated Function
ansi.sys	Controls screen colors and the position of the cursor.
driver.sys	Creates drive letters which are assigned to physical devices
emm386.exe	Provides access to upper memory & emulates expanded memory.
himem.sys	Manages the extended memory area.
setver.exe	Manages the DOS version table.
smartdrv.exe	File used by various hard drives.
power.exe	Advanced Power Management (APM) reduces power consumption during idle times.
ramdrive.sys	Driver that simulates a logical hard drive in RAM (memory).

COMMON DEVICE DRIVERS

DOS

The following is an example of a **CONFIG.SYS** file.

device=C:\dos\himem.sys

device=C:\dos\emm386.exe

files=40

buffers=25

dos=high,umb

stacks=9,256

lastdrive=E

In the above example . . .

· The first line, **device=C:\dos\himem.sys,** will manage the extended memory area in the system RAM.

· The second line, **device=C:\dos\emm386.exe,** will make **emm386.exe** active so that upper memory will be available and will simulate expanded memory for programs that can use it.

· The **files=40** statement provides that 40 files can be open concurrently.

· **Buffers=25** will assign 25 buffers for transferring information to and from the hard disk.

· The **dos=high,umb** statement will load DOS into high memory and will also make upper memory blocks available.

· The **stacks=9,256** statement will provide nine 256-byte stack handlers available for use by the interrupts.

· The **lastdrive=E** statement indicates the last local drive available.

AUTOEXEC.BAT

The **AUTOEXEC.BAT** contains commands that customize a DOS installation. It runs automatically when the system is started. Listed below are some of the more common DOS commands that can be used in the **AUTOEXEC.BAT** file:

Common DOS commands in an AUTOEXEC.BAT file	
path	Sets a logical path to directories containing executable files.
set	Defines DOS variables.
prompt	Establishes and sets the command prompt.
mode	Specifies options for the monitor, printer ports and keyboard.
echo off	Instructs DOS not to display each command as it executes.
call	Will run a second batch file.
rem	Used to add a documentation statement in the AUTOEXEC.BAT file

The following is an example of a **AUTOEXEC.BAT** file.

> **echo off**
>
> **cls**
>
> **prompt=pg**
>
> **path=c:\;c:\dos;c:\wp**

In the above example . . .

· The **echo off** statement will tell DOS not to display each command as it executes.

· The **cls** statement will clear the screen.

· The **prompt=pg** command will set the user's prompt to display the current drive followed by the "greater than" sign (>).

· The DOS **path=c:\;c:\dos;c:\wp** statement in this example tells DOS to search for files in the following order starting with the root directory, the DOS directory, and finally, the **WP** directory.

DOS

DOS Batch Programs

DOS batch files or programs are short cuts that allow a user to place frequently used commands into one file. These commands will execute when the file name is typed. A DOS batch file could be very simple, issuing one or two commands, or it can be very complex, issuing an entire series of commands. Any valid DOS command can be included in a batch command or any third party application compatible with DOS can also be included as the batch file. The list below includes some of the most frequently used batch file commands:

call

goto

if then

echo

choice

pause

rem

MindWorks © 2000

Creating Batch Files

A DOS batch file can be created within a DOS text editing program, but the files should always be saved with a **.bat** extension. The names of the batch files should always be unique and should never be named the same as any other DOS commands. An example of a name to avoid would be **format.bat** because the DOS operating system would not have any way of differentiating between the **format.bat** and **format.com** files.

To execute a batch file, the user types the batch file name followed by the enter key. The extension is optional and does not need to be typed. The execution of the batch file may be halted by typing **Ctrl + C** or touching the **Ctrl + Break** keys. Another command that can be used to temporarily suspend the process of a batch file is the DOS **pause** command. It is very useful for troubleshooting or testing a batch file.

Exercise 6.3: Creating a DOS Batch File.

Objectives

When you've completed this section, you will be able to:

- Describe the use of DOS batch files.
- Create a DOS batch file.
- Execute a DOS batch file.

Preparation

DOS batch commands can be very useful and can save you time. For example, let's say that as part of your job you need to create multiple directories and subdirectories on every new machine that comes into your office. You also have to copy files to these directories. You could use the **md** and **copy** commands repeatedly each time you configure a new system, or you could create a batch file that will do this for you.

In this exercise, you will create a batch file to do the following: create five directories, copy your current **AUTOEXEC.BAT** and **CONFIG.SYS** file to a directory called **backup**, and copy all DOS files to a directory called **c:\save**.

Step 1 -   Change the root directory and view the directory.

- Type **cd** to change to the root directory.
- Press **Enter.**
- Type **dir** to display the contents of the directory.
- Press **Enter.**

Step 2 - **Create a DOS batch file called** repeat.bat.

·   Type **edit repeat.bat**

·   Press **Enter**

·   Enter the following commands:

```
cd\
md backup
md save
md word
md common
md test
copy c:\dos\*.* c:\save
copy c:\autoexec.bat c:\backup
copy c:\config.sys c:\backup
```

Step 3- **Now exit and save the file.**

·   Press the **ALT** key

·   Press **Enter.**

·   Press **X** to exit.

·   Press **Enter** again when the system asks if you want to save.

DOS

Step 4 - **Run the batch file you just created and view the results.**

· Type **repeat.bat** to run the batch file.

· Press **Enter**.

· Type **tree** to verify that the directories have been created.

· Move into the **save** directory.

· Type **dir** to view the contents of the directory.

· Press **Enter** to verify that you have a backup of the DOS files.

List of DOS Commands

The following is a list of common DOS commands organized by their function. A brief description of the command is included.

Directory Commands	
CD or CHDIR	Changes the current directory of a disk drive.
DELTREE	Deletes a directory, including all the files and sub-directories it may contain.
MD or MKDIR	Creates a new sub-directory on a disk.
RD or RMDIR	Deletes an empty sub-directory on a disk.
TREE	Displays the sub-directory structure present on a disk.

Batch File Commands	
CALL	Executes a batch file from within another batch file.
CHOICE	Accepts a single keystroke from the keyboard.
COMMAND	Runs a second copy of the MS-DOS command interpreter.
ECHO	Echoes text to the screen from a batch file.
FOR	FOR-IN-DO loop for batch files.
GOTO	Jumps to a labeled line in a batch file.
IF	IF-THEN decision structure for a batch file.
PAUSE	Waits for a keystroke before continuing.
REM	Inserts a remark into a batch file.
SHIFT	Shifts batch file parameters down one place.

Disk Commands	
CHKDSK	Checks a disk for errors and provides information on the amount of space in use.
DEFRAG	Defragments the files on a disk. This can cut down on the time it takes your computer to find files on your hard disk.
DISKCOMP	Compares two floppy disks to see if they are identical.
DISKCOPY	Makes an exact copy of a disk.
FDISK	Hard disk partitioning program. Prepares a new hard disk to accept DOS, or partitions a single drive into two or more logical drives.
FORMAT	Formats a hard or floppy disk for MS-DOS.
LABEL	Creates, edits, or deletes the volume label on a disk.
SCANDISK	Analyzes disks and repairs errors. The ScanDisk utility can repair DoubleSpace compressed drives as well as normal disks.
SUBST	Creates a disk drive letter that refers to a sub-directory of another drive.
SYS	Installs the MS-DOS system files on another disk.
UNFORMAT	Returns a disk to its previous state before FORMAT was run.
VERIFY	Controls whether DOS will read everything written to disk to ensure that no errors occurred.
VOL	Displays the volume label of a disk.

DOS

File Commands	
ATTRIB	Views or changes file attributes.
COPY	Copies or concatenates a file or group of files.
DEL or ERASE	Deletes a file or group of files.
DIR	Displays a listing of the files in a sub-directory.
EXPAND	Expands (uncompresses) files on the MS-DOS 6 distribution disks.
FC	Compares two files for differences.
FIND	Finds matching text in a file.
MOVE	Moves a file from one sub-directory to another or renames a sub-directory.
REN or RENAME	Renames a file or group of files.
REPLACE	Replaces or adds files to a sub-directory.
SHARE	Provides file sharing and locking capabilities for DOS.
TYPE	Displays the contents of a file on-screen.
UNDELETE	Undeletes a file or group of files.
XCOPY	Copies files and sub-directories.

Full-Screen DOS Applications	
DBLSPACE	Program that compresses information on a disk, providing up to twice the amount of space you previously had.
DEBUG	Programmer's debugger.
DEFRAG	Defragments the files on a disk. Running this program can cut down on the time it takes your computer to find files on your hard disk.
DOSSHELL	Graphical shell program for DOS.
EDIT	A full-screen ASCII text file editor.
MSAV	Checks your computer for viruses.
MSBACKUP	Backs up files on your hard disk to a series of floppy disks.
MSD	Provides information about a computer's configuration.
QBASIC	Provides access to the MS-QuickBASIC development environment, which enables users to write and run programs written in the QuickBASIC language.

Help Commands	
FASTHELP	Displays a short description of what each DOS command is for and the correct syntax for its use.
HELP	A full-screen, on-line help system that provides descriptions and examples of every DOS command.
/?	Not an actual command. If you include a /? on the command line with a DOS command, a short description is displayed of what the command does and how you can use it.

International Commands and Device Drivers	
CHCP	Changes the active country code page.
KEYB	Sets the active keyboard layout.
MODE	Configures standard DOS devices, including changing the active code page for the keyboard, display, and printer.
NLSFUNC	Contains code page switching support required by CHCP and MODE.

Miscellaneous Commands	
MEM	Displays how memory in your computer system is being used.
MEMMAKER	Utility to optimize memory usage on your computer.
APPEND	Establishes a DOS search path for data files.
BREAK	Turns on or off extended Ctrl-Break checking.
CLS	Clears the screen.
DATE	Sets or views the system date.
DOSKEY	Provides enhanced command-line editing and macros capability.
GRAPHICS	Provides support for a graphics mode Print Screen function.
MSCDEX	Provides support for CD ROMs.
MODE	Configures standard DOS devices such as serial ports, parallel ports, the display, and the keyboard.
MORE	Pauses display output when the screen is full.
PATH	Establishes a DOS search path for executable files.
PRINT	Print spooler for ASCII text files.
PROMPT	Customizes the prompt used by DOS at the command line.
RESTORE	Restores files backed up with the DOS 5 version of BACKUP
SET	Sets, clears, or displays environment variables.
TIME	Sets or views the system time.
VER	Displays the version of DOS running on the computer.
VSAFE	Resident program that watches for viruses.

DOS

Exercise 6.4 (Optional): Formatting and Partitioning a Hard Disk

Objectives

When you've completed this exercise, you will be able to:

- Use the **fdisk** command to create primary and extended partitions.
- Create logical drives.
- Set the active DOS partition.
- Delete primary and extended partitions.

Preparation

Obtain a bootable DOS diskette that contains at least the following files: **FORMAT.COM, FDISK.EXE** and **SYS.COM.**

Part One: *Creating new partitions.*

Step 1 - **Reboot your system.**

- Insert a diskette into drive A and reboot your system.

Step 2 - **View the existing partitions on your hard disk.**

- At the **A:** prompt type **fdisk** to view the partitions on your hard disk.

- Press **Enter.**

- Choose Option 4 from the **fdisk** main menu. How many partitions currently exist?

Step 3 -   **Delete the existing partitions.**

·   Press the **Esc** key to return to the **fdisk** main menu.

·   From the main menu, select **Option 3**.

·   Select **Option 1** to delete the primary partition.

·   Press **Enter** to accept **1** as the partition you wish to delete.

·   When prompted for the volume label, enter its name. If there is no volume label, press **Enter** to continue.

·   Answer **Yes** to confirm the deletion.

·   Press **Esc** to return again to the main menu.

Step 4 -   **Create a primary DOS partition using about 50% of the total hard disk space.**

·   Select **Option 1** to create a DOS partition.

·   Select **Option 1** again to create a primary DOS partition.

·   When prompted with **Use the Maximum Size**, click **No**.

·   Enter **50%** for the size.

·   Press **Esc** to return to the main menu.

Step 5 -   **Create an extended DOS partition.**

·   From the **fdisk** main menu, click **Option 1** to create a DOS partition or logical drive.

·   Select **Option 2** to create an extended DOS partition.

·   Press **Enter** to accept the size in megabytes.

·   Press **Enter** again to continue.

·   After a short pause, you will see the command: **Create Logical DOS Drive in the Extended DOS Partition.**

·   Press **Enter** to accept the total space and create the first logical drive. Note which letter is assigned to the first logical drive.

·   Press **Esc** to return to the main menu.

Step 6 -   **Set the active boot partition.**

·   From the **fdisk** main menu, select **Option 2**.

·   Select **Partition 1** as the active partition. Notice now that status is set to **A** to indicate that this is the active partition.

Step 7 -   **Exit the** fdisk **program**

·   Exit the **fdisk** program by pressing the **Esc** key until you are back to the DOS prompt.

Part Two: *Format the new partitions.*

    Step 1 -   **Format the C drive with the** SYSTEM **option.**

- Type **A:** to change to the A drive.

- Press **Enter**

- Type **format C: /S**

- Press **Enter.**

    Step 2 -   **Format the logical drive D.**

- Type **format D:**

- Press **Enter.**

    Step 3 -   **Verify that you can access each drive.**

- Type **C:** to switch to the C drive.

- Press **Enter.**

- Type **dir** to view the contents of the C drive.

- Press **Enter.**

- Type **D:** to switch to the D drive.

- Press **Enter.**

- Type **dir** to view the contents of the D drive.

- Press **Enter.**

Summary

This section provides an overview of DOS. Introduced in the early 1980s, DOS has become the most widely used operating system in the world. Literally hundreds of thousands of programs have been written for it. This section has focused on the key concepts and functions of DOS that will prepare you for *A+ Certification*.

DOS allows the user to organize the hard drive for storing and retrieving files. It does this through a hierarchical file system that uses directories, subdirectories and files. In order to identify files, DOS follows certain rules called "naming conventions." These rules set limitations on the length of file names and the characters that can be used for naming files.

Before DOS can run on a system, the hard drive or disk that will be used must be formatted. Formatting prepares a disk to accept data by creating sectors, tracks and clusters on the disk. In addition, certain files must be present within DOS that tell the system how DOS will be configured. The two most important files for DOS configuration are the **CONFIG.SYS** and the **AUTOEXEC.BAT** files.

Review Questions

1. Choose the correct load order sequence of the following files:

     ✗ A.   CONFIG.SYS, AUTOEXEC.BAT
        B.   AUTOEXEC.SYS, CONFIG.SYS
        C.   AUTOEXEC.BAT, CONFIG.SYS
        D.   AUTOEXEC.BAT, COMMAND.COM

2. To bypass both the **CONFIG.SYS** and the **AUTOEXEC.BAT** you would type:

        A.   F6
        B.   F8
     ✳ C.   F5
        D.   F3

3. The acronym **POST** stands for:

        A.   Power On Start Test
     ✳ B.   Power On Self-Test
        C.   PC Over Start Test
        D.   Power Off Self-Test

4. Which of the following file names is invalid?

        A.   money1.txt
     ✗ B.   com1.txt
        C.   12345x.doc
        D.   back.xxx

5. What three required files are placed on a diskette after formatting it with the **/s** option?

        A.   COMMAND.BAT, IO.SYS, MSDOS.SYS
        B.   AUTOEXEC.BAT, CONFIG.SYS, COMMAND.COM
     ✗ C.   IO.SYS, MSDOS.SYS, COMMAND.COM
        D.   AUTOEXEC.BAT, CONFIG.SYS, COMMAND.EXE

MindWorks © 2000

6. You can always unformat a disk that has been formatted with the **/u** option.

    A. True

 ✳ B. False

7. The **himem.sys** command will manage extended memory.

 ✳ A. True

    B. False

8. What does the **$G** command do in the following statement: **PG**?

    A. Displays the path.

 ✳ B. Displays the "greater than" sign.

    C. Displays DOS.

    D. Displays the C:

Section 7

DOS Memory Optimization

Section 7: DOS Memory Optimization

Introduction

In a perfect computer world, only one configuration of DOS would be needed for all computers. In the real world, however, no two computers are exactly alike. Therefore, one default configuration is not practical.

In order to get the best performance from a computer, it is often necessary to optimize the installation. For the most part, optimization relates to memory and how it is allocated. As mentioned in the previous section, DOS and DOS programs are limited to the first 640K of memory (conventional memory), so the process of managing or optimizing memory under DOS usually involves freeing up as much of that memory as possible.

Objectives

When you've completed this section, you will be able to:

·   Describe the different types of PC memory areas.

·   Identify which programs are located in these areas.

·   Use the DOS Memory Optimization Program (**MEMMaker**).

DOS MEMORY OPTIMIZATION

Memory Optimization

In order to discuss memory optimization, it is first important to understand the different terms associated with the optimization of memory. These terms generally describe the different types of memory available to the PC.

The graphic below depicts the different memory locations.

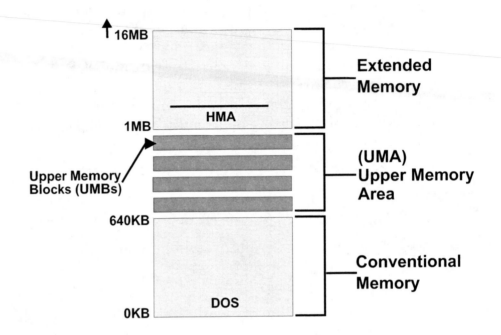

MEMORY LOCATIONS

Conventional Memory

Conventional memory is the first 640KB of system memory. This is all the memory DOS has for running programs. Traditionally, this was the only memory available to DOS applications. Even if your computer has 16MB of RAM, you only have 640KB in which to run DOS programs. This is sometimes referred to the 640KB barrier. In addition to DOS programs, the DOS command processor, TSR, and BIOS information table reside in this area.

Upper Memory Area (UMA)

The UMA, upper memory area, is located between 640KB and one megabyte. This area of memory contains ROM BIOS, video ROM and RAM, and device controllers. It will also contain the expanded memory page frames.

Upper Memory Blocks (UMB)

The UMB are free blocks of memory within the upper memory area. They can be used to contain things like TSR (terminate and stay resident) programs and device drivers. To gain access to the upper memory blocks, you must use **HIMEM.SYS** and **EMM386.EXE**.

Extended Memory (XMS)

The extended memory can range from 1MB to 16MB for 80286-based machines, and up to 4GB for 80386 and above based machines. The use of the extended memory requires that the **HIMEM.SYS** program be loaded in the **CONFIG.SYS** file.

DOS MEMORY OPTIMIZATION

High Memory Area (HMA)

The high memory area, or HMA, is the first 64KB of extended memory. DOS requires a program such as **HIMEM.SYS** to access the HMA area. This area of memory is most commonly used for loading DOS components. However, only one program at a time may reside in the high memory area.

Expanded Memory Area (EMS)

Expanded memory is extra memory located in the PC. It was originally developed as a way of working around the limitation of DOS. It requires the use of the LIM (Lotus-Intel-Microsoft) specifications. This is generally referred to as the LIM4.0 memory manager. Very few programs will actually make use of the expanded memory area.

Managing Memory

Memory management is something unique to the DOS operating system. Other operating systems do it automatically. With DOS, you need to use an additional program. There are many products on the market that help you manage and optimize memory. Some examples are: *QuarterDeck's* QEMM, or the **MEMMaker** program that comes bundled with DOS 6.

The DOS **MEMMaker** utility will help you configure, manage, and optimize all the memory in your PC. This program will analyze all the currently loaded programs and device drivers on your PC and then determine the best possible memory configuration. The **MEMMaker** program is fairly straightforward and easy to use. Unfortunately, **MEMMaker** will not run on all systems. It requires at least an 80386 microprocessor or above and extended memory.

The **MEMMaker** program can be run in two ways. The express setup works for most systems without any problems. The custom setup may be necessary if you have a monitor or device driver that may interfere with the **MEMMaker** program.

Viewing Memory

While the DOS **MEMMaker** program allows you to optimize the system memory, the DOS **mem** command allows you to view memory usage and availability. The DOS **mem** command can be a useful tool when you need to diagnose a memory problem or for optimizing memory manually. The **MSD** (Microsoft Diagnostic Program) will also allow you to view current system memory usage.

Exercise 7.1 : Viewing and Optimizing System Memory

Objective

View and optimize system memory usage with the DOS **mem** command and the DOS Optimize Program (**MEMMaker**).

Preparation

Rename your current **AUTOEXEC.BAT** and **CONFIG.SYS** to **AUTOEXEC.BAK** and **CONFIG.BAK**.

- Type **ren autoexec.bat autoexec.bak** to rename your current **AUTOEXEC.BAT** file.
- Press **Enter.**
- Type **ren config.sys config.bak** to rename your current **CONFIG.SYS** file.
- Press **Enter.**

Part One

Step 1 -   Create a new AUTOEXEC.BAT **file.**

- Type **edit autoexec.bat** to modify your **AUTOEXEC.BAT** file.

- Press **Enter.**

- Enter the following commands:

  echo off

  path c:\;c:\dos

  prompt PG

- Save the new file by pressing the **Alt** key.

- Press **Enter.**

- Type **X** to exit.

- Press **Enter** to save.

Step 2 - **Create a new** CONFIG.SYS **file.**

· Type **edit config.sys**

· Press **Enter.**

· Enter the following Remark (REM) Statement
rem **This is my config.sys file**

· Save the **CONFIG.SYS** file by pressing the **Alt** key.

· Press **Enter.**

· Press **X** to exit.

· Press **Enter.**

Step 3 - **Reboot your system.**

Step 4 - **From the C: prompt view your current memory statistics.**

· Type **msd** to start the MSD utility.

· Press **Enter.**

· Press **M.**

· Press **Enter** to view memory.

· Record the following:

Total Conventional Memory   _638 K_

Available Conventional Memory _576 K_

Total Extended Memory   _65,535_

Step 5 -   **Exit the** MSD **program by pressing function key** F3.

Step 6 -   **Edit your** CONFIG.SYS **file:**

   ·   Type **edit config.sys**

   ·   Press **Enter.**

   ·   Add the following line by typing:

      device=c:\dos\himem.sys

   ·   Save the file.

Step 7 -   **Reboot your computer by pressing** CTRL + ALT + DEL **simultaneously.**

Step 8 -   **Run the** MSD **program and record the amount of Available Extended Memory.**

   ·   Type **msd** to start the MSD utility.

   ·   Press **Enter.**

   ·   Press **m.**

   ·   Record the amount of Available Extended Memory _65,404 K_ .

   ·   Exit **msd** by pressing the function key **F3.**

Step 9 - **Add the Expanded Memory Manager** (EMM386.EXE) **to your** CONFIG.SYS **file.**

·   Type **edit config.sys**

·   Press **Enter.**

·   Add the following line to your **CONFIG.SYS**, immediately following the **HIMEM** line by typing **device=c:\dos\emm386.exe**

·   Save the new file by pressing the **Alt** key.

·   Press **F**

·   Type **X** to exit.

·   Press **Enter** to save.

Step 10 - **Reboot your computer and note the addition of Page Frame in the Upper Memory Area.**

·   Type **msd** to start the MSD utility.

·   Press **Enter.**

·   Press **m** and notice Page Frame Memory.

·   Exit **msd** by pressing the function key **F3.**

Step 11 -   **Load DOS into High Memory by adding** dos=high **to the** CONFIG.SYS **file.**

·   Type **edit config.sys**

·   Press **Enter.**

·   Add **dos=high** as the last statement in the **CONFIG.SYS** file.

·   Save the changes.

Step 12 -   **Reboot your computer to view the changes.**

Step 13 -   **View the effects of the** dos=high **statement, using the DOS** mem **command.**

·   Type **mem /c |more**

·   Press **Enter.**

·   Record the amount of **Total Conventional Memory** _____.

·   Compare this to the results of Step 4.

DOS MEMORY OPTIMIZATION

Step 14 - **Add the** noems **command to the end of the**
device=c:\dos\emm386.exe **statement in the** CONFIG.SYS **file.**

· Type **edit config.sys**

· Press **Enter.**

· Add **noems** to the end of the **emm386.exe** line.
The line should read:

device=c:\dos\emm386.exe noems

· Save the changes.

· Reboot your computer.

Step 15 - **Run the** MSD **Program to see your changes and
note that the Page Frame is now gone.**

· Type **msd**

· Press **Enter.**

· Press **m** and notice that the **noems** prevented **Page
Frame** from being created.

· Exit **msd** by pressing the function key **F3.**

Step 16 -   **Add the** umb **statement to the** CONFIG.SYS **file to create Free Upper Memory Blocks.**

·   Type **edit config.sys**

·   Press **Enter.**

·   Add the **umb** statement to the **dos=high** statement. The line should read **dos=high, umb**

·   Save the changes and reboot your PC.

Step 17 -   **Run the** MSD **Program and look for the creation of Upper Memory Blocks. (These are the areas designated by FF.)**

·   Type **msd**

·   Press **Enter.**

·   Press **m** and look for the Free Upper Memory Blocks.

·   Exit **msd** by pressing the function key **F3.**

Step 18 -   **Loading a program into the** umb **area.**

·   Type **lh doskey**

·   Press **Enter..** (This will load the **DOSKEY** Program into Upper Memory.)

·   Type **msd**

·   Press **Enter.** View where the **DOSKEY** Program was loaded. (You should see four U's in the Upper Memory Area. This is the **DOSKEY** Program.)

·   Exit **msd** by pressing the function key **F3.**

Part Two: *Running the* MEMMaker Program *to optimize memory.*

Preparation

Rename your **AUTOEXEC.BAT** and **CONFIG.SYS** files to **autoexec.xxx** and **config.xxx**.

Step 1 -   **Create a new** AUTOEXEC.BAT.

·   Type **edit autoexec.bat**

·   Press **Enter.**

·   Add the following lines:

         echo off

         path=c:\;c:\dos

         prompt=PG

         vsafe

         doskey

·   Save the new **AUTOEXEC.BAT** file.

Step 2 - **Create a new** CONFIG.SYS **file.**

· Type **edit config.sys**

· Press **Enter.**

· Add the following line:
   device=c:\dos\setver.exe

· Save the new **CONFIG.SYS** file.

Step 3 - **Reboot your computer.**

Step 4 - **Using the** mem **command to view and record the location (conventional or Upper Memory area) and size of the following** doskey **and** vsafe **programs.**

· Type **mem /c /p**

· Press **Enter.**

	LOCATION	SIZE
DOSKEY:	Conventional	4,144 K (4K)
VSAFE:	"	45,024 K (44K)
SETVER:	"	480 (0K)

How much Conventional Memory is Available? _540,480_

How much Extended Memory is Free? _0_

How much Upper Memory is Free? _0_

Part Three : *Running the* MEMMaker Program *to optimize the system.*
Compare the results with the information listed above.

Step 1 - **Run the MS DOS** MEMMaker **Program.**

· Type **memmaker**

· Press **Enter.**

· Choose **Custom Setup.**

· Respond **No** to **EMS Support.**

· Respond **No** to **Support Windows.**

· Toggle all the rest of the **Advanced Options** to **Yes**

· Press **Enter** to accept the **Windows Default Directory.**

· Respond **Yes** to optimize **setver** and **doskey.**

· Respond **No** to optimize **vsafe.**

· Press **Enter** to allow **MEMMaker** to **Optimize System.**

Step 2 - **The computer will automatically reboot twice.**

· Press **Enter** after the first reboot.

Step 3 - **If the computer boots the second time, respond** Yes.

Step 4 -   **Note any changes that MEMMaker has made.**

·   Press **Enter** to exit.

Step 5 -   **View the** AUTOEXEC.BAT **and** CONFIG.SYS **and note the changes that were made.**

·   Type **type autoexec.bat**

·   Press **Enter.**

·   Note changes.

·   Type **type config.sys**

·   Press **Enter.**

·   Note changes.

Step 6 -   **Use the** mem **command to compare this to the results that you recorded in Part Two.**

Summary

In this section, we discussed the reasons for optimizing memory and conducted hands-on labs. No one memory configuration will work for all computer systems. In fact, optimizing a computer's performance is the process of finding and establishing settings that are unique to that particular system.

Most optimizing is a process that involves manipulating a computer's memory. As mentioned in the previous section, DOS and DOS programs are limited to the first 640KB of memory (conventional memory), so the process of managing or optimizing memory under DOS usually involves freeing up as much of that memory as possible.

Review Questions

1. HMA is the first 64KB of _____ Memory.

    A. Conventional

    B. Expanded

    C. Base

    ✗ D. Extended

2. Conventional Memory starts at __0__KB and ends at __640__KB.

3. Which MS DOS Program will optimize your system's memory?

    A. **DOSKEY**

    B. **MEM**

    ✗ C. **MEMMaker**

    D. **MEMORY**

4. Which of the following statements from the **CONFIG.SYS** file depicts the correct load order?

    A. **DEVICE=C:\DOS\EMM386.EXE**
       DEVICE=C:\DOS\HIMEM.SYS

    ✗ B. **DEVICE=C:\DOS\HIMEM.SYS**
       DEVICE=C:\DOS\EMM386.EXE

    C. **DEVICE=C:\DOS\SETVER.EXE**
       DEVICE=C:\DOS\EMM386.EXE
       DEVICE=C:\DOS\HIMEM.SYS

    D. **DEVICE=C:\DOS\HIMEM.COM**
       DEVICE=C:\DOS\EMM386.SYS

5. Using the **NOEMS** switch with:
    DEVICE=C:\DOS\EMM386.EXE NOEMS
    will not create Page Frame Memory.

    ✗ A. True

    B. False

6. The UMA Memory Area is located between _____ and _____.

    A. 0   - 640KB

   ✱ B. 640 - 1024KB

    C. 1024 - 16MB

    D. 640 - 740KB

7. What device will manage the Upper Memory Blocks?

    A.   **HIMEM.SYS**

    B.   **EMM387.EXE**

  ✗ C.   **EMM386.EXE**

    D.   **DOSKEY**

8. Extended Memory ranges from __1 MB__ to __16 MB__ on a 80286 machine, and __1 MB__ to __4 GB__ on a 80386 and above machine.

9. When using **MSD**, Free Memory Blocks are depicted by:

    A. BB

  ✱ B. FF

    C. UU

    D. FB

10. As a general rule of thumb, one set of optimized configuration files will work for most machines.

    A. True

  ✗ B. False

Section 8

Printers

Section 8: Printers

Introduction

A printer is a computer whose sole purpose is to convert electronic pulses into images on paper. Although printers come as a separate unit, they are an integral part of a computer system. Printer technology has kept pace with newer computers. Today's printers are able to handle increasingly large amounts of data and produce extremely high quality outputs for a variety of different applications. This section will focus mainly on electrophotographic printers (commonly called laser printers), their different components and how they produce a printed page. We will also briefly examine the other categories of printers, as there is a wide variety of printers in use today.

Objectives

When you've completed this section, you will be able to:

· Identify and describe the different parts of a laser printer.

· Identify and describe the different parts of the Image Formation System.

· Troubleshoot and diagnose common printer problems.

· Perform preventive maintenance.

Electrophotographic (EP) Printer

The term *laser printer* has become a generic name to describe printers that utilize an electrophotographic process to produce images on paper. The fact is there are many "*laser printers*" on the market which do not use laser beams to write image data.

Instead, they utilize a bar of microscopic *light-emitting diodes (LEDs)* or arrays of *liquid crystal shutters (LCS)* to accomplish the same task. There is a big difference between *electrophotographic (EP)* printers and their more inexpensive counterparts. EP printing is a process that involves the interaction of many areas within the printer. Dot matrix and ink-jet printing, on the other hand, are the result of a single event: the printing head creating an image directly on paper.

The collection of parts that produce EP prints is known as an Image Formation System (IFS) and it consists of several distinct components:

BASIC COMPONENTS OF AN IMAGE FORMATION SYSTEM

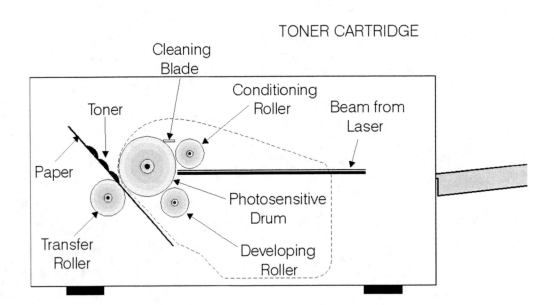

The Parts of an Image Formation System	
The photosensitive drum (PS drum)	An aluminum cylinder coated with a photoconductive material, which conducts electricity when exposed to light. This is a very delicate instrument. It can be permanently damaged if exposed to unfiltered light.
The erase lamp assembly	Clears or erases images from the PS drum by shining a strong beam of light across the drum's surface.
The primary corona	A thin wire located in the disposable toner cartridge. A highly negative charge is applied to the wire creating an electrical corona effect that is used to condition the PS drum. The static charges in the corona may reach -6000 Volts, making it the highest electrically charged component of the printer.
The writing mechanism	Writes images onto the PS drum by producing and directing light to its surface. There are three types of writing mechanisms for EP printers: a laser beam or scanner; bars of light emitting diodes (LEDs), or arrays of liquid crystal shutters (LCS)s.
Toner	An extremely fine powder composed of plastic resin and organic compounds bound to iron particles.
The transfer corona	Operates in the same way as the primary corona, except that this wire carries a positive charge. Its function is to place a positive charge on paper.
Fusing assembly	Consists of two rollers that apply a combination of heat and pressure to fuse toner to the paper. As the paper goes between the two rollers, heat from the top roller melts the toner while pressure from the bottom roller squeezes it into the paper fibers. A lot of heat is generated at this station. Make sure that the material you are printing on will not melt below 180°F.

EP Printer Components

All printers have to process electronic data to produce images. An **interface controller** is the printer's motherboard. It performs several functions:

- Communicates with the host computer via one of three installed interface ports (parallel, serial, or direct video interface).

- Manipulates incoming data for translation to the print engine.

- Monitors the control panel for user input.

- Provides information on printer status at the display and through various LED's.

- Stores configuration and font information.

The interface controller is very similar to the motherboard in the PC. It contains a CPU, memory (RAM) and a System Bus.

Electromechanical Components	
AC power supply	Provides energy for the fusing assembly heaters and the erase lamp assembly.
DC power supply	Converts AC into the various levels of DC needed to power electronics and electromechanical devices.
High-voltage power supply	Used to create and dissipate the powerful static charges (1000 V or more) needed to move toner within the printer.
Main motor	Provides the mechanical force needed to support mechanical activity within the printer.
Paper control assembly	Provides sensors that monitor and detect the presence of paper at every area in the IFS.
Main logic assembly	Consists of most of the circuitry that operates the printer and the electronics that interface with the host computer.
EP cartridge	A replaceable cartridge that contains the toner supply. It also includes delicate, wear-prone parts such as the primary corona, the EP drum, and the developer roller.
Control panel assembly	Provides the user with the means to select different printer's operating modes.

Printing Process

As mentioned earlier, printing is a series of events combined to produce a printed page. This complicated process creates sharp printed images in extremely high resolution. But it also increases the potential for problems. It is important that you understand each of the steps in the printing process, not only to prepare for the *A+ Certification* test, but also so you will be able to troubleshoot laser printers. Understanding each step in the process will enable you to more efficiently identify, diagnose and isolate potential laser printing problems.

SPECIAL NOTE:

A+ Certification candidates must know these steps.

Step-by-Step Description of the Laser Printing Process

Know 6 steps for exam

Step 1: Drum Preparation (Cleaning)

Before a new page can be printed, the *photosensitive drum* must be cleaned. (This process could be listed as the last or the first step of the printing process.) The cleaning process is accomplished by a rubber cleaning blade that gently scrapes any residual toner from the drum. The drum is then exposed to a lamp (the erase lamp) that will completely remove the last image.

Step 2: Conditioning (Charging)

After the cleaning/erase process, the drum is no longer light sensitive and it needs charging. This is done by applying a uniform negative charge (about 6000 volts) to the drum's surface. This is accomplished by a very thin solid wire called the *primary corona* located very near the drum's surface.

Step 3: Writing

During the writing process a latent image is formed on the drum surface. The uniform negative charge from the previous step becomes discharged at precise points where the image is produced. The actual writing is done with the *laser*. Where the laser strikes the drum will now become less-negatively charged.

Step 4: Developing

After the writing process the image is no more than an invisible array of electrostatic charges on the drum's surface. The *toner* is used to develop it. When the toner is ready to be applied, it is exposed to a cylinder (*developer roller*) that contains a permanent magnet. It is here that the toner receives a strong negative charge. The areas of low charge on the drum now attract the toner from the cylinder. This will fill-in the electromagnetic image. The other areas repel the equally negatively charged toner. The drum now holds an image that is ready to be transferred to the paper.

Step 5: Transfer

At this point, the developed image is transferred to the paper. The paper is exposed to the *transfer corona* which fixes a powerful positive charge to the paper that allows it to pry the negatively charged toner particles from the drum.

Step 6: Fusing

After the transfer process, the toner image is only laying on the surface of the paper, held by a small charge. It must be permanently bonded to the paper before it can be touched. The *fuser assembly*, along with the *pressure roller*, melts and presses the image into the paper's surface.

Servicing Laser Printers

As previously stated, the *Image Formation System* of a printer consists of several distinct components. If any one of these components fails to function properly the quality of the printed material suffers. Because of the number of components involved in the printing process, the potential for problems is high. Diagnosing a problem requires some intuition, the proper equipment and a logical troubleshooting approach.

Troubleshooting Cycle

The need for a logical troubleshooting approach cannot be overstated. No matter how complex the system may be, a simple four step procedure should help you to pinpoint the cause of the printer's problems.

Step 1: Define the Symptoms

In order to diagnose an illness, a doctor must first study the symptoms. The same concept applies here. If a printer is not working properly, take a close look at what it is (or is not) doing. This will make it easier for you to trace the problem to the right cause. Remember: it is always a good idea to take notes.

Step 2: Identify and Isolate

Never assume the printer is the cause of the problem. Remember, the printer is one piece of a larger system, which includes the computer and the cable connecting them. You could try connecting the suspect printer to a different computer, or try connecting a similar printer to the computer. Once you've determined that the printer is at fault, then you can start examining the components to find the cause of the problem.

Step 3: Repair or Replace

When you determine which component(s) is failing, you will then need to determine if you should replace them, or whether you should attempt to repair them. The solution could be as simple as cleaning the component in question. Or, if the problem is more severe, it may require replacing parts.

Depending on your level of expertise and knowledge, you may decide to replace small electronic components within the different subassemblies. NOTE: This can be a risky undertaking since many small parts are only obtainable through the manufacturer who may refuse to sell to anyone other than their authorized distributors.

If you are able to obtain new parts, there is nothing wrong with replacing a defective subassembly with a new one. However, be sure to keep the pieces well organized. Labeling may be tedious but, in the long run, it will save you the anxiety and frustration of not remembering how the components should to be reassembled.

Step 4: Re-Test

After the repair is completed and the unit is reassembled, test the printer to ensure that you have successfully solved the problem. If the problem persists or new problems surface, you will need to repeat the troubleshooting process.

Things to Check Before You Open Your Tool Box

The following is a list of potential causes for printer problems to consider before performing any disassembly.

Electricity Supply

Laser printers consume a lot of energy and require a reliable and dedicated source of power. It is always a good idea to check the wiring schematic for the outlet feeding the printer to be sure it is not being shared with another device. The outlet wiring should be checked to make sure it is in good condition. Laser printers are also susceptible to device interference (electrical line pollution). Try to keep printer cables isolated.

Reset

Just as a computer may be rebooted when it stops responding to commands, the printer can be reset or powered down when it stops responding to commands. This will provide only a temporary solution. You will still need to get to the cause of the problem. When you reset the printer, any downloaded fonts or macros will be lost.

Cables

Cables that are not properly secured can be a source of problems. Any movement may loosen them enough to cause print errors. Cable length is another consideration. Parallel cables should not be longer than 10 feet. A serial cable, on the other hand, can extend up to 50 feet. If the printed material shows typographical errors that do not appear on screen, it may be due to a break in a parallel cable data pin. Switching cables should correct the problem.

Environment

Much of the energy a printer consumes is transformed into heat, so it is important to place it in a well-ventilated area to allow the heat to dissipate. Ventilation is also important to dissipate small amounts of ozone gas produced during the printing process. Aside from being a mild irritant to humans in small concentrations, ozone is also an oxidizer which may corrode components. Light is another factor that could shorten the life of the printer. The light used to write the image on the PS drum is red filtered. Do not expose the PS drum directly to light unless you intend to replace it.

Paper

Every printer manufacturer will recommend a specific type of paper to be used with the printer. Follow these recommendations. Using a cheaper lower grade paper may cause paper jams and distortion problems. Do not forget that damp paper may also affect the quality of the printout. Make sure to keep paper dry.

Preventive Maintenance

Shipping

Never ship a printer with a toner cartridge still inside. Depending on how the printer is handled during shipping, there may be a lot of toner to clean upon arrival. Toner is very difficult to remove from clothing. You may want to try cold water and soap to remove toner stains. Strong chemicals or hot water (heat) may only cause the toner to bond to the cloth fibers.

Periodic Cleaning

The following parts require some periodic cleaning:

Corona wires - A long cotton swab, some alcohol, and a good deal of care and patience are required to clean the coronas. Above all, be very gentle with the wires.

Registration and feed guide assemblies - Most of the time, the only thing that may collect on these assemblies is residual toner and paper fragments. A damp cloth should be enough to do the job.

Fusing assembly - Things have a tendency to stick to the fusing assembly due to the amount of heat generated by it. You must remove all contaminants very carefully to prevent scratching the surface of the roller. Use a little bit of alcohol and a soft cloth to clean the fusing assembly. (Let the assembly cool down before you clean it.)

Separation pawls - The pawls facilitate the separation of the paper from the fuser. They have a claw-like appearance and are located behind the fuser assembly. Contaminants attach to them creating a buildup that may scratch the Teflon-coated surface of the fuser assembly rollers. Once again, a cotton swab dipped in alcohol should be enough to remove any buildup.

Common Printer Problems and Solutions

Vertical white streaks on the page

This is a problem that generally occurs when any part of the two corona wires is covered with toner. Since the job of the coronas is to transfer an electric charge, any toner covering the wire will cause uneven charges to be transferred to the drum or the paper. The drum's surface would be improperly conditioned to attract sufficient toner, or, in the case of the transfer corona, the paper would be inadequately charged to bring about a full toner transfer, causing the vertical streaks on paper. A simple solution to this problem is to clean the corona wires. Some printers come equipped with a small brush or attachment specifically for this purpose.

Horizontal streaks

Take a look at the printed material. If the lines appear at regular intervals, then the problem lies with one of the rollers the paper passes by. To identify which roller, measure the distance between the marks and use that as an indication of the circumference of the roller is causing the problem

Smearing

Remember that toner remains loose on paper until it reaches the fusing rollers. Smearing could be the result of the roller not applying enough heat to fuse the toner. Although the fusing roller is covered with a Teflon-like substance to prevent anything from sticking to it, sometimes it may get scratched or something may get baked onto it. A good way to get rid of the problem is to inspect and clean the rollers with a soft cloth and some alcohol. Keep in mind that the roller generates heat (a lot of it) and alcohol is a flammable fluid. When heat and a flammable fluid socialize, they produce fire. Let the rollers cool down before you attempt to clean them. Smears can also be caused by trying to print on both sides of the same paper. Not all printers are designed to do this.

Faded prints

This is another problem caused by a dirty corona wire. Simply clean the coronas as described previously.

Printer picks up multiple sheets

In this case the problem may lie with the paper in use and not the printer. Dry, good quality laser printer paper is required for a proper feed. Also, if paper is exposed to humidity, chances are that it will not work very well with the printer. Always store paper in a dry area.

Paper jams

There are various causes to this problem. Double-sided printing is one cause or you may be using the wrong side of the paper to print. There are two different sides to a sheet of paper, the wax and the wire sides. The paper wrapper has an arrow indicating which side to print first. Again, it is always best to follow the manufacturer's suggestion to use specific paper types. Low grade paper may also cause jams. Check the paper wrapper or label to make sure that it is suitable for laser printer use.

Error 20 appears on the control panel display

This is an insufficient memory error. Adding memory to the printer is generally a good solution, but don't overlook the possibility that this may be a software-related problem.

Error 55 appears on the control panel display

This is an error flag that appears during start up. This problem can be traced to two circuit boards inside the printer, one that controls the charging and discharging of the corona wires (the *DC controller board*), and one that controls the serial and parallel interfaces (the *interface controller board*). When the printer starts up, the two boards run a communications test; if the test fails, the error signal is displayed. This may be an indication of a bad interface controller board that will need to be replaced. Before replacing the controller, try connecting the printer to a different outlet. Power noise is strong enough at times to cause interference between the two boards, and this may also trigger an error message.

Stalled print spooler

Windows creates a temporary file called a "spool" file on your hard disk where it stores the document information prior to printing the document. If the printer becomes stalled for some reason (out-of-paper, printer offline,etc.), click on the **Print Manager** icon on your desktop (Windows 3.x) or the **Printers** folder (Windows 95). The stalled printer should be clearly identified. Click **Resume** to clear and jump-start the printer to resume printing.

Wrong printer driver

If you receive an "*incompatible printer driver*" error message, contact your software manufacturer to obtain the most current driver for your particular printer if your printer is not listed when you installed the printer. To update the driver;

Window 3.x

· Click the **Control Panel** icon in the Main Program Group.

· Double-click the **Printers** icon.

· Click the **Add** button.

· Click on the first line **Install unlisted or updated printer driver**.

· Put the disk from the manufacturer with the new driver in your floppy drive.

· In the **Add** dialog box, type **A:** to direct the computer to your floppy drive and the disk with the new driver file.

· Click **OK.**

Windows 95

- Click **Start**, then **Settings.**

- Click **Printers** (or, from the **Control Panel**, click the **Printers** folder).

- Double-click the **Add printer** icon and the **Add Printer Wizard** will appear.

- Click **My Computer** to make changes to only *your* printer configurations not for the entire network.

- Click **Next>**

- Click the box next to the port the printer is directed to.

- Click **Next>**

- If your printer is not listed and you wish to install the printer driver from a disk, click **Have Disk**.

- If the correct drive is displayed, click **OK**. Otherwise, type in the letter for your floppy drive, then **OK**.

The new printer driver will be installed into the correct Windows directory.

Other Printers

Laser printers are not the only type of printer that you will encounter in the real world. There are at least two more categories of printers you will need to be aware of as an A+ Certified Technician. These two categories are impact printers (dot matrix) and non-impact printers (ink jet).

Dot Matrix Printers

Dot matrix printers fall under the broad heading of impact printers. This is the family of printers that uses a print head containing pins (generally 9 to 24) that are forced to strike an inked ribbon against the paper to form a character. The character is actually formed by a series of dots. The more dots, the better the print quality. This is why a 24-pin printer will cost more than a 9-pin printer.

Just as with laser printers, dot matrix printers have various components that are more likely candidates for failure than others. Some of the most common components that are prone to fail are listed below:

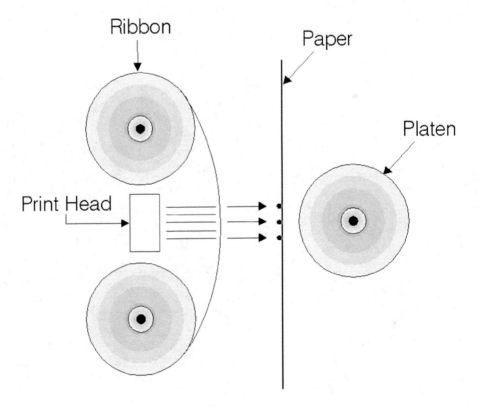

**DOT-MATRIX PRINTER
(IMPACT PRINTER)**

COMMON DOT-MATRIX PROBLEMS

Problem	Possible Cause
Light then dark print.	Most likely caused by a defective ribbon drive motor.
Consistent light, patchy print.	Could be caused by a dry or old ribbon.
Printer shuts down after getting hot, then restarts after a short while.	Replace the thermistor, a device that will shut down the printer after it reaches a certain temperature.
Characters not fully formed.	Could be a defective print head or broken pin.
Printer does not print.	Check to see if the printer is on-line and connected to the PC.
Prints continuously on the same line.	Check and replace the stepper motor (linespace).

Non-Impact Printers

Unlike impact printers, nothing is forced against the paper in non-impact printers. For the most part, non-impact printers use a technology called ink-jet to form the image on the paper. The print head in this case actually sprays a narrow stream of ink on the paper. Generally, ink-jet printers will yield a more fully-formed character than the dot-matrix. They are also much quieter than impact printers.

A disadvantage of ink-jet printers is that the cartridges tend to clog resulting in partial or no print at all. Another potential problem is that there is little warning when the cartridge is running out of ink. An ink-jet printer can go from perfect print to no print in just a few lines. With the dot-matrix, the ribbons progressively get lighter, giving you a little warning.

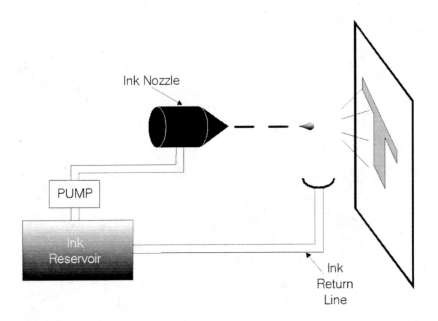

Ink Nozzle

PUMP

Ink Reservoir

Ink Return Line

NON-IMPACT PRINTER

Summary

A printer is a computer in itself that converts electronic pulses into images on paper. Printers are an integral part of a computer system. Today's printers are able to produce extremely high quality outputs for a variety of different applications. Laser printers are perhaps the most common in the business environment. It is important that you understand the components integral to the laser printer and the electrophotographic process. Regardless of the brand, most laser printers use this six-step process to produce the image on the paper:

- Cleaning
- Conditioning (charging)
- Writing
- Developing
- Transfer
- Fusing.

Laser printer technology is not the only process for printing. There are also two other categories of printers:

- Impact (dot-matrix)
- Non-impact (ink-jet).

Both of them have advantages and disadvantages over the other. When choosing between them, it is important to define what type of print jobs that you will be doing.

Review Questions

1. Which laser printing step puts a uniform negative charge on the drum's surface?

    A.   Cleaning

    B.   Developing

  ✳ C.   Conditioning

    D.   Transfer

2. During the laser printing process, what happens in the transfer stage?

    A.   Residual toner is removed.

    B.   The image is transferred to the drum.

    C.   A negative charge is transferred to the drum.

  ✳ D.   The image is transferred to the media.

3. In a laser printer, which component will least likely cause a paper jam?

    A.   The drum

    B.   The fuser roller

    C.   The sheet feeder

  ✳ D.   The laser scanner unit

4. Which laser component should never be exposed to sunlight?

  ✗ A.   The photosensitive drum

    B.   The corona wire

    C.   The toner cartridge

    D.   The paper

5. Which of the following laser components should be cleaned or replaced during preventive maintenance?

    A.   Scanner

    B.   Cleaning blade

  ✳ C.   Ozone filter

    D.   Toner cartridge

page 8-14

6. Light then dark print on a dot-matrix printer would typically be caused by:

    A. Print head alignment

    B. Print head overheating

  ✳ C. Erratic ribbon drive advancement

    D. Paper advancement

7. During preventive maintenance you should never lubricate:

    A. Paper advancement gears

  ✳ B. Print head pins

    C. Print head pulley

    D. Gear bus hinge

8. Your printer's power lamp LED is on, but the printer will not print. What should you do first to attempt to correct the problem?

    A. Replace the fuse.

    B. Replace the ribbon.

  ✳ C. Ensure printer is on-line.

    D. Turn the printer off.

9. Which of the following printers would be the best choice for printing on multipart forms?

    A. Ink-jet

  ✳B. Dot-matrix

    C. Thermal

    D. Bubble-jet

10. When storing laser paper which of the following should be considered? (Choose all that apply.)

  ✳ A. Location

  ✳ B. Temperature

  ✳ C. Humidity

    D. Ream size

Section 9

Networks

Section 9: Networks

Introduction

A network is a group of computers linked together for the purpose of sharing resources. More than half of all PCs in the world are connected to a network. Businesses not only need to share resources among personnel, but also need to manage and protect data by controlling and limiting access to information. Networks address these needs in various ways. In this chapter we will discuss different network set-ups and look at the parts that combine to form a network.

Objectives

When you've completed this section, you will be able to explain the following concepts:

· What is a Local-Area Network?

· Identify the components of a network.

· Describe the LOGON process.

· Identify the types of networks.

· Identify topology.

LAN (Local-Area Network)

A Local-Area Network is a group of computers that share information and other resources through a system of cables and network interface cards that links them together. As the name implies, a LAN links computers that are located relatively close to each other, as would be the case with a group of computers located in offices in the same building. Networks with widespread coverage linking cities or even countries are known as Wide-Area Networks (WAN). Networks address the need to share data and resources and also allow for the protection of data by controlling and limiting access to the information contained in them.

Components of a Network

Networks consist of two major areas, a physical and a logical. The physical network is the collection of hardware and peripherals linked together to build the network. The logical network is the software that manages the information going through the physical network. Here is a look at some of the components:

LAN
(Local-Area Network)

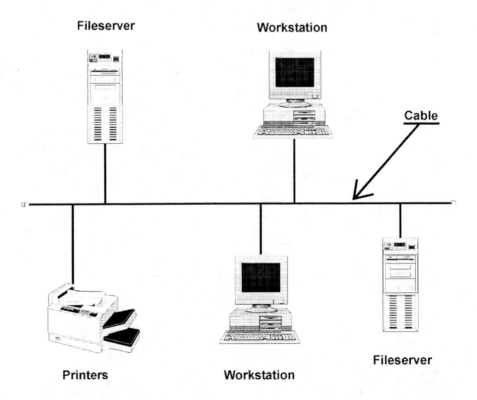

COMPONENTS OF A LOCAL-AREA NETWORK

Physical Components

Network Servers

The *server* is the heart of a network. It is a computer containing the network's operating system and it controls all LAN operations.

Workstations

The individual computers are called *workstations*. They connect independently to the server to retrieve applications and files as needed. To be part of the network, workstations need to have a Network Interface Card (NIC) to allow the PC to attach to the network cable. The workstation must also have enough memory (RAM) to support network applications.

Peripherals

Peripherals are the different components such as printers, modems, scanners, etc. shared by the workstations. The server controls the order in which the different workstations are serviced by peripherals.

NETWORKS

Network Cabling

Network cabling is a very specialized field. Cabling requirements vary depending on the protocol in use and the topology of the network. There are four major types of cable used in network installations:

- Unshielded Twisted Pair Wire (UTP)

- Shielded Twisted Pair Wire (STP)

- Coaxial Cable

- Fiber Optic Cable

Protocol

Before any communication can take place between computers, they first must agree upon a common language to speak. In the world of networks, this is referred to as the *protocol*. Some common LAN protocols are:

TCP/IP (Transmission Control Protocol/Internet Protocol)

TCP/IP is the major language used to communicate across the Internet. It is ideal for this task because of its ability to cross routers and connect different networks together.

NetBeui (Net BIOS Extended User Interface)

NetBeui, unlike TCP/IP, is called a non-routable protocol and is not suitable for large networks. However, NetBeui is a fast, reliable choice for small networks and workgroups. NetBeui support is built into Microsoft's networking products.

IPX (Internetwork Packet Exchange)

IPX is Novell's default protocol choice for its networking products.

Topology

The topology is the cabling pattern used to form the network. Examples of topologies are:

- Bus
- Star
- Ring

Bus Topology

The bus topology will typically consist of one main cable, referred to as the *backbone*. The individual computers and components of the network are attached to this main cable via shorter cables, called drop cables. It's important to note that if the cable breaks anywhere, the entire network will be affected. Each end of the main cable must include a device called a *terminator* to remove any signals from the wire after passing all workstations.

BUS TOPOLOGY

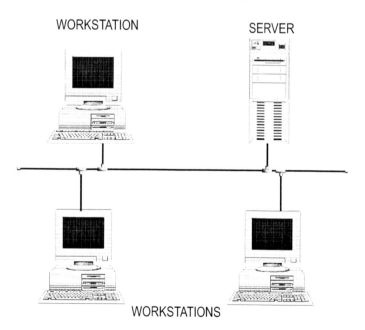

Star Topology

A star topology uses a central wiring device to connect all the individual computers to the network. Each device is connected to the network by a cable from the PC to a central device called a *hub* or *concentrator*. Multi-hubs and concentrators can be linked together to accommodate growth. A key advantage of the star topology as compared to the Bus is if a cable breaks between the PC and the hub, only that station is affected. This also facilitates the troubleshooting process.

STAR TOPOLOGY

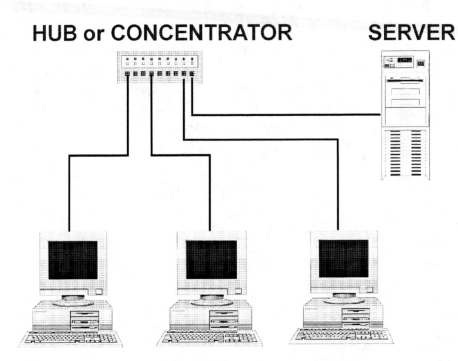

HUB or CONCENTRATOR　　　　　SERVER

USER WORKSTATIONS

NETWORKS

Ring Topology

As the name would imply, the ring topology connects the devices of the network in a circular fashion. Each network device connects directly to the ring or indirectly via a drop cable. Unlike a Bus topology, where the electrical signal can pass in both directions, the ring topology passes the signal from one device to the next, in one direction only.

RING TOPOLOGY

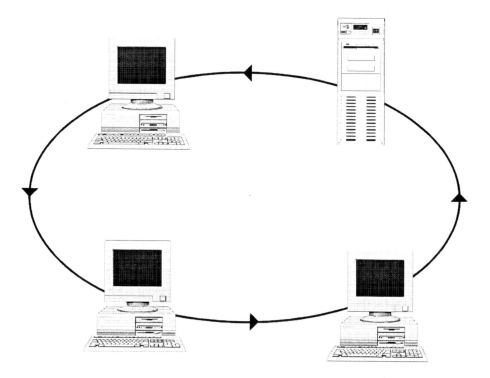

Logical Components

Network Operating System

A Network Operating System (NOS) is a group of programs that run on networked computers. It can be divided into two areas: *server* and *client* software.

Server Software

The *server software* has various functions: it manages the network, it prioritizes the applications' requests for network hardware resources, and it provides network security by controlling access to files. The NOS is also responsible for the *Logon* process. It's during the *Logon* process that a user sitting at a workstation will enter his/her unique *user ID* (*Logon name*) and *password* to gain initial access to the resources of the network.

LOGON

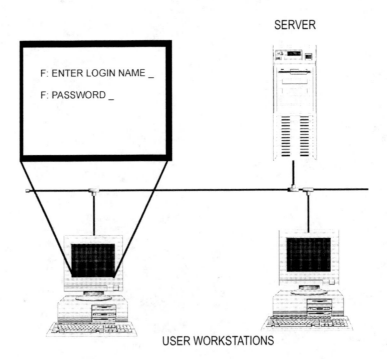

Client Software

The softwareloaded on the user's individual workstation is called the *client software*. Unlike the server software that controls overall access to the network, the client software is just responsible for making the connection between the workstation and the server.

The following are some of the different network operating systems available in today's market:

AppleShare   LAN Manager

IBM LAN Server   LANtastic

Banyan VINES   Novell NetWare

MS Windows 95   MS Windows NT

MS Windows for Workgroups

Different Types of Networks

Server-Based LAN

The concept behind a server-based LAN is that a single, dedicated computer provides all server functions to the network. The server runs a specialized multitasking operating system and stores the files and applications the workstations use. Information is retrieved or written to one or many hard drives inside the file server. This centralized approach allows the server to offer security and excellent data management. It also provides an almost unlimited capacity for expansion. Because of their complexity, server-based LANs represent a considerable investment in equipment, software and training. Novell and Microsoft both provide this type of platform.

Peer-to-Peer Networks

This type of network is simple and economical. Peer-to-peer networks utilize the resources of existing hardware to create the network. Instead of relying on one centralized server, peer-to-peer networks rely on many computers to provide server functions. All of the computers in the network share their resources (files, hardware and peripherals) with others. Windows 95 and *Artisoft's* LANtastic are both examples of peer-to-peer networks.

Summary

A LAN (Local-Area Network) is a group of computers that communicate through a cabling system. The goal of local-area networking is to provide a means of sharing common resources such as hard drives, files, printers and applications.

The LAN can be broken down into two major components: the physical (hardware) component, and the logical (software) component. The network hardware is made up of the server and workstation PCs, and peripherals such as printers and modems. The network operating system and the client software, along with any applications, comprise the logical components of the network.

The two basic types of networks are the server-based network and the peer-to-peer network.

NETWORKS

Review Questions

1. A LAN is a group of dumb terminals attached to a mainframe.

   A. True

   ✳ B. False

2. The acronym NOS stands for:

   A. Network On System

   B. Net Op System

   ✳ C. Network Operating System

   D. New Operating System

3. Which of the following are networking topologies: (Choose all that apply.)

   ✳ A. Ring

   B. Open

   ✳ C. Star

   ✳ D. Bus

   E. Road

4. The _____ determines the language that the server and workstation will use to communicate.

   A. Rule

   B. TCP

   ✳ C. Protocol

   D. Topology

5. The letters TP, when used in reference to computer cabling, stand for:

   A. Two Pair

   B. The Pair

   ✳ C. Twisted Pair

   D. Three Pair

6. *Microsoft's* Windows 95 would be an ideal choice for this type of workgroup:

      A. Client server

      B. WAN

    ✱ C. Peer-to-peer

      D. MAN

7. This type of topology connects every device to the network via a point-to-point connection to a central HUB or concentrator:

      A. BUS

      B. RING

      C. RANG

   ✱ D. STAR

8. The LOGON process typically would require the user to enter a unique:

      A. number and password

      B. phone number

      C. name

   ✱ D. user-name and password

9. A Novell client server network would most likely use which of the following protocols?

      A. TCP/IP

      B. NetBeui

      C. SOFAST

   ✱ D. IPX

NETWORKS

Section 10

Preventive Maintenance

MAINTENANCE

Section 10: Preventive Maintenance

Introduction

Have you ever heard the saying, "An ounce of prevention is worth a pound of cure?" This saying certainly holds true for computer equipment. Electronic equipment is delicate. If you want it to last and provide you with peak performance during its life, then you need to maintain it properly and protect it from potential harm. The focus of this chapter is two-fold. First, we will talk about things you can do to minimize or eliminate damage from outside sources. Then we will outline the steps for developing a good Preventive Maintenance program.

Objectives

When you've completed this section, you will be able to do the following:

- Recognize harmful external influences for computer equipment.

- Understand the possible damage that could be caused by stray electromagnetism, power-related problems, water and other liquids and corrosive elements.

- Run a comprehensive preventive maintenance program.

- Review the recommendations for cleaning the parts of a PC.

MAINTENANCE

Harmful Influences

In order to better understand what steps to take to better care for a PC, we need to know what things affect it adversely.

Internal Heat

Chips and other internal components are continuously generating heat. This is why most computers are equipped with fans. The fan helps to dissipate heat as quickly as possible. If the fan fails, the heat continues to build and there is a strong likelihood that the chips will suffer damage. Computer manufacturers spend large amounts of time and money engineering case design to create optimal air flow. Always replace slot covers over empty slots. The air flow may change enough to cause heat related problems if the slots are left open.

Heat from Direct Sunlight

If the computer sits under direct sunlight, it adds an additional heat source for the fan to combat. It may cause the fan to fail, or it may cause the system to overheat. Hardware manufacturers recommend specific operating temperature ranges for their products. A typical range would be a minimum of 60° F and a maximum of 85° F. Individual components are rated for much higher temperatures. Circuit boards, for example, are rated for a maximum of 125° F and hard drives for 110° F These may sound like safe numbers, but typically the interior of a computer will run approximately 40° F higher than the room temperature. On a hot summer day, you may well exceed the operating range for these parts.

Thermal Shock

Thermal shock occurs as a result of rapid cooling or rapid heating of computer components. This occurs most often during the winter months when an office computer may be exposed to cold temperature settings during a weekend and then rapid heating as the office is heated again during the week.

Dust

When dust settles on a surface it may act as a thermal insulator, helping to create a larger heat build up. It may also permeate sensitive areas like the space between the disk drive heads and the disk, causing mechanical failure.

Magnetism

Magnetism could cause you to loose data on the hard drive or on floppy disks. The following is a list of common objects in an office that are a source of magnetic fields:

- Small electric motors from office equipment.

- Magnetic screwdrivers.

- Magnetic clip holders.

- Magnetic paper holders.

MAINTENANCE

Stray Electromagnetism

Electromagnetic Interference (EMI)

Electromagnetic interference is particularly problematic in network environments. Wires carry electronic pulses that produce magnetic fields as a side effect. When two or more wires are in close proximity to each other, their magnetic fields cross and produce additional electronic pulses or echoes. These echoes are then carried by the wires causing interference.

Radio Frequency Interference (RFI)

Radio frequency interference is radiation emitted in the frequency range of radio waves. Have you ever taken a portable radio into a car and heard it hum in synch with the engine? This is radio frequency interference. Additional sources are:

- High speed digital circuits (like the ones in your computer)
- Nearby radio sources
- Cordless telephone
- Power line intercoms
- Electric motors

Power-Related Problems

Electric utility companies are supposed to provide users with a constant and regular supply of energy all the time. But for many reasons, the energy that comes out of your outlet does not always flow evenly. Power suffers very brief variations in the form of drops (sags) and surges. These power fluctuations cause very harmful effects on your PC, both in the short-term and over time.

Voltage Surges and Sags

Surges and sags in voltage are the most common type of power-related problems. The nature of surges may be such that they slip past the built-in protection in your computer's power supply and go directly to the chips. Damage may not become evident the very first time a voltage surge passes into your system. More than likely it will have a cumulative effect that will slowly destroy one or more components.

Sags, on the other hand, have a different effect, especially if they endure for an extended period. Extended drops in voltage are commonly known as brown-outs. When these occur, the power supply tries to compensate for the loss of voltage by drawing more current. This causes chips and other components to heat up and may even cause them to overheat.

MAINTENANCE

Electrostatic Discharges

We've already talked about the causes and dangers of ESD. But since the subject is a very critical one, here are a few more tips on how to control electrostatic potential build up.

- Install a static-free carpet.

- Raise the humidity level in a room through the use of an evaporative humidifier, (ultrasonic humidifiers create dust) or by adding some plants to the environment.

- Make use of anti-static mats under your PC.

Water and Other Liquids

Most liquid damage caused to computer equipment occurs when the computer user spills a beverage on the keyboard, the mouse, or even the monitor. The computer case has a nice flat surface that some people may find suitable for resting a soda or cup of coffee. These and other fluids will oxidize and corrode metals, and can diminish their conductive properties.

A second, more hazardous problem occurs when fluids mix with electricity. At the very least, this combination could cause a component to short. The most dangerous effect of combining water and electricity is the possibility of electric shock. Remember, the system is plugged into an electrical outlet!

The best way to avoid fluid damage is to provide a secure spot for the computer. Rest the case on a stand above the floor to preclude the possibility of flood damage. The keyboard can be protected by covering it with a plastic "keyboard skin."

MAINTENANCE

Corrosive Elements

The major problem with corrosion is that it affects the conductive properties of metals. Household cleaners contain chemicals such as ammonia, various acids, sulfurs, etc. that have a corroding effect on any metal they come in contact with. Mist particles from spray bottle cleaners may find their way inside a computer case, causing some damage. When cleaning your computer, use a damp cloth with a mild mix of soap and water. You may also want to dust off components with compressed air. However, be careful not to do it in the vicinity of other equipment otherwise you'll be moving dust from one component to the other.

Implementing a Preventive Maintenance Program

Let's summarize the previous section by outlining the steps necessary to provide a safe environment for PCs.

- Preferably, computers need to be in a cool, constant environment. But if changes in temperature are inevitable, take steps to ensure that the maximum operating temperature does not exceed 110° F and does not fall below 65° F.

- Eliminate the possibility of dust buildup on components. Regular internal component cleanups may help to alleviate this problem. Another way would be to utilize power supplies that come equipped with a filtered fan. This type of fan creates an opposite airflow pattern by filtering the air first, compared to regular fans, which filter the air after pulling it through the fan.

- Remove any magnetic sources from the computer's vicinity.

- Instruct computer operators on ESD damage and prevention. Provide an environment less conducive to ESD and make use of anti-static materials around the computer.

- Make sure the computer does not share the same electrical line that may supply energy to large electric motors such as the ones found in refrigerators or air conditioners and other smaller appliances. This may have the effect of causing power sags and surges as the appliances and motors turn on and off.

- Instruct operators on the potential dangers of liquid spills.

- Remove corrosive chemicals from the list of suitable computer cleaners and provide some other options.

MAINTENANCE

Troubleshooting/Repair Tools & Maintenance Procedures

Cleaning Tools

Your troubleshooting/repair toolbox should contain the following to clean and maintain computer equipment:

- Can of compressed air
- Dust-free cloth
- Glass cleaning liquid (Windex, etc.)
- Small brush
- Cotton swabs
- Hand-held vacuum cleaner
- WD-40 or teflon-based lubricant like Tri-Flow to lubricate the head rails of floppy drives
- A commercial connector cleaning product, such as TexWipe, to clean contacts and connections

Wear and Tear

Dust can clog air-intake areas which will result in excessive wear and heat-buildup within the CPU. Dust can also clog spaces such as the area between the floppy disk drive head and the disk. When you're installing a new peripheral card or performing other tasks inside the CPU, take the time to blow out the interior of the case with compressed air, being careful to aim the compressed air away from the machine. Otherwise, you're blowing the excess dust right back into the system.

PCs attract dust -- much the same as your television screen does. Don't smoke around your PC and be sure users are warned about consuming food or beverages while working at the computer. Nothing can damage a keyboard quicker than a spilled "Big Gulp" or that morning cup of coffee. A plastic skin can be used over a keyboard to protect it in high traffic areas where spills may occur.

To control ESD and EMI, don't plug heating elements into the same outlet as the PC. Keep the PC away from any vibration source, such as an impact printer.

When transporting or storing circuit boards or other components, always use anti-static protective tubes or bags. Be careful not to touch the fragile pins on a circuit board.

MAINTENANCE

Preventive Maintenance/Cleaning Recommendations

- **System Case -** Clean the system case, inside and out, on an annual basis. Wipe the case with a damp cloth but don't spray cleaning liquids directly on the case. Clean the inside by either blasting with compressed air or using a small vacuum with a PC cleaning attachment. Be sure to replace any slot covers that may have been removed. Slot covers are a good way to keep dust from the interior of the case.

- **Power Supply -** The main enemy of a power supply is overheating caused by excessive dust and dirt clogging the fan and coating the components. Inspect the fan regularly to ensure it is providing good ventilation and is not dirty. Clean it with the vacuum or compressed air. Also check the power protection devices to see that they are working properly.

- **Motherboard -** As part of the annual cleaning, clean the motherboard and expansion cards with a vacuum or compressed air to improve the cooling of the motherboard components. DO NOT clean the gold contacts on expansion cards with a pencil eraser. Over time, the abrasion can cause damage. Check the board for connectivity problems. Are all cards and cables making good contact. On older boards, check for "Chip creep" - chips that work their way out of their sockets due to repeated thermal expansion and contraction. Back up the system BIOS settings as a part of your annual maintenance routine.

- **Processor -** The system processor requires no maintenance, however, during the annual cleaning, touch the edge of the processor (or the edge of the heat sink as close to the processor as possible). If it's too hot to leave your finger on for more than a second, it's too hot. Consider adding a larger heat sink or a better cooling fan to improve the cooling level. Inspect and clean the heat sink and fan with a vacuum or compressed air.

- **System Memory** - SIMMs and DIMMS do not require maintenance, other than as part of the overall cleaning of the inside of the system. Check to be sure all memory modules are seated correctly in their slots.

- **Video Cards** - Clean the video card just as you did the expansion cards on the motherboard, with a vacuum or compressed air.

- **CRT** - Clean the monitor's screen weekly. Just like on a TV, the screen accumulates dust more quickly because of the static charge generated by the CRT. Wipe it with a soft cloth. Using the wrong cleaner can damage the special coatings used on many newer screens to reduce glare and improve image quality. Some cleaners may also leave smudges and streaks. Never use an abrasive cleaner on the screen. A damp, soft cloth is the best choice. Clean the outside of the CRT including the vents to prevent the cooling vents from becoming clogged with dirt.

- **Hard Disk Drives** - Newer hard drives generate a lot of heat. Be sure the system's interior has adequate cooling and ventilation. The annual general cleaning will reduce excessive dust buildup on the sealed hard drive unit. When the case is opened, check the hard drive for excessive vibration and heat. (Be sure the PC has been running for at least a half-hour before you open the case.)

- **Floppy Disk Drives** - Unlike hard disk drives, floppy drives are not sealed and are thus exposed to the outside air. Clean these drives quarterly, or more often if they are used often. Clean the read/write heads with either a Q-tip and alcohol or a special cleaning kit. Clean the inside of the drive with a vacuum or compressed air, just as you did the other components. Also check and adjust the alignment of the drive. A misaligned drive will lose its ability to read and write data.

MAINTENANCE

·   **CD-ROM Drive** - Most CD-ROMs can tolerate a good deal of dirt and dust. If you are experiencing errors reading disks that can be read in other CD-ROM drives, you can use a CD-ROM lens cleaner.

·   **Peripheral Ports** - Clean and check all connections as you perform the annual cleaning.

·   **Keyboards** - Over time, dirt and the natural oils from fingers accumulate on the keycaps and dirt and debris fall between the keys. Clean the keyboard with compressed air and/or the PC vacuum at least annually. Check for cable and connector damage.

·   **Mouse** - Clean the mouse on a monthly basis, including the mouse ball and the rollers on the inside of the unit. Check for cable and connector damage.

Safety/Environmental Repair Considerations

High-Voltage Equipment

NEVER attempt to repair a monitor or a power supply. If you were to open a power supply or a monitor while the computer was plugged in (even if the power was OFF), you could receive a charge of the full 120 volts. Even if the PC is OFF, the capacitors store power and can shock you.

Laser Beams

When repairing a laser printer or other component that uses laser technology, avoid looking directly at the laser beam. Lasers have the potential to cause blindness.

Disposal of Used Materials

Consult your city's environmental regulations for the proper disposal procedure for potentially harmful materials such as batteries, monitors, toner kits/cartridges, circuit boards, cables and chemical cleaning solvents. You should always check your local laws concerning disposal of batteries or toxic cleaning supplies.

Material Safety Data Sheets (MSDS)

Ask the vendor or manufacturer of a cleaning solvent or other chemical product you use regularly for the product's MSDS. These sheets provide specific handling procedures and safety precautions to minimize the risk to health and environment when they are used and disposed of in the workplace.

MAINTENANCE

Summary

Computer equipment is delicate and expensive. If you want it to last and function properly, you need to conduct regular maintenance on your equipment. Take steps to protect it from potential harm. By recognizing those elements which may damage or interfere with a PC's performance, you will be able to create a safe operating environment for your computer.

Review Questions

1. What is the term for the rapid cooling or rapid heating of computer components?

    A. Shock

    B. Hot/cold transfer

✸ C. Thermal shock

    D. Thermal reduction

2. Magnetic screwdrivers are very helpful and safe when working with computer components.

    A. True

✸B. False

3. When some electrical equipment produces undesirable magnetic fields, it is called what?

    A. EMB

✸ B. EMI

    C. Field Shock

    D. Stratus noise

4. Electronic components are not sensitive to dust because they are hermetically sealed.

    A. True

✸ B. False

5. Which of the following describes the sudden drop of voltage on an AC line?

✸A. Sag

    B. Drop

    C. Surge

    D. Null

MAINTENANCE

Section 11

Windows 3.1

Section 11: Windows 3.1

Introduction

Windows (versions 3.1 and 95) presents applications and functions in a user-friendly, colorful, and consistent graphical environment. Through the use of menus and dialog boxes, Windows 3.1 enables you to manage the information on your hard disk without the hassle of remembering and typing multiple commands.

This very familiar characteristic of the Windows operating system is known as the graphical user interface (GUI). All programs and accessories are organized and represented through windows or icons.

For *A+ Certification*, there are some key concepts you will need to understand about Windows 3.1. First, you will need to know how Windows is installed and what preparations should be made before installing.

You will need to know how Windows 3.1 works with DOS-based programs and understand how Windows uses Program Information Files (PIFs) to properly operate these programs. You must also know how to use the main Windows 3.1 applications that control Windows to manage files, printers and other devices.

Finally, because Windows' graphical interface is so memory-intensive, you will need to know how to effectively manage memory in the Windows environment.

Objectives

When you've completed this section, you will be able to:

· Install Windows 3.1.

· Discuss and create a Windows **.PIF** file.

· Work with the Windows 3.1 applications.

· Discuss and modify **.INI** files.

· Manage memory in the Windows 3.1 environment.

Installing Windows

Prior to Windows, the most common application installation program was **INSTALL.EXE**. Windows 3.x and Windows 95 both use **SETUP.EXE** as the default installation program file.

To run efficiently, Windows 3.1 must have access to the following hardware and software:

- An 80486 processor. (The minimum requirement is an 80286.)

- 8 MB of RAM. (The minimum requirement is 2MB.)

- MS DOS 6 or higher.

- A mouse.

- A hard drive with enough space to accommodate your choice of software, plus some additional space for temporary and swap files.

Some hard drive maintenance is recommended and desirable prior to installing Windows 3.1. This may be accomplished by using the **SCANDISK** utility contained in MS-DOS. A hard drive is analogous to a filing cabinet: computer files are easier to access when they are well organized.

Occasionally, file pieces may become separated or lost during use, and lay scattered on the hard drive's surface taking up unnecessary space. After awhile, this situation may contribute to decreased hard drive performance. Windows performance is tied to the hard drive's performance, so it is a good idea to fine-tune the drive before the installation.

The First Step

·   Browse through the directory tree on your hard drive and delete all programs and files that you no longer need.

·   Once those unwanted files are removed, type **scandisk** at the prompt.

·   Press **Enter.** This utility will check the hard drive for errors, remove all lost file fragments, and reorganize the rest of the files.

·   To begin the install of Windows 3.1 on your system, switch to the appropriate disk drive in your PC.

·   Insert the installation disk.

·   Type **setup** at the prompt.

The Windows **SETUP** is a colorful and graphics-oriented environment. Throughout the installation process, it will prompt you make choices about how you want Windows to work.

Express or Custom Installation

You will be asked to choose between an Express or a Custom installation. The Express option does not require a lot of Windows or PC knowledge. It automatically determines the settings and hardware configuration on your computer and proceeds to install system defaults that logically match your PC.

The **AUTOEXEC.BAT** and **CONFIG.SYS** files are automatically modified and saved. Express Setup is not very flexible and utilizes many system defaults which may not always be optimal for your computer.

The Custom installation requires a more in-depth knowledge of your PC. Setup will ask you to confirm that the hardware it detected, such as the video adapter and the mouse, are correct. It allows you to select which printers and what Windows components you wish to work with. It will also ask you to select which installed software will have windows and icons.

The **AUTOEXEC.BAT** and **CONFIG.SYS** files are modified but they are not saved until you manually edit or accept the changes. A custom installation allows much greater flexibility and enables the user to install only those files that are needed.

Exercise 11.1: Installing Windows 3.1

Objective

When you've completed this exercise, you will be able to install Windows 3.1 using the custom installation option.

Preparation

You will need at minimum an 80286 computer with at least 2MB RAM and the Windows setup diskettes.

Step 1 - **Boot your computer to DOS and run the Windows setup program.**

· Insert Windows 3.1 Disk 1 into drive A.

· Change to Drive A

· Type **setup**

· Press **Enter.**

· Press **Enter** again to bypass the Welcome Screen.

Step 2 - **Select option C to run the custom installation.**

Step 3 - **Press Enter to accept the Default Windows Location.**

Step 4 - **Review the system list, making changes as necessary**

· Press **Enter** to accept and continue.

The setup program will now copy Preliminary Files to your hard disk. This will take a few minutes. Be patient.

Step 5 - **When prompted by the system, insert Windows Disk 2.**

· Press **Enter** to continue.

WINDOWS 3.1

Step 6 -   **Insert other Windows diskettes as prompted.**

Step 7 -   **Personalize your copy of the Windows program.**

- When prompted, enter your name and any company name you want.

- Press **Enter** to continue. You will be asked to verify the information.

- Press **Enter** to continue.

Step 8 -   **You will now see the components that Windows will install.**

- Press **Enter** to accept the defaults.

Step 9 -   **Press Enter to accept the Default Windows Groups.**

Step 10-   **Press continue to create a Permanent Swap File. Window setup will now do a file copy. Be patient.**

Step 11 -   **When prompted, insert the Windows Disk 4.**

- Press **Enter** to continue.

Step 12 -   **When prompted, insert the Windows Disk 5.**

·   Press **Enter** to continue.

Step 13 -   **Allow Windows setup to modify your** AUTOEXEC.BAT
and CONFIG.SYS **files.**

·   Press **Enter** to continue.

Step 14 -   **Install a printer.**

·   Select **HP Desk Jet**

·   Click **Install**. (This can be changed later.)

Step 15 -   **Insert Disk 6.**

·   Click **OK**.

Step 16 -   **Select** Continue.

Step 17 -   **Select** Cancel **when you are asked to setup
Applications.**

Step 18 -   **Choose** Skip Tutorial.

Step 19 -   **Click** Reboot the System.

MindWorks, *a BrightStar Company* © 1999

Starting Windows

Once the installation is complete, you must reboot the computer to activate the changes. Windows may then be started by typing **WIN** at the DOS prompt.

The Windows 3.1 command program is invoked (**WIN.COM**) and it starts by loading the Windows logo and checking the computer's hardware configuration to determine if Windows 3.1 starts in Standard or 386-enhanced mode.

Next, it takes control of the computer's memory resources. After that, Windows goes through a long list of configuration commands contained in the **SYSTEM.INI** file.

Among other things, the **SYSTEM.INI** file contains device drivers to access the keyboard and the mouse. Other **.INI** files are read and loaded depending on the hardware and peripherals required by the different applications. Finally, the **Program Manager** is loaded with all applications and is displayed on screen ready to work.

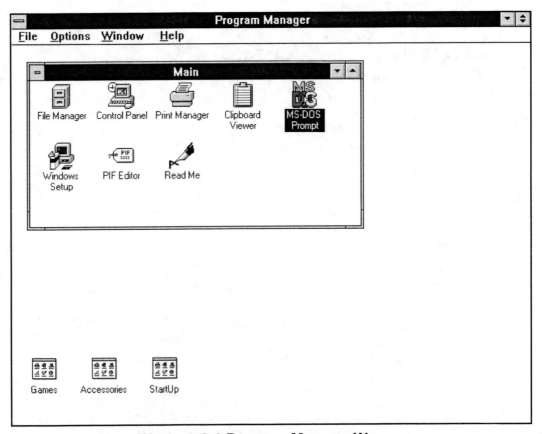

WINDOWS 3.1 PROGRAM MANAGER WINDOW

Installing Non-Windows-Based Applications

Non-Windows-based applications (DOS applications) may be installed during the Windows 3.1 installation process or at a later time. For any new application, the best option is to run Windows **Setup** (included in the **Main** group from **Program Manager**). **Setup** creates groups and icons, and if available, it also creates a **.PIF** (Program Information File) for the new program. Once groups and icons are created, the program may be started by selecting the application's icon.

WINDOWS 3.1

Creating and Using Program Information Files (.PIFs)

A **.PIF** is a file that contains information about a DOS application. Any time a DOS program is started, Windows 3.1 refers to the application's **.PIF** file to obtain information such as memory and video mode requirements. If Windows is unable to locate the application's file, it uses a **DEFAULT.PIF**. Most DOS applications will work with the default set up, but if required, the **.PIF** may be modified to accommodate the particular needs of an application. This can be accomplished through the use of the **PIF Editor** located in the **Main** group window.

.PIFs may be set up in three ways:

1. Through the Windows **Setup** program.

2. Using or modifying the **DEFAULT.PIF**.

3. Using the **.PIF** that came with the DOS application

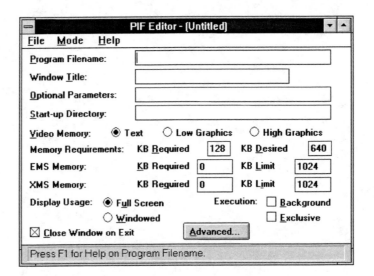

WINDOWS 3.1 PIF EDITOR

Exercise 11.2: Creating a PIF (Program Information File)

Objectives

Uses of the Windows PIF Editor to create a Program Information File for a non-Windows application.

Preparation

Ensure that the system is loaded with Windows 3.1 and a copy of the MS DOS Diagnostic Program (**MSD**).

Step 1 - **Open the Main Program Group**

· Double-click the **PIF Editor** icon.

Step 2 - **Create a PIF to run the MSD (Diagnostic Program).**

· Enter the following information:

Program File Name: **MSD.EXE**

Window Title: **Microsoft Diagnostic**

Start-up Directory: **C:\DOS**

XMS Memory KB Limit: **1024**

Leave all others at default.

WINDOWS 3.1

Step 3 - **Name and save the file.**

- Click **File**

- Click **Save As.**

- Name the file **DIAG.PIF**

- Click **OK.**

- Click **File.**

- Click **Exit.**

Step 4 - **Now create a Program Item for the newly created PIF.**

- Click **File.**

- Click **New.**

- Click **OK** to **Create Program Item.**

- Enter **Microsoft Diagnostic** for description.

- Press the **TAB** key.

- Click the **Browse** Button and locate the **DIAG.PIF.**

- Click **OK.**

- Click **OK** again.

Step 5 - **Double-click your new Program Icon. Does the Program start?**

Windows 3.1 Applications

There are many applications that are included in a Windows 3.1 installation. The most frequently used applications are the **Program Manager**, the **Control Panel**, the **Print Manager**, and the **File Manager**. You will need to be familiar with the functions that can be performed by these programs.

Program Manager

Program Manager is the environment through which the user interacts with the applications and hardware in the computer. It starts when Windows 3.1 starts and remains active as long as you are working with Windows. It allows the user to control and organize Windows applications and files.

The **Program Manager** window contains the following elements:

Program Manager Window	
Group Icons	Windows 3.1 creates an icon for each application it controls. All applications appear on the Program Manager as a small window. The name of the application is at the bottom of the window.
Group Windows	These are separate windows inside the Program Manager window. Once a program or group icon is selected, the window for that particular application opens up and displays program-item icons or icons that start applications.
Program-Item Icons	These icons are located inside the Group windows and represent documents, accessories or applications. If an icon is selected, it will activate the utility that it represents. An icon can exist in any or all program groups any number of times.

WINDOWS 3.1 PROGRAM MANAGER WINDOW

WINDOWS 3.1

Control Panel

Control Panel is the application that allows you to customize Windows to your needs. The **Control Panel** window is included in the **Main** group window from **Program Manager**. The following listing provides a brief description of the utilities contained in **Control Panel**.

WINDOWS 3.1 CONTROL PANEL

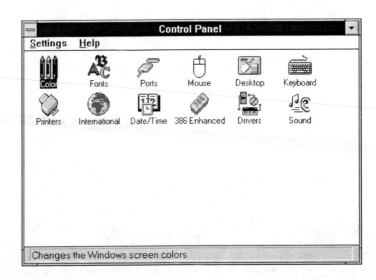

Control Panel	
Color	Changes the colors of the Windows environment.
Fonts	Adds or removes fonts.
Ports	Configures communications ports and establishes IRQ interrupt settings.
Mouse	Allows adjustments to the speed of the pointer and configures mouse button operation (left or right hand).
Desktop	Configures the screen saver operation and allows changes to the desktop patterns.
Keyboard	Controls the keyboard rate of repeating.
Printers	Adds or removes printer drivers and defines the appropriate ports.
Internat'l	Controls date, time and currency formats, also resets the keyboard layout for different languages.
Date/Time	Resets the computer's date and time.
386 Enh	Configures Virtual Memory and determines how applications run in 386 enhanced mode.
Drivers	Installs and configures Multimedia drivers such as sound boards, CD audio, and MIDI.
Sound	Assigns sound to different Windows events.

Print Manager

This special program manages all printing for Windows applications. When a print command is issued, the **Print Manager** intercepts the command and sends it to a buffer where these files are organized (queued) for printing. The files are sent to the printer in the order they were received. One of the main advantages of the **Print Manager** is that it works in the background. In other words, all printing takes place without interrupting your work. **Print Manager** may also be turned off. You would normally do this when print jobs are being sent through a network, or when you want an application (such as a word processor) to take over the printing process.

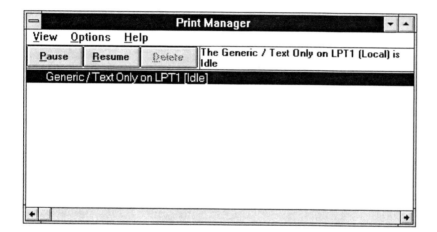

PRINT MANAGER WINDOW

WINDOWS 3.1

Print Manager allows you to perform the following operations:

Print Manager	
Install/remove printers	Any time a new printer is connected to the computer, it must be configured to operate under Windows. This is accomplished by installing the corresponding printer driver.
Assign printer ports	By default, Windows assigns port LPT1 for printer operations. This port may be changed if necessary.
Printer default settings	Settings such as paper size, print resolution, default font, and others can be changed by activating this dialog box.
Pause/resume printing	Pauses and resumes print jobs.
Change print order	This help in case you change your mind about the order in which documents are scheduled to be printed.

File Manager

File Manager is the tool that helps you organize and manage all the files in your hard drive. This is a very powerful utility and you must be careful using it, especially when using commands such as **Delete** and **Format**. A simple oversight could wipe out very important files. Or worse yet, you could start formatting your hard drive.

The **File Manager** window is divided into two parts. The left side shows you an expanded view of the directories and subdirectories (directory tree) on the selected drive. Each directory is graphically represented by a miniature folder with its name next to it. The right side shows a complete list of files contained in the selected subdirectory. At the bottom of the **File Manager** window appears a status bar displaying information such as the number of files and their size on the selected subdirectory.

FILE MANAGER WINDOW

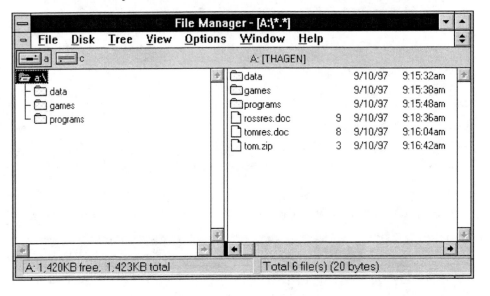

File Manager menus contain an extensive list of commands:

File Manager	
Disk utilities	Includes commands such as disk drive selection, disk copying, disk formatting, creation of system disks, and disk labeling.
File utilities	Used for directory creation, opening, moving, copying, deleting, renaming and printing files.
File Manager options	Customizes the way in which File Manager operates.
Directory Tree options	Customizes the way in which directory trees are presented on-screen.
Viewing options	Controls the amount of information presented on-screen to the user and also contains a file sort utility.
Windows settings	Customizes the Windows environment.

WINDOWS 3.1

Files and Type Formats

If you take a look at the contents of the Windows directory and subdirectories, you'll notice that there is a long list of files. These files can be recognized by Windows 3.1 and the different applications through their extensions. A file extension is the three character (alphanumeric) combination at the end of a file's name (name.xxx). Each application has its own kind of file extension.

Drivers

In Windows 3.1, applications and devices communicate through the use of device drivers. Drivers are software written to allow the operating system and interface to communicate with the hardware devices. Windows is a device-independent program. In the past, all programs had to directly control devices such as printers, modems, etc. Today, hardware and peripheral manufacturers provide device drivers with their products that act as translators between Windows and the device. New or modified versions of a device may be installed without upgrading to a new Windows version.

The following are some examples of device drivers:

System drivers	**SYSTEM.DRV**
Keyboard drivers	**KEYBOARD.DRV**
Display drivers	**VGA.DRV**

Accessories and Utilities

Windows 3.1 comes equipped with certain accessories and utilities like games, a calculator, a clock, etc. If you run Express Setup at the time of installation, all the utility files will be loaded. If you run a Custom Setup, only those files that you select will be loaded into your computer. Like all program files, the files that contain these application have an **.exe** extension.

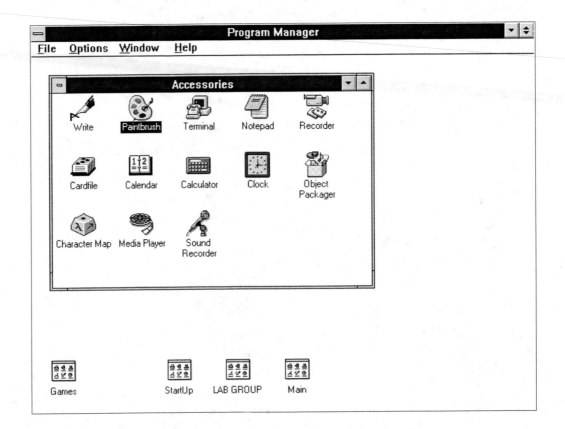

Common Windows Configuration Files

*.BAT	Batch files to start applications.
*.BMP	Wallpaper bitmap files that contain a wide assortment of wallpaper files.
*.CAL	Calendar files include a daily appointment book and a month-at-a-glance calendar.
*.CLP	Clipboard files that are used as temporary information storage files.
*.COM	Command files used to start applications.
*.CRD	Card files can be used to keep track of names, addresses, phone numbers, etc, just like a set of index cards.
*.GRP	Program Group Files contain information about the objects included in a program group.
*.PIF	Program Information Files contain information such as memory requirements, communications ports, etc. for non-Windows applications.
*.SRC	Source files that are used in the installation of Windows. These files contain source information for creating the initialization files.
*.SCR	Screen Saver files that contain different types of graphical animation used to prevent motor burn-in.
*.WAV	Wave files are sound files that can be used by Windows or other programs.
*.WRI	Write files. Write is a word processing application.
*.TMP	Temporary files.

WINDOWS 3.1

Windows 3.1 System Files

WINDOWS 3.x SYSTEM FILES		
WINDOWS 3.x	**Where Located**	**Function**
WIN.INI	\windows\	Controls Windows environment setting during start-up
SYSTEM.INI	\windows\	Controls system hardware settings and their associated information. Contains list of drivers for installed hardware.
WIN.COM	\windows\	Loads WIndows logo and checks hardware configuration to determine if Windows 3.x starts in Standard or 386-enhanced mode.
PROGMAN.EXE	\windows\ i	A standard program in Windows 3.1; replaced with the Windows 95. desktop. However, Windows 95 can be configured to use Program Manager in place of the standard Windows 95 desktop.
PROGMAN.INI	\windows\	Contains configuration information. Used by Windows 3.1 to save information about your preferences for Program Manager.
USER.EXE	\windows\system	Dynamic Link Libraries which make up the Windows "core." *USER.exe* is responsible for keyboard, mouse, sound, communication hardware, timer hardware. *GDI.exe* is responsible for graphics and printing; and *KRNLxxx.exe* is responsible for memory management, loading and executing programs on startup.
GDI.EXE		
KRNLxxx.EXE		

Optional Files

If you are running out of hard drive space, there are some files that may be removed to create more room. Before you delete any files, make sure you know their specific function and that you will no longer need them. If you are not sure about the purpose of a particular file, it is safest not to delete it.

Standard Mode Files

These files may be deleted if you only run Windows 3.1 in 386 Enhanced mode.

DOSX.EXE	**DSWAP.EXE**
KRNL286.EXE	**WINOLDAP.MOD**
WSWAP.EXE	

Any file with the extension **.2GR**

386 Enhanced Mode Files.

Remove only if you run Windows 3.1 in Standard mode.

CGA40WOA.FON	**CGA80WOA.FON**
EGA40WOA.FON	**EGA80WOA.FON**
CPWIN386.FON	**DOSAPP.FON**
WIN386.EXE	**WIN386.PS2**
WINOA386.MOD	

Any file with the extension **.386 or .3GR**

WINDOWS 3.1

Non-Windows Application Files.

There are many files used to provide support for DOS-based programs. If you only utilize Windows-based applications, then you may delete the following files:

APPS.INF	CGA40WOA.FON
CGA80WOA.FON	EGA40WOA.FON
EGA80WOA.FON	DOSAPP.FON
DSWAP.EXE	WINOLDAP.MOD
WINOA386.MOD	

Any files with the extensions **.2GR or .3GR**

Miscellaneous

If you do not plan on using the following files, you may delete them also:

Game files	Wallpaper and sound files
Screen savers	Unused Drivers
Font files	

Accessory files such as the Card file, Write, and Calendar

Windows 3.1 Initialization Files

When Windows or any of its applications start, there are files that control start-up settings such as the position and size of Windows, the printer configuration, etc. These are the initialization files, which are sometimes referred to as **.INI** files.

.INI files are created during the Windows installation setup. When a new application is added to Windows, it creates its own **.INI** file. Usually the file's name will be the application name followed by the extension **.INI** (Application **.INI**)

All Windows **.INI** files are standard ASCII text files. They can be changed, edited, or modified with any DOS text editor program or through the Windows operating system itself. The following is a list of Windows **.INI** files:

Windows .INI Files		
Windows 3.1 Initialization	WIN.INI	This file controls Windows environment settings during start-up.
System Initialization	SYSTEM.INI	Controls the system hardware settings and their associated information. SYSTEM.INI contains a list of drivers for the hardware installed.
Control Panel Initialization	CONTROL.INI	This file is responsible for color scheme, patterns, printer setting and installable driver settings.
Program Manager Initialization	PROGMAN.INI	Defines the Program Manager information such as the location of the program group files, their size and location of the Program Manager window.
File Manager Initialization	WINFILE.INI	Defines the appearance of the File Manager objects and components.

WINDOWS 3.1

Exercise 11.3: Modifying Windows .INI Files

Objective

Use the Windows **SYSEDIT** Program to modify Windows Initialization Files.

Preparations

Windows 3.1 must be loaded on your computer. Make back up copies of your original Windows **.INI** files before you start.

Step 1 - **From the DOS prompt, make copies of your original Windows** .INI **files.**

- Type **cd\windows** to change to the Windows directory.

- Press **Enter.**

- Type **copy *.ini *.xxx**

- Press **Enter.**

*You now have copies of your .INI Files. If you need to restore them, reverse the above procedure.

Step 2 - **Launch Windows.**

Step 3 - **Run the Windows** Sysedit **Program.**

- Click **File** in **Program Manager**

- Select **Run...**

- Type **Sysedit**

- Press **Enter.**

- Click **OK.**

Step 4 -   **Open the Windows .INI file.**

· Click the **WIN.INI** window.

Step 5 -   **Edit the line to load the Calculator Program.**

· Locate the **RUN=** keyword.

· Retype the line so that it reads **RUN=CALC.EXE**

· Close the **Sysedit** program by holding down the **Alt** key while pressing the **F4** function key.

· Exit and restart Windows.

Did the Calculator Program automatically start?

· Close the **CALC.EXE** Program.

MindWorks, *a BrightStar Company* © 1999

Step 6 -   **Use the** Sysedit **Program again to change the wallpaper type.**

- Click **File** to display the **File** drop-down menu.

- Click **Run...**

- Type **Sysedit** to open the program.

- Press **Enter.**

- Click **OK.**

- Click the **WIN.INI** window.

- Find the **Desktop** section heading.

- Change the **Wallpaper=** line to **WALLPAPER = HONEY.BMP**

- Click **File**

- Click **Save**

- Close the **Sysedit** program by holding down the **Alt** key while pressing the **F4** function key.

- Exit and Restart Windows.

  Did the wallpaper change? Did the Calculator Program automatically start?

Step 7 -   **From the** Main **program group, use the** Control Panel **to reset the wallpaper to the original setting.**

- Double-click the **Control Panel** icon.

- Double-click the **Desktop** icon.

- Change the wallpaper setting.

- Click **OK**

How Windows 3.1 Manages Memory

Memory is Window's most important resource. Memory availability will determine how many applications can run at the same time, and to an extent, it will also determine how fast applications operate. The ability to run several applications consecutively is called multitasking. Its performance is directly affected by the way in which memory is configured.

As a general rule of thumb, the more memory (RAM) you make available to Windows, the better the performance. This performance gain typically is accomplished by adding more physical (RAM) to the system board. Sometimes adding more RAM is restricted by physical limitations of the motherboard or cost. Windows allows you to set aside space on the hard disk that will emulate physical RAM. This process is known as Virtual Memory. Virtual Memory allows for the creation of a file on the hard disk that will simulate actual system RAM. This is used by applications when they require more memory than is physically installed in the machine.

This is accomplished through the use of swap files. Information is moved in blocks from memory to a swap file that Windows creates on the hard disk. This swap file can either be permanent or temporary.

WINDOWS 3.1

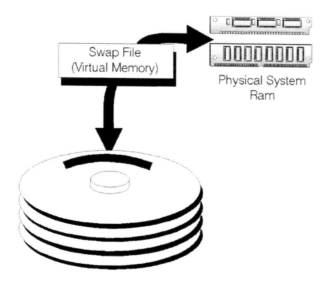

Swap File
(Virtual Memory)

Physical System
Ram

SWAP FILE

Permanent Swap Files

A permanent swap file will generally provide the best performance. Having said this, you might be tempted to ask, "Why not always use a permanent swap file?" There are some limitations to a permanent swap file.

- A permanent swap file *cannot* be created on a network drive.
- A permanent swap file *cannot* be used on a disk that is running any type of compression program.
- A permanent swap file *cannot* be used on a badly fragmented drive.

When Windows creates a permanent swap file, it actually creates two hidden files in the root and Windows directory of the hard disk. These hidden files are **386SPART.PAR** (located in the root directory) and **SPART.PAR** (located in the Windows directory).

Temporary Swap File

The temporary swap file, as the name implies, is created when you start Windows and is deleted when you exit Windows.

A temporary swap file can be useful in environments that will not allow for the creation of the permanent swap file. Some advantages of the temporary swap file are:

- A temporary swap file *can* be created on a network or restricted drive assignment.
- A temporary swap file *can* be created on disks that are too fragmented for a permanent swap file.

A temporary swap file is not static, and can change dynamically in size to adjust to the Windows environment.

SmartDrive

Later versions of DOS and Windows 3.1 included a disk caching system for faster access to data on a hard disk. **SmartDrive** allows you to monitor how the cache is used and change the cache size to optimize performance.

Starting with Windows 95, **SmartDrive** was replaced by a disk caching system called **VCACHE**.

The System Configuration Editor (**SYSEDIT.EXE**) utility included in Windows 3.1 was designed to simplify the task of editing system files (**WIN.INI, SYSTEM.INI, AUTOEXEC.BAT and CONFIG.SYS**). The application file is located in the **Windows\system** subdirectory. Most users find it helpful to create an icon for **SYSEDIT** in Program Manager to quickly find and start the program when editing is necessary.

In Windows 95, **SYSEDIT** is located in the **Win95\System** subdirectory.

Exercise 11.4: Modifying the Windows Swap File

Objective

When you've completed this exercise, you will be able to explain the steps required to modify the Windows swap file.

Preparation

You should have Windows 3.1 running on your computer.

Step 1 - **Open** Control Panel **from the** Main **program group.**

- Double-click the **Control Panel** icon.

- Double-click the **386 Enhanced** icon.

Step 2 - **Check the type of your current swap file.**
- Click the **Virtual Memory** button.

Step 3 - **Change the swap file size to 5000KB and make it temporary.**

- Click the **Change** button.

- Click **Type** and change it to **Temporary**.

- Set the size to **5000KB**.

- Click **OK**.

- Click **Yes** to save changes.

- Click **Restart Windows.**

Step 4 - **After Windows restarts, confirm the changes.**

- Double-click the **Control Panel** icon.

- Double-click the **386 Enhanced** icon.

- Click the **Virtual Memory** button.

- After confirming, click **Cancel**

- Exit **Control Panel.**

Summary

Windows 3.1 provides a Graphical User Interface (GUI) that allows the user to manage the information on the system drives without the hassle of remembering and typing multiple commands. All programs and accessories are organized and represented through windows or icons.

For *A+ Certification*, there are some key concepts you will need to understand about Windows. First, you will need to know how to prepare for and perform a Windows 3.1 installation. You will need to know how Windows uses Program Information Files (**PIF**s) to run DOS-based programs.

You must also know how to use the main functions of the **Program Manager**, **Control Panel**, **Print Manager** and **File Manager**. These are the primary Windows applications that control Windows and allow you to manage files, printers and other devices. Finally you will need to know how to effectively manage memory in the Windows 3.1 environment.

Review Questions

1. A Windows 3.1 program icon:

    A. Must only exist once in a program group.

    B. Can exist in any or all program groups a number of times.

    C. May exist more than once as long as they do not call up the same program.

    D. Can exist only once.

2. Windows group information can be located in files with ___ extensions.

    A. .GPP

    B. .GPR

    C. .GRP

    D. .GUP

3. What is the minimum memory (RAM) requirement for installing Windows 3.1?

    A. 4MB

    B. 2MB

    C. 8MB

    D. 16MB

4. What is a **PIF**?

    A. Program Initialization Program

    B. Program Information File

    C. Permanent Information File

    D. Primary Information File

5. To run Windows, which file must be loaded?

    A. **mouse.sys**

    B. **msdex.exe**

    C. **himem.sys**

    D. **setver.exe**

6. After clicking on a program icon, Windows reports the following error message: **Invalid Working Directory**. What should you do first?

    A.   Run **fdisk**.

    B.   Click icon's properties.

    C.   Check the path statement.

    D.   Check group properties.

7. You need to create a batch file. Which Windows program automatically will save it in ASCII file format?

    A.   Write

    B.   Notepad

    C.   Paintbrush

    D.   MS Word

8. Windows generates an error message stating that it cannot open enough files. What file needs to be modified?

    A.   **AUTOEXEC.BAT**

    B.   **SYSTEM.INI**

    C.   **WIN.INI**

    D.   **CONFIG.SYS**

9. Which Windows **.INI** file contains the boot section?

    A.   **WIN.INI**

    B.   **SYS.INI**

    C.   **SYSTEM.INI**

    D.   **BOOT.INI**

10. The clock program can be automatically launched by adding it to the **RUN=** line in which file?

    A.   **WIN.INI**

    B.   **BOOT.INI**

    C.   **SYSTEM.INI**

    D.   **SETUP.INI**

WINDOWS 3.1

11. Which files can you edit with the **Sysedit** program? Choose all that apply.

    A.   **SYSTEM.INI**

    B.   **AUTOEXEC.BAT**

    C.   **WIN.INI**

    D.   **CONFIG.SYS**

    E.   **BOOT.INI**

Section 12

Windows 95

Section 12: Windows 95

Introduction

All the work started around 1992 in what was to become the glitziest and most heavily advertised release of any Windows product to date. Finally released in August 1995, Windows 95 was a far cry from any previous versions of Windows. The new Windows 95 release attempted to make obsolete the old work-horses of the Microsoft stables. To accomplish this, Microsoft incorporated DOS and many of the features from Windows 3.x into one completely new product.

Objectives

When you've completed this section, you will be able to identify the following:

· Understand the Windows 95 design philosophy.

· Identify the differences between Windows and Windows 95, including the many new features and tools of Windows 95.

· Differentiate between FAT16 and FAT32.

· Understand Windows 95 Plug & Play capabilities.

· Perform a Windows 95 upgrade.

· Understand the function of the specific troubleshooting tools in Windows 95.

Windows 95 Design

When the work began on Windows 95, the design team at Microsoft had some pretty clear-cut design goals to guide them, including the following:

- Backward compatibility
- Ease of use
- Reliability
- Built-in networking capabilities
- Speed considerations

Backward Compatibility

One of the most important priorities for the design team was creating a product that could run on existing hardware and run existing programs better than Windows 3.x.

The Windows 95 operating system still supports **.INI** files for backward compatibility. Most of the information stored in the Windows 3.x **.INI** files is imported into the Registry during a Windows 95 upgrade. However, some of these configurations were left in the **System.ini, Winfile.ini** and the **Win.ini** to facilitate the compatibility issues. The **Win.ini** files contain the **RUN=** line that will automatically run a program when Windows is started. The syntax to automatically start the calculator program would be **RUN=C:\windows\calc.exe.**

Ease of Use

The look and feel of Windows 95 was designed to be easier to use than Windows 3.x. Gone would be the days of one window hiding another! Windows 95 was also written to the Plug and Play standard, which makes hardware configuration much less time-consuming.

Built-in Networking Capabilities

Like the Windows for Workgroups product before it, Windows 95 was also designed to include peer-to-peer networking capabilities. Windows 95 also would include support for network drivers and protocols to facilitate attaching to heterogeneous networks.

Speed Considerations

Windows 95 was expected to run at least as fast as Windows 3.x and, given the new 32-bit software capabilities, actually outperform its predecessor. This mandate would also have the effect of driving the 32-bit software market as well. Windows 95 is neither a 16-bit nor a 32-bit operating system, but rather a hybrid mixture of 16-bit and 32-bit components.

WINDOWS 95

Upgrading Windows 3.x to Windows 95

Upgrading to Windows 95 from the Windows 3.x environment can be accomplished in two ways. You can do a complete new install, which will not add any of your existing applications, or you can perform an upgrade. The upgrade option of Windows 95 will detect your existing applications and add them to the new platform.

When you install Windows 95 from a Windows 3.x machine, the Upgrade version of Windows 95 will search your hard disk for a current version of Windows. If it cannot find it on the disk, Windows 95 will ask you to insert a Windows 3.x Installation disk.

Windows 95 requires that all older 16-bit programs share the same memory space to ensure backward compatibility with Windows 3.x. Because of this sharing, it is possible that one program can step on (overwrite) the memory area of another. This will usually generate a general protection fault error code.

There are advantages and disadvantages associated with both upgrading and installing new. The upgrade version tends to leave a number of old files on the disk that take up valuable space. Installing new avoids this problem, however the new installation will not add existing applications to your desktop, therefore making it a more time consuming install.

Before starting either method you should insure that your computer meets at least the minimum hardware requirements. The following is a list of **minimum** hardware requirements:

· 386DX or better (486 or Pentium is recommended)

· 4MB of RAM (16MB is recommended)

· 3.5 floppy drive or CD-ROM

· Minimum of 60MB of free disk space (200MB is recommended.)

· VGA video adapter

It should be stressed that these are bare minimum requirements to install Windows 95. (more is always better...more RAM, bigger Disk.

Exercise 12.1: Performing a Windows 95 Upgrade

Objectives

To upgrade an existing Windows 3.x system to Windows 95 platform.

Preparation

You will need a minimum of a 386 with at least 4MB RAM (16MB is recommended) currently loaded with Windows 3.x.

*Note: The Windows 95 Installation Wizard will respond differently depending upon what type hardware is installed in your PC. This procedure assumes that you do **not** have a modem or network interface card (NIC) installed and that you are installing from a CD-ROM drive.*

Ask your Instructor for a copy of the Windows 95 CD-ROM software and the **CD KEY: #**.

Step 1 -   Start Windows 3.x.

· Insert the Windows 95 Upgrade CD ROM into the drive.

Step 2 -   Initiate the Setup program

· In the **Program Manager** window, click **File.**

· Click **Run...**

· Type **<DRIVE>:SETUP** (i.e. **D:SETUP**, if "D" is the letter assigned to your CD-ROM)

· Press **Enter**.

Step 3 -   From the Windows 95 WELCOME **screen, click** Continue.

Step 4 -   Click YES **to accept the software license agreement.**

Step 5 -   The Windows 95 Setup Wizard **will now collect information about your machine.**

· Click **Next** to continue.

WINDOWS 95

Step 6 - **Choose a directory for Windows 95**

· Click **Next** to accept the default location.

Step 7 - **Save the system files.**

· Click **Yes** to save the file.

· Click **Next** to continue.

Step 8 - **Choose a drive to save system files if necessary.**

· Click on **OK** to accept the default drive.

Step 9 - **Select Setup options**

· Choose **Typical**.

· Click **Next** to continue.

Step 10- **Verify name and company information**

· Click **Next** to continue.

Step 11- **Enter the CD-ROM key #. (See Instructor for the key)**

· Click **Next** to continue.

Step 12- **Select the appropriate hardware settings for your PC. (Ask your Instructor for details)**

· Click **Next** to continue.

Note: The Wizard will now analyze your machine. Be patient. This may take awhile.

Step 13- **Accept the default Windows components.**

· Click **Yes** to accept.

· Click **Next** to continue.

Step 14-   **Create an Emergency Startup Diskette.**

· Click **Yes** to create the diagnostic startup disk.

· Click **Next** to continue.

Step 15 -   **Begin the process to copy Windows 95 files to your hard disk.**

· Click **Next** to start the copy process, then follow the instructions on your screen.

Be patient, this may take awhile.

Step 16 -   **Complete the installation process.**

· Click on **Finish** to continue.

Windows will now reboot your PC and display the Windows 95 first time screen. ***Be patient.***

Step 17 -   **Set the Time**

· Select your appropriate time zone

· Click **Apply**.

· Click **OK**.

Step 18 -   **Click** OK **to restart the computer**

Step 19 -   **Optional**

· Click the **Windows Tour** button in the **Welcome to Windows 95** window.

· Complete the tour.

Windows 95—The Differences

Perhaps the most obvious difference between Windows 95 and Windows 3.x is the look. The Windows 95 desktop appearance has been completely redesigned from Windows 3.x. The new desktop is automatically launched when you boot the PC. You are no longer required to type a separate command to start it.

The first thing you see on the new desktop is a few icons on the left side of your screen and a task bar on the bottom of the screen with a **Start** button. **Program Manager** and the other groups are all gone in favor of a less cluttered desktop.

The **Start** button is a new feature to Windows 95. It allows you easy access to some of the more commonly used functions of the software, including searching the system for files and folders. By clicking the **Start** button and choosing **Find,** then **Files** or **Folders**, you can then enter a specific file name or search for all files having a common extension by using the * wild card switch.

WINDOWS 95 DESKTOP

Configuring The Desktop

As you have already seen, the Windows 95 desktop is dramatically different from Windows 3.x. At first glance the long time 3.x user might be a bit intimidated, but with a little practice most will agree that the new desktop is much cleaner and easier to use.

To create an interface that was more intuitive to use, Microsoft took an object-oriented approach to the Windows 95 desktop. This basically means that everything in Windows 95 is treated as an object. The icons on your desktop, the folders, documents and even the desktop itself are all considered objects. Even the various pieces of hardware, like your keyboard, mouse, and hard disk, are also viewed as objects. All objects have properties, so to change something like the mouse speed, you change the mouse's properties. If you wanted to change the wallpaper on your desktop, you would modify the desktop properties.

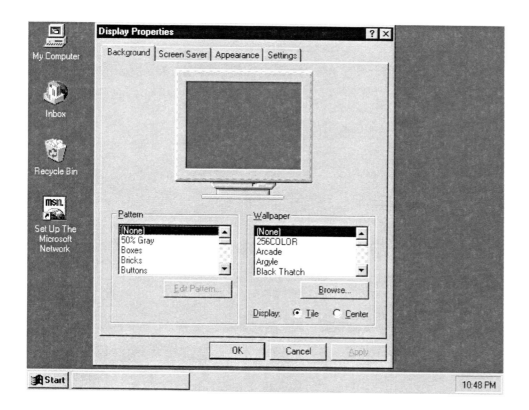

WINDOWS 95 DISPLAY PROPERTIES

Exercise 12.2: Configuring the Desktop

Objectives

Modify the Windows 95 desktop. Change the wallpaper settings, enable the screen saver and modify the task bar and mouse properties.

Step 1 - **Change the wallpaper settings**

- Place the pointer to any open area on the desktop.

- Click the alternate mouse button.

- Click **Properties**.

- Select a wallpaper and mark the tile box

- Click **Apply**.

- Click **OK**.

Step 2- **Modify mouse properties to display pointer trails**

- Double-click on the **My Computer** icon on the desktop.

- Double-click on **Control Panel.**

- Double-click the **Mouse** icon.

- Click on the **Motion** tab.

- Click the **Show pointer trails** box.

- Click **Apply**.

- Click **OK**.

- Close **Control Panel**, by clicking on the **X** in the upper right-hand corner.

- Close **My Computer**.

- Move your mouse and notice the trails.

Step 3-　　**Modify the task bar options, to** Auto hide

- Place the pointer anywhere on the **Taskbar** and alternate-click.

- Click **Taskbar Properties**.

- Click the **Auto hide** box.

- Click **Apply**.

- Close the **Properties** box

Notice that your **Taskbar** is now hidden from view. Move your pointer toward the bottom of the screen to display **Taskbar**.

Step 4-　　**Enable the Screen Saver program**

- Place the pointer anywhere on the open desktop and click the alternate mouse button

- Select **Properties**.

- Click the **Screen Saver** tab.

- Select a screen saver.

- Set the **Wait Time** to 1 minute.

- Click **Apply**.

- Click **OK** and wait 1 minute, without touching the keyboard or mouse.

WINDOWS 95

Windows Explorer

Long time Windows users will notice another difference the first time they look for files. The old mainstay **File Manager** is gone and its replacement is the new Windows 95 **Explorer.** One of the design challenges faced by the programmers was to create a file browser program that was easy for the novice computer user to learn and use.

The Windows 95 **Explorer** lets you view and search the file system for folders, subdirectories and files. If a folder contains other subdirectories and files, it is denoted by a plus sign enclosed in a small box to the left of the folder.

Windows 95 **Explorer** can be accessed in two ways:

- Double-click on the **My Computer** icon and open the **C Drive** icon. A window with folders and documents is displayed.

- Or, alternate-click on any resource and get a double window. One of the options listed is **Explorer.**

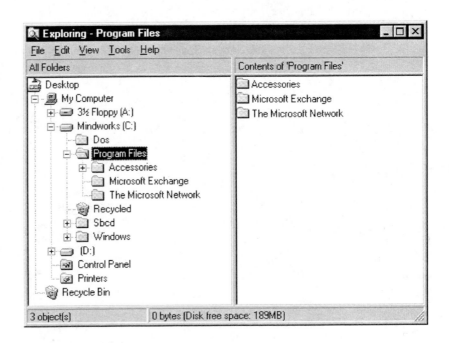

WINDOWS 95 EXPLORER

Recycle Bin

Another very noticeable feature on the Windows 95 desktop is the addition of the **Recycle Bin**; at least new to PC users. (Macintosh people might disagree.) In previous versions of Windows, if you deleted a file it wasn't easy to get it back. The DOS **Undelete** feature or some third party utility was your only option.

With Windows 95, things are a bit easier. When a file is deleted within Windows 95, it is actually just moved to the **Recycle Bin**. If you find that you have just deleted a file accidentally, you can open the **Recycle Bin** on your desktop. This will display all files that have been placed there since the **Recycle Bin** was last emptied. You can now click on the file and restore it. The file will be restored to the location it was deleted from.

The addition of the **Recycle Bin** was a long-awaited feature in Windows. However, if your ultimate goal is to free hard drive space by deleting files, you must empty the recycle bin. Remember that the files in the **Recycle Bin** are still taking up space on the hard disk.

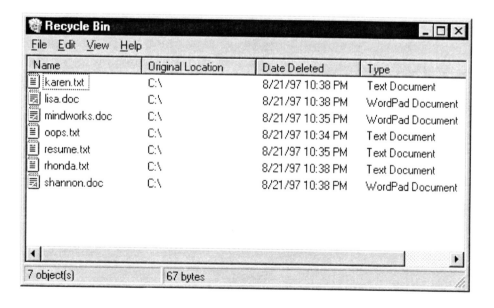

WINDOWS 95 RECYCLE BIN

Right Click →

Alternate-Click Function

The alternate-click function in Windows 95 allows you to modify an object's properties. In the case of a folder, you can set attributes like **Read-only** or **Hidden** and also enable sharing of a folder.

In Windows 95, you can alternate-click the printer icon and from the pull-down menu, choose **Set as Default**. This default printer will then be used by all your Windows-based applications. You can also **Pause** and **Purge** print jobs from this same pull down menu.

Long File Names

Not all the new features of Windows 95 are so obvious as the desktop changes. Unlike previous versions of DOS, Windows 95 supports long file names, up to 255 characters including spaces. For all these years we have been stuck with the infamous DOS 8.3 rule for naming files. A file name can be no longer than eight characters, with an optional three character extension. Well, no more. Windows 95 supports long file names for both files and folders. True, it's not unlimited—the names can not exceed 255 characters and spaces included. But who's counting?

Windows 95 will truncate long file names for any programs that do not know how to handle the long file convention. When Windows 95 needs to truncate a name, it will only use the first six characters, no spaces, and adds a tilde (~) followed by a sequence number beginning with 1. The long file name **my resume.txt** would be displayed as **myresu~1.txt.**. These restrictions apply to both files and folders. The following characters are considered illegal and cannot be used:
/ \ * ? " : < > | .

Windows 95 file and folder names are case preservative, but not case sensitive. An example might be if you named a file **Resume.doc**. The capital "R" would be preserved, but could be referenced as **resume.doc**.

Exercise 12.3: Windows 95 Explorer Lab

OBJECTIVE:

Use Windows 95 Explorer to create, view, rename and move files and folders.

PART 1   *Creating, renaming and deleting folders (directories).*

Step 1:   **Creating Folders**

· Click **Start.**

· Click **Programs, Windows Explorer**

· Highlight the "**C**" drive (click on it)

· Click **File, New**

· Select **Folder**

· Name the new folder with your first name and press **Enter**

· Repeat the above procedure to create another folder called **Sub1**

· Highlight the **Sub1** folder in the left pane of **Explorer**

· Click **File, New, Folder**

· Name it **Sub2** and press **Enter**

NOTE: Notice the plus (**+**) sign next to the **Sub1** folder indicating that it now contains a sub-directory or folder

· Double-click the **Sub1** folder

NOTE: Notice that the plus (**+**) sign now changes to a minus (**-**) and displays the **Sub2** folder.

Step 2:   **Renaming a Folder**

·   Locate the folder corresponding to your first name.

·   Alternate-click that folder, select **Rename.**

·   Change the name to **Copytwo**.

·   Press **Enter**.

NOTE: This folder will be used in the copy exercise.

·   Locate the renamed folder.

Step 3:   **Deleting a Folder**

·   Locate the **Sub1** folder in the left pane in **Explorer**.

·   Double-click the **Sub1** folder.

·   Alternate-click on the **Sub2** folder and select **Delete**

·   Click **Yes.**

NOTE: Notice that the **Sub1** folder no longer has a **+** sign next to it.

PART 2   *Creating, renaming and moving files*

Step 1:   Creating files in your SUB1 Folder

NOTE: To view the DOS (**.txt**) extensions, you must unhide the DOS file extensions.

·   Highlight the **Sub1** folder

·   Alternate-click in any open area in the right pane of **Explorer**.

·   Select **New, Text Document**.

·   Name it **RED.TXT**.

·   Repeat the above procedure creating two more files named **WHITE.TXT** and **BLUE.TXT**.

Step 2:   Renaming a file

·   Alternate-click the **WHITE.TXT** file.

·   Choose **Rename** and name it **BLACK.TXT**.

·   Press **Enter**.

WINDOWS 95

Step 3:   **Copying a File (BLACK.TXT)**

· Alternate-click the **BLACK.TXT** file.

· Click **Copy**.

· Alternate-click the **COPYTWO** folder.

· Click **Paste**.

· Double-click the **COPYTWO** folder to verify that the file was copied into the folder.

Question: Is the original **BLACK.TXT** file still located in the **SUB1** folder?

Step 4:   **Moving a File**

· Click on the **SUB1** folder in the left pane of **Explorer**

· Alternate-click the **RED.TXT** file and choose **Cut**.

· Alternate-click the **COPYTWO** folder and choose **Paste**.

· Double-click the **COPYTWO** folder to verify that the file was copied into the folder.

Question: How many copies of the **RED.TXT** file exist?

Question: What is the difference between the **Copy** and **Cut** commands?

PART 3: *Viewing long file names and attributes*

Step 1: **Create a file and name it LONGFILENAME.TXT**

· Open the **SUB1** folder by double-clicking it

· Alternate-click any open space in the right pane of **Explorer**.

· Select **New, Text Document**.

· Name it **LONGFILENAME.TXT**

NOTE: Notice that the full file named is displayed.

Step 2: **Viewing the long file name from a DOS based environment using Windows 3.x file manager.**

· Click **Start, Run**.

· Enter **WINFILE** in the open dialog box.

· Click **OK**.

· Locate and open the **SUB1** folder.

· Locate the long file name you created.

NOTE: Notice that a DOS-based program truncated the name to the first six characters followed by a tilde and a sequence number starting from 1.

· This now conforms to the DOS eight character limitation.

PART 4: Close File Manager

Step 1: **Viewing file attributes**

- Open **Windows 95 Explorer**.

- Open the **SUB1** folder.

- Alternate-click on the **LONFILENAME.TXT** file.

- Choose **Properties.**

NOTE: Notice that file attributes are now displayed and can be changed or modified. This box also displays both the DOS and long file names.

SCANDISK and DEFRAG Utilities

Windows 95 ships with two very useful disk-related tools: **Defrag** and **Scandisk**. The **Defrag** utility, as the name implies, will organize and optimize a badly fragmented hard disk. The **Scandisk** program will search the hard disk for errors and attempt to repair and flag them. Windows 95 will run the **Scandisk** tool automatically as required if, for example, Windows was shut down improperly. However, you can start **Scandisk** or **Defrag** from the Desktop by clicking **Start** and choosing **Programs, Accessories,** and **System Tools.**

Windows 95 System Files

Know for
Exam

WINDOWS 95 SYSTEM FILES		
WINDOWS 95	**Where Located**	**Function**
COMMAND.COM	C:\Windows	The DOS command interpreter which allows you to use simple DOS commands.
MSDOS.SYS	C:\	Unlike the MSDOS.SYS file in MS-DOS, this file is a text file. It contains a [Paths] section that lists the locations for other Windows 95 files (such as the registry file) and an [Options] section that you can use to personalize the boot process.
IO.SYS	C:\	A new system file which replaces the MS-DOS system files (IO.SYS and MSDOS.SYS). This real-mode operating system file contains the information needed to start the computer. Computer no longer needs CONFIG.SYS and AUTOEXEC.BAT to start the Windows 95 operating system (although these files are preserved for backward compatibility with certain applications and drivers). Loads HIMEM.SYS, IFSHLP.SYS, SETVER.EXE, DBLSPACE.BIN or DRVSPACE.BIN drivers.
REGEDIT.EXE	C:\Windows	The program file for the Registry. A database of all the settings for Windows95. It is contained in two hidden files in your Windows directory, called USER.DAT and SYSTEM.DAT.
SYSTEM.DAT	C:\Windows (hidden file)	The Registry system file that takes care of hardware and software. These files keep up to date on what's on your computer.
USER.DAT	C:\Windows (hidden file)	The Registry user file that takes care of user specific settings such as wallpaper settings, whether profiles are used and who gets what profile. Normally, the Registry user files are not changed when resetting the Registry.

Registry

Part of what makes the Plug and Play feature feasible is something called the **Registry**. The **Registry** is a database that holds all the settings and configurations that 95 uses for both hardware and software. The **Registry** replaces most of the **.INI** files that were part of previous versions of Windows. Some of the **.INI** files are still used by Windows 95 for compatibility reasons. The **SYSTEM.INI** and the **WINDOWS.INI** are still present. Information from all the **.INI** files have been incorporated into the registry data base.

This database is divided into two separate files for ease of administration. The files are **user.dat** and **system.dat.** and are typically located in the Windows folder. Windows 95 will create backup copies of these two files every time the computer is rebooted. The **user.dat** file is copied to a file called **user.da0** and the **system.dat** file is copied to the **system.da0** file. Both the **.dat** files and the backup files (**.da0**) are hidden read-only files.

Regedit

Under Windows 3.x, if you needed to edit the **.INI** files, you could use the **SYSEDIT** program. In Windows 95, a program called **REGEDIT** is used to view or modify the information in the registry.

The **REGEDIT** program is powerful and mistakes can be made. *Always have a backup of the registry before making any modifications.* By default, the **REGEDIT** program is not displayed on the desktop or **Start** menu. If your Windows 95 was installed from floppies, **REGEDIT** will not be available, it only shipped on the CD-ROM version of the software.

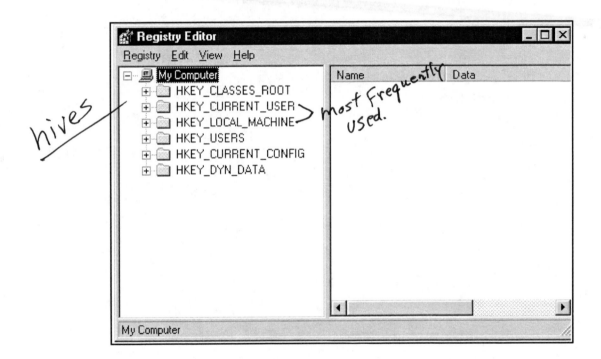

WINDOWS 95 REGISTRY EDITOR

To launch the **REGEDIT** program,

- From the **Start** menu, click on **Run...**
- Type **REGEDIT**. This will display the different sections of the **Registry**. These sections are referred to as **KEYS**. There are six major keys:

Hot Key	Function
Hkey_local_machine	This includes the hardware settings.
Hkey_current_config	Stores hardware profiles
Hkey_classes_root	File linkings and associations.
Hkey_dyn_data	Buffered hardware settings in RAM, for speedy access.
Hkey_users	Individual software settings for all users.
Hkey_current_user	The system settings for the current user.

Each of the different sections (KEYS) above can also contain subsets to better organize data.

WINDOWS 95

Exercise 12.4: Windows 95 Regedit LAB

OBJECTIVE:

In this exercise, you will use the **Regedit** utility to search and modify key values.

PART 1   **Searching the registry for the "RUNONCE" key value using the** Regedit **utility program.**

Step 1   **Starting the Regedit program**

· Click **Start, Run**.

· In the open dialog box, type **Regedit** then click **OK**.

· Click the **HKEY_LOCAL_MACHINE** in the left pane of the **Registry Editor** window.

· On the **Edit** menu, click **Find**.

· In the **Find What** box, type **RUNONCE**.

· Click **Find Next**.

NOTE: Note, this should locate and open the **RUNONCE** key

· In the **Edit** menu, point to **New**, then click on **String Value**.

· Type **SOLITAIRE** for the value name, then click the **Enter** key

· Double-click on the new value **SOLITAIRE**.

· In the value data dialog box, type the following path.

C:\windows\sol.exe

NOTE: Check with your Instructor for the exact location of **SOL.EXE**.

· Click **OK** and close the **Regedit** program

· To view the results of the **Registry** change, restart your system. (Click **Start, Shut Down, Restart the Computer.**)

FINAL NOTE: Any value placed in the **RUNONCE REGISTRY** key is executed the next time you restart the computer and is then deleted from the **REGISTRY KEY**.

System Tools

The **System Monitor** utility is a Windows 95 tool for tracking memory and other resources for possible problems, including 16 memory-management items such as **Swapfile in Use**; **Free Memory** and **Maximum Disk Cache Size**. The **System Monitor** can help with problem or performance determination on a local or a remote computer.

To install the **System Monitor**:

· Click on the **Control Panel**.

· Double-click the **Add/Remove Programs** icon.

· Click on the **Windows Setup** tab.

· Double-click **Accessories**.

· Click **System Monitor**.

· Click **OK**.

To run the **System Monitor**:

· Click **Start**.

· Select **Programs**.

· Select **Accessories**.

· Select **System Tools**.

· Select **System Monitor**.

Also from the **System Tools** drop-down menu, you can track system resource usage by selecting the **Resource Meter** utility. The **Resource Meter** dialog box will display usage for the following three categories: System resources, User resources and the GDI (graphics-related) resources.

The GDI (Graphical Device Interface) provides Windows 32-bit programs with an interface and services to interact with graphical devices, like the CRT and printers.

Windows 95 includes a **Backup** utility that lets you backup important files from your hard disk to floppy diskette or tape. The **Backup** utility is also located in the **System Tools** folder.

WINDOWS 95

EXTRACT Tool

You can use the **EXTRACT** tool (**EXTRACT.EXE**) to decompress Windows files from the original media.

First copy the **EXTRACT.EXE** file from disk 1 of the Windows program diskettes or from the Windows 95 CD-ROM to the root folder of drive C. Type the following command at the MS-DOS prompt:

copy a:\extract.exe c:

(Drive A = your floppy diskette drive with the Windows Program files disk #1 - or you can target your CD-ROM drive.)

The **EXTRACT** tool has only a command-line interface (there is no GUI interface). Because Windows does not allow you to delete or overwrite a file that is in use, you may have to restart your computer in **Command Prompt Only** mode before you can use the **EXTRACT** tool.

If you receive an **Access denied** error message when you try to delete a file before using the **EXTRACT** tool, or when you use the **EXTRACT** tool to overwrite an existing file, follow these steps to restart your computer in **Command Prompt Only** mode and then use the **EXTRACT** tool:

· Click **Start**, and then click **Shut Down**.

· Click **Restart The Computer**, and then click **OK**.

· When you see the **Starting Windows 95** message, press the **F8** key

· Choose **Command Prompt Only**.

Adding/Removing Applications

When a new application is added in Windows 95, it usually will be installed to a new directory created by the application. It is very important to remember that if you must remove an application, do not simply delete the folder. The preferred method is as follows:

- Open the **Control Panel**.

- Choose **Add/Remove Programs**.

- Select the program.

- Click **Remove**.

This procedure will ensure that the operating system will search for and remove all references to the program. If you delete just the folder that contains the application, there still could be hooks and links in other locations.

MSD.EXE

The Microsoft Diagnostics (**MSD.EXE**) is a small DOS utility that takes a brief inventory of your PC and displays it in a text-based format. **MSD.EXE** is very useful in seeing what disks are in your system, how much memory is installed and checking system resource usage such as LPT ports and IRQs. It will show you what type of BIOS you are using and what UART chip you have in your serial ports. **MSD.EXE** is included in Windows 95 but is not usually installed as part of the normal installation. The utility is located on the Windows 95 CD-ROM. Copy the file to the **C:\Windows\Command** directory.

NOTE: **MSD.EXE** will give incorrect information if run within the Windows environment. Go into the DOS mode before running it.

EDIT.COM

Windows 95 contains a DOS-based text editor called **EDIT.COM**.

Plug & Play

Perhaps one of the most exciting and functional new features of Windows 95 is the way it takes advantage of the Plug & Play (PNP) technology. This is especially true if you ever have tried to install a new piece of hardware, only to be thwarted by IRQ and DMA conflicts.

In order for a Plug & Play system to function, the BIOS, Operating System, and hardware must all be capable of working together. That is why it is very important to ensure that your hardware is Plug & Play compliant.

With Plug & Play enabled, Windows 95 can automatically detect and configure hardware installed in the machine. It is most important to note that PNP will only be successful if the hardware and associated drivers are PNP compliant.

Windows 95 was written to use Plug & Play technology, which makes the process of adding and configuring new hardware much easier and faster. Under Windows 95, when you add a new piece of hardware, it is automatically detected by the software. The IRQs and DMA are then configured for you by the operating system. There is a catch though. The hardware has to also be designed to conform to Plug & Play standards. If you attempt to install an older non-Plug & Play device, Windows 95 will prompt you to make the changes manually.

Windows-Specific Troubleshooting Tools

Device Manager

Device Manager is a useful tool to get troubleshooting information about devices connected to your system and your system's configuration settings. If you're having a hardware problem, check **Device Manager** first.

- Click **Start** menu.
- Select **Settings**.
- Select **Control Panel**.
- Double-click **System**.
- Click the **Device Manager** button.

You can also open **Device Manager** by alternate-clicking on **My Computer** and choosing **Properties**, then **Device Manager.**

In the list shown, find the device that's giving you problems and click the **+** sign for that device to see what's installed. If Windows 95 has detected a configuration problem or conflict, you'll see an exclamation point in a yellow circle over the name of the device. Double-click the device's icon and look at the **General** tab. If the wrong driver was installed or if it's not working properly, you'll see it here.

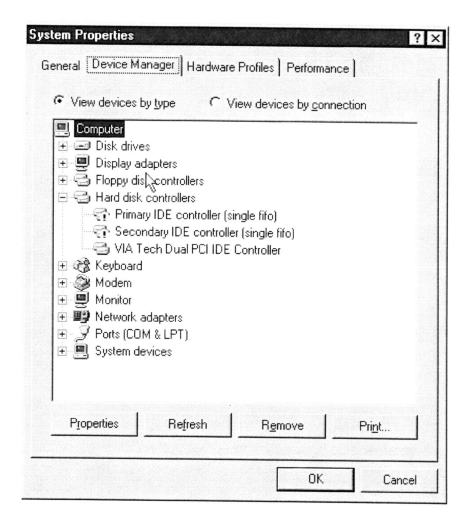

A handy resource guide is the **System Resource Report** feature of **Device Manager**. This comprehensive summary of your hardware is available in printed form or in a **.prn** file for later printing. It's a good idea to keep a hard copy of this report for later reference in an emergency. It lists IRQ assignments, I/O addresses, hard disk parameters and other resources. To print the report:

· Click **Print** button at the bottom of the **Device Manager** screen.

· Select **All Devices**

· Select **System Summary** under **Report Type**.

WINDOWS 95

Windows 95 Boot Sequences

Creating A Startup Disk

During the installation, the Windows 95 **Setup** program will ask you to create an **Emergency (Startup) Diskette**. It is always a good idea to say **YES** to this option. You will need a blank floppy diskette before starting.

The system will copy all the necessary boot files to this diskette, which can then be used to boot and troubleshoot any problems that could occur in the future.

The Emergency Repair Disk can be used as an aid in trouble-shooting situations. The "startup disk" is not only a boot disk but also includes several utility and diagnostic programs. If the disk was not created during the initial installation, you can create a startup disk:

- Double-click the **Add/Remove Programs** icon in **Control Panel**.

- Click the **Startup Disk** tab.

- Click **Create Disk**.

Boot Process Shortcut Keys

Windows 95 has configured several shortcut keys that can be pressed during the boot process to aid in troubleshooting. The following is a list of these special function keys:

F8	**Startup** menu
F4	Previous version of MS-DOS
F5	**Safe** mode
Ctrl+F5	**Safe** mode without compression
Shift+F5	**Safe** mode command prompt only
Shift+F8	Step by step confirm
F6	**Safe** mode ....with network support loaded

The proper time to press a function key is after your machine has finished running **POST**. This is usually when the **Starting Windows 95** message appears on the screen.

There are many types of viruses that will attach to and corrupt the **MBR** (master boot record) which may cause Windows to fail during the boot process. If this should happen, you can usually boot to a "clean" floppy and run the **fdisk /MBR** command which will restore the master boot record and eliminate the virus.

Boot in Safe Mode

If your system hangs up when you boot up because of some changes you've made to the system or if you suspect a device driver may be causing a problem, you can have the system boot up in **Safe Mode**. Then, make the necessary changes to your configuration settings and reboot to solve the problem.

·   When you turn on your computer and the system says **Starting Windows 95**, press **F8**.

·   Select **Safe Mode** from the options menu. This allows only the mouse, keyboard and standard VGA device drivers to be loaded.

·   Make the necessary changes to your configuration settings.

·   Shut down the system and reboot as normal.

Once Windows 95 has rebooted in **Safe Mode**, try to shut it down. If your PC shuts down without an error message, then the device driver was causing the conflict.

When a Windows 95 machine is booted in **Safe** mode, it will load just the minimal set of drivers needed to function. This is very akin to the "good old days" when a DOS machine was booted with a clean floppy (loading no **CONFIG.SYS** or **AUTOEXEC.BAT**). In the case of the above example, the mouse, keyboard and standard VGA driver are the minimum requirements to perform a successful boot.

Boot To Command Prompt

If you want to boot up to a DOS command prompt:

- When you turn on your computer and the system says **Starting Windows 95**, press **F8** .

- From the options menu, select **Command Prompt**.

- Shutdown the system and reboot as normal. Your system will display the DOS prompt when it boots up instead of the Windows start screen.

Log Files

Windows 95 will also create a log file during the installation process, called **BOOTLOG.TXT.** This file will keep a record of all the devices and drivers that the system attempts to load, and will note if the devices loaded successfully. This will only be created once after the first successful setup, After that you must specify the log option from the **Startup** menu.

Study !

- To access the **Startup** menu, press **F8** during the boot process as soon as the **Starting Windows 95** message appears (you have to be quick).

- The **Startup** menu will then display a list of options, **logged (BOOT.TXT)** will be one of them.

This file then can be opened and examined with any text editing program, like **Notepad**.

Windows Log Files

The Windows 95 installation program creates two text files during installation that can be very useful in troubleshooting any problems that occur during the setup phase. These files are **detlog.txt** and **setuplog.txt**. The **setuplog.txt**. file contains information about what happened during the setup phase.

The **detlog.txt** file contains information about hardware components and their parameters.

Windows Installation Files

The Windows 95 installation files found on the installation CD are compressed. During installation they are decompressed to the target drive location. The installation files on the CD have a **.cab** extension. They are referred to as cabinet files.

Summary

Windows 95 is an extremely feature-laden new operating system. Virtually every detail of Windows 95 is an improvement over the Windows products that came before it.

Windows 95 is the first real step in addressing the legacy of problems that have plagued the DOS operating systems in past years. The days of memory management and hardware configuration problems have all been greatly simplified.

The greatly enhanced Windows desktop has also made learning the new operating system a joy as well.

Review Questions

1. Where is the information now embedded that was recorded in the Windows 3.1 **.INI** files?

    A. **CNI** files

    B. **RegBase**

    ✷ C. **Registry**

    D. **Regedit**

2. Windows 95 has built-in networking capabilities.

    ✷ A. True

    B. False

3. Which of the following is a new feature in Windows 95?

    A. Trash can

    B. Bin

    C. Garbage can

    ✷ D. Recycle bin

4. The Plug and Play feature of Windows 95 allows new hardware to be automatically detected.

    ✷ A. True

    B. False

5. What is the program used to configure and modify the **Registry** called?

    A. **SYSEDIT**

    ✷ B. **REGEDIT**

    C. **REZEDIT**

    D. **CONEDIT**

6. The **Registry** section headings are referred to as what?

    A. Classes

    B. Folders

    ✷ C. Keys

    D. Locks

7. The alternate mouse button has little or no functionality
   in Windows 95.

        A.   True

   ✳ B.   False

8. What should you click to shut down your computer from
   the desktop?

        A.   **Down** button

        B.   **Close** button

   ✳ C.   **Start** button

        D.   **Exit** button

9. Windows 95 supports file names longer than 8.3
   characters.

   ✳ A.   True

        B.   False

10. The files located in the **Recycle Bin** take up space on the hard
    disk.

    ✳ A.   True

         B.   False

WINDOWS 95

Section 13

Windows 98

Section 13: Windows 98

Introduction

If you were a Windows 95 user, you should be right at home with the Windows 98 product. It isn't that Windows 98 doesn't offer any thing new...it does! There are many improvements, most of which are internal enhancements that are only noticed by the most technical of users. These are the tweaks that help your system run faster and more efficient with less down time. There is, however, a fair amount of new goodies that the average user will appreciate as well. Most of the more obvious improvements are in the area of "Web Integration." The Microsoft programmers have put some life into all those Web-related icons, which were there in Windows 95 but lacked any real functionality.

Objectives:

· Discuss Windows 98 System requirements

· Discuss the Windows 98 setup and installation features

· Perform a Windows 98 upgrade

· Describe the Web Integration tools

· Create a Web page using FrontPage Express

· Troubleshooting Windows 98

WINDOWS 98

Windows 98 System Requirements

The system requirements for Windows 98 are not much different than they were in Windows 95. The table below describes the minimum hardware requirements for running Windows 98 on a local computer. The Windows 98 code was specifically designed to run on an Intel platform or at the very least "Intel compatible." It cannot be installed on any other processors.

DEVICE	MINIMUM REQUIREMENT	RECOMMENDED
Hard Disk Space	120 MB free hard disk space	
Processor	486 DX/66 MHz	Pentium or higher
Memory	16 MB	32 MB or more
Monitor	VGA "16 color"	Super VGA "16 or 24-bit color"
Mouse	Windows 98 compatible pointing device	
Floppy Disk		At least one 3.5 HD drive
CD-ROM	1x speed or faster	Fast as you can get!
Sound card and speakers	Sound Blaster or (compatible)	

It should probably be noted that when in doubt, always try to install components that have the "Designed for Microsoft" logo. These products have been tested to ensure compatibility with the Microsoft operating systems.

Software Requirements

Besides the hardware requirements, Windows 98 can be installed in a dual boot-mode with other operating systems. Windows 98 will install on a computer that is currently running the following systems:

- MS-DOS Ver. 5.x and later

- Windows 3.1x

- WFW Windows for Workgroups 3.1x

- MS-DOS / OS2

- Windows NT / MS-DOS

You should notice something missing from the above list. You can **NOT** dual boot Windows 98 and Windows 95. It would get just a bit confusing for you and the operating system!

Windows 98 setup and installation features

The Windows 98 setup program has been streamlined from the Windows 95 days. Windows 95 had been shipped with two supplemental releases referred to as OEM Service Releases. The OSR-1 and OSR-2 provided support for the newest hardware and Internet software. Windows 98 includes all of the OSR-1 and OSR-2 updates as well as support for the USB (Universal Serial Bus).

The new Windows setup makes the entire installation process more streamlined than ever before. The following setup enhancements are featured in Windows 98:

- Reduced installation steps (five)

- The addition of a setup information bar

- Improved organization of setup files (CAB files)

- Improved Plug and Play detection

- Anti-virus checks

Reduced installation steps

The actual amount of user input has drastically been reduced in the Windows 98 setup program. The number of steps to install Windows 98 has been reduced from about twelve steps in Windows 95 to just five steps. The setup program will request user input at the beginning of the install, then will complete the installation unattended. Windows 98 will automatically restart the computer as necessary.

The following table summarizes and compares Windows 95 and Windows 98 installation steps:

Windows 95 Setup Steps	Windows 98 Setup Steps
Setup Initialization	Preparing to run Windows 98 setup
Smart Recovering preparation	Collecting information about your computer
Processing the **setuplog.txt** file	Copying files to your computer
Gathering computer information	Restarting your computer
Hardware detection	Initializing hardware and finalizing settings
Locating Windows components	
Preparing to copy files	
Finishing setup	
Configuring hardware	
Completing configuration options (first restart)	
Windows Message "Restarting your Computer" (second restart)	

Setup Wizard Information Bar

Windows 98 now makes it easier than ever to monitor the installation progress. This is accomplished with addition of the new **Setup Wizard Information Bar** located on the left side of the setup screen. The information bar also includes a timer that indicates the estimated time to completion.

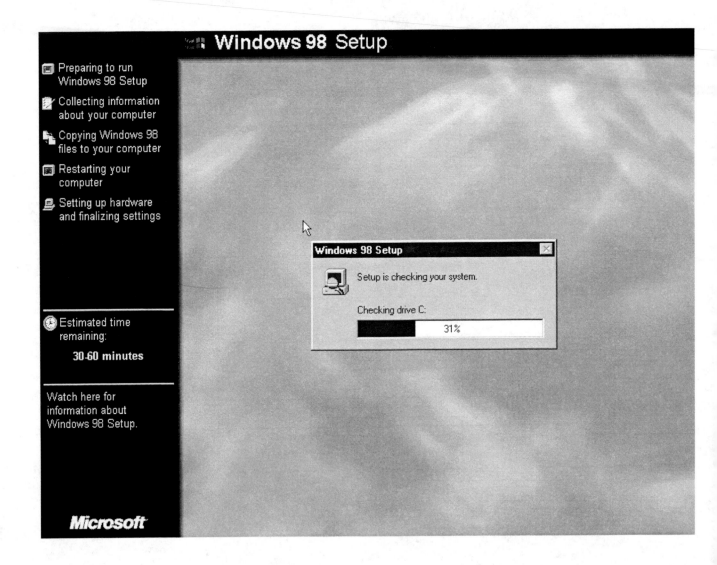

New Cabinet Files Organization

Like Windows 95, Windows 98 also uses **.CAB** files (cabinet files) for installation. The cabinet file is just an ordinary file that contains setup information. These files are included with the Setup CD and are usually in a compressed format.

The Windows 98 files are separated into different folders by function. This makes the overall installation process much faster.

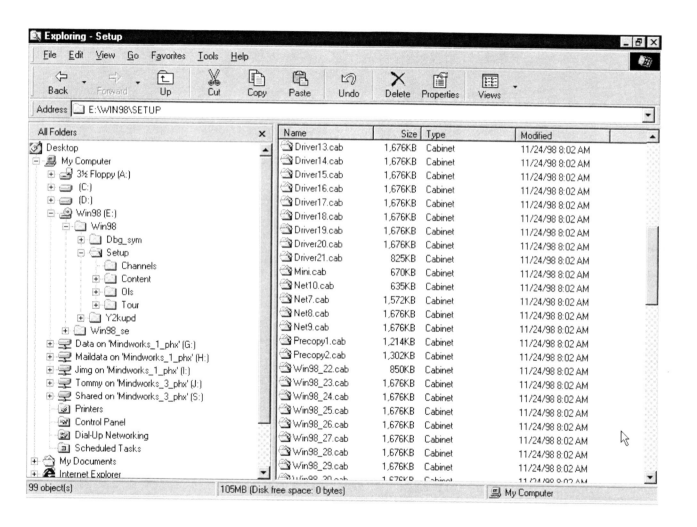

Improved Plug and Play Detection

Inventory of your computer's plug and play hardware has now been moved to the beginning portion of the installation. This inventory is completed before detection to limit problems and errors in the middle of an install.

Windows 98 will also use existing (current) system configuration information to identify any legacy hardware components.

Anti-Virus Checks

This feature is not what you might think! It doesn't check for viruses. It checks to see if there are any virus protection programs currently running before beginning. If there are, the setup dialog box will inform you to disable the software.

Installation programs don't like those little TSRs running as a background process during setup. Windows 98 will make changes to the boot sector during the install process. Most virus protection programs are designed to prevent this, therefore it could cause the installation to fail. It is better to stop before you begin rather than half way into the install only to be halted because of TSR conflicts.

Windows 98 upgrade

The key to any successful installation or upgrade is preparation. One of the most important steps in the preparation process is backing up your current system configuration (if one exists) and any personal or mission critical business data you may have on the disk.

Uninstall option

If, for any reason, you need to uninstall Windows 98, you can then return to your previous Windows 95 environment if you backed up the Windows 95 system files during the Windows 98 install. To uninstall Windows 98 and return to your previous configuration the following items must be checked:

- Click **Yes** to **Save System Files** in the dialog box that appears when you install Windows 98.

  This will create two files called **winundo.dat** and **winundo.ini** located in the root directory of the partition that you selected during setup. These two files contain all the saved Windows 95 system files.

- Be sure you have not compressed your system or boot partition after completing the Windows 98 install. This includes any partition that stores the **winundo.dat** file.

- Be sure you have not converted any system files to FAT32 if your Windows 95 was released before OSR-2.

Windows 98 Upgrade Checklist

The following checklist should be used as a guideline prior to doing any upgrade. You should complete all of the following before starting an upgrade:

Decide on which installation configuration best meets your needs.

This would include decisions like retaining your existing Windows 95 settings also deciding if you want Windows 98 to dual-boot with some other operating system. Another decision would be the type of components to install for a Typical, Compact, or Custom Installation. This would also be the time to decide to install locally (from CD-ROM) or from a network drive or disk.

Is your hardware supported?

This is a big one. Try to determine in advance if all the hardware installed in your computer is supported by Windows 98. Perhaps the easiest way to do this prior to the upgrade is to go to the Microsoft Web site, ***www.microsoft.com*** and check the hardware compatibility list. This link will be more up to date than any other published list that is available.

Does your computer meet the minimum system requirements?

It is very important to verify that your computers meet the minimum system requirements. You can get this information on the side of the Windows 98 box.

Are all TSR programs disabled?

It is important to disable all **Terminate and Stay Resident** (TSR) programs that may be running in the background. The only exception would be those that are required for partition or hard drive control and those used for CD-ROMs and network interface cards (NICs).

The **setup.txt** file located on the Windows 98 CD includes more information on using Terminate and Stay Resident programs.

WINDOWS 98

Hard disk cleanup

This is a perfect time for some hard disk cleanup and maintenance. Now is the time to delete any old or temporary files. Then run scandisk to check the integrity of the disk. You should also defragment the entire drive before starting the upgrade.

Check to ensure that all system files are backed up

· All business files

· All personal data

· All password files in the windows directory (**PWL**) files

· All **INI** files in the Windows directory

· All **DAT** files in the Windows directory

· Any proprietary network configurations (drivers or logon scripts)

· Any **config.sys** or **Autoexec.bat** in the root directory

Disable all MS-DOS programs

Make sure to disable all DOS programs running on your PC. You can use **Alt+Tab** to find out which programs are currently running. Exit all these except for the setup program.

Locate the Windows 95 boot disk

You will need this disk to recover in the event of a Windows 98 Setup failure.

Choosing the Setup option

You can choose from four different Windows 98 installation options. The type you choose will determine the amount of disk space the installation will require. The following options are available:

Typical

This is the Windows 98 default option, recommended for most users. It installs with a minimum of user input. *This type of installation will require about 205 MB of hard disk space.*

Portable

This is the recommended option for mobile users with laptop computers. This includes the "briefcase" feature to facilitate file synchronization and support software for direct cable connections to exchange files. *This installation will require approximately 177 MB of hard disk space.*

Compact

This option is designed for those users who have a limited amount of free disk space. The setup program will install the minimum files needed to operate. No optional components are installed. *This installation will require about 164 MB of hard disk space.*

Custom

This option is designed for advanced users, who want to have control over all available setup options. The setup utility will install the necessary components based on the selection of options. *This type of installation will require about 205 MB of hard disk space.*

Exercise 13.1   Performing a Windows 98 Upgrade

OBJECTIVES

Upgrade an existing Windows 95 system to the Windows 98 operating platform.

PREPARATION

- This exercise assumes that you will be running setup from the Windows 98 CD. If not, check with your instructor for the location of the source files and setup program.

- Secure from your instructor a copy of the Windows 98 CD-ROM software and the CD-ROM product key number.

- Ensure that your Windows 95 computer is running correctly!

Step 1   **Start Windows 95**

- From the desktop, insert the Windows 98 CD.

- If it autostarts, click on the **Install Windows 98** button. If it does not autostart, click on the **Start** button.

  - At the **Start** menu, click on **Run**.
  - At the **Run** menu, click on **Browse**.
  - At the top of your **Browse** menu go to the top where it says **Look In** and click on the down indicator.
  - Now select your CD-ROM drive (most likely the **D** drive).
  - Locate the **Win 98** folder and double-click it.
  - Locate the **Setup** folder and double-click it.
  - Then click on the **setup.exe** file and click **Open**.
  - This should now take you back to the **Run** menu window with the **setup.exe** file selected.
  - Now click **OK** to proceed.

Step 2   **Windows 98 Setup Window opens and the system starts to copy files for the setup process.**

Step 3   **The Microsoft License Agreement window appears.**

·   You can scroll down to the end of the agreement.

·   To continue, you MUST click the **I Accept the Agreement** statement.

·   Click **Next** to continue.

Step 4   **The product key window appears.**

·   Enter the product key number supplied to you by your instructor.

·   Click **Next** to continue.

Step 5   **The Select Directory window appears.**

·   Accept the default of **C:\Windows.**

·   Click **Next** to continue.

Step 6   **The Preparing Registry windows opens and checks the current Windows 95 Registry and the disk space available.**

Step 7   **The Save System Files window opens.**

·   This will allow you to save the files necessary to return to Windows 95 if for some reason Windows 98 is not right. If **Yes**, it will take approximately 50 MB of disk space for these files.

Step 8   **The Setup option window opens and asks what kind of setup you want.**

·   Typical

·   Portable

·   Compact

·   Custom

Note: Choose **Typical** *for this installation.*

·   Click **Next** to continue.

WINDOWS 98

Step 9   **The User Information Window is displayed.**

·   Enter your name and company or other identification here.

Note: This information will be used for identification in the future.

Step 10   **Check for Windows components.**

·   This will allow Windows to check for your components and load the necessary drivers.

·   Click **Next** to continue.

Step 11   **Establish your location.**

·   Select your location

·   Click **Next** to continue.

Step 12   **Create a Windows Startup Disk**

·   This will allow you to create a Startup Disk , used to boot your system in the event of a Windows 98 boot failure.

·   Click **Next** to continue. It will load the files for the startup disk. If you want a startup disk, insert a clean floppy diskette in your **A** drive at this time. If you choose not to create a startup diskette, click **Cancel** at the **Insert disk** prompt.

·   Otherwise, click **OK**. It will copy the necessary files.

·   When completed, click **Next** to continue.

Step 13   Windows will now start the copy process

Note: This may take a little time, so be patient.

Step 14   When the file copy is complete, the system reboots.

Step 15   After the system restarts, it displays the Windows Password Dialog Box.

- If you don't want a password, just click **OK**. If you enter a password, the system will ask you to verify it by entering it again.

Step 16   Windows 98 continues to load.

- The setup program may ask you to load drivers (depending on your PC configuration and in-stalled devices).

- Click **Next** to continue.

- If Setup ask you where you would like to search, select CD-ROM. *Note: If you have the manufacture's disk with the necessary drivers, you can specify it as the destination.*

- Click **Next** to continue.

- When the drivers have installed, click **Finish**. *Note: Windows 98 should load with the new desktop and display the Welcome Screen.*

WINDOWS 98

Web Integration Tools

Perhaps one of the hottest new features of Windows 98 is in the area of Web Integration. The Web Integration tool allows you to browse your personal computer just like pages on the World Wide Web. Depending on how your computer was originally setup, the Web integration feature may be active or inactive. When the Web Integration is active it will drastically change the way you access information on your PC.

A summary of Web Integration is presented below:

Hyperlinks

With web integration turned on, icons take on a whole new look. Your desktop icons now are presented as Web page hyperlinks. The icon title is underlined and when you hover over them with the mouse pointer the text turns blue.

The One-Click option

This feature allows you to launch anything with a single click. There are only a few areas that still require a double click.

The No-Click option

Now you can select an icon by simply moving your mouse pointer over it and in a few seconds Windows 98 will highlight the icon to show that it has been selected. You can also use this feature to select multiple icons without having to click anything. That will be covered in more detail in the lab at the end of this section.

Web Integration

Microsoft has made it quite easy to enable or disable the Web Integration feature. To enable Web Integration, choose Start, Settings, Folders Options. This will open the Folder Options dialog box shown below:

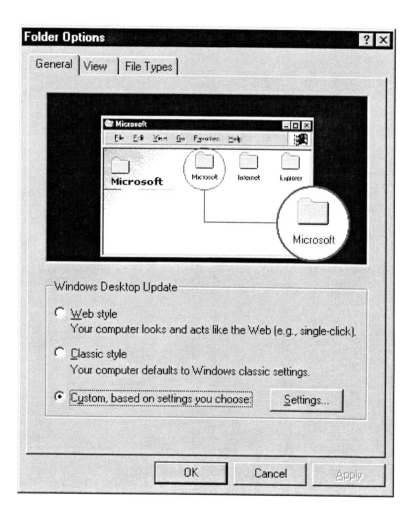

Notice that the general TAB includes three options:

· Web Style

· Classic Style

· Custom Style

Web Style

This choice will enable the Web Integration feature. If you choose this method it will then ask if you want to use the single click mode to open icons. If you say **Yes**, then all icons and folders on your desktop will be presented as an underlined hyperlink.

Classic Style

The Classic style presents icons just the way they were in the Windows 95 product requiring that you double-click an icon to launch it.

Custom Syle

The **General** tab in the dialog box also supports a third option, the custom style. As the name implies, this option allows the user to customize the settings to a point somewhere between the Classic style and the Web-based style. An example of the custom dialog screen is shown below:

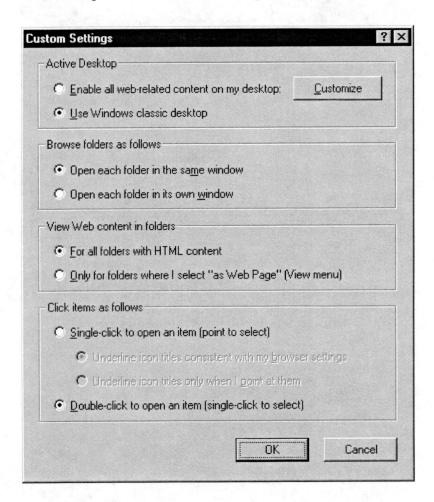

Custom option	Description
Active Desktop	This setting allows you to turn on/off the active desktop feature. The active desktop feature permits you to use a web page to replace your static background used in Windows 95.
Open each folder in the same window	With this feature active you navigate folders by viewing a single window that will change with each opened folder.
Open each folder in its own window	This option will allow you to leave all previous folders you display open.
For all folders with HTML content	Windows 98 will display every folder window as a Web page. The exception to this is, folders are not shown as Web pages in the explorer view.
Only for folders where I select "as Web Page" (View menu)	With this feature active you must display each folder as a Web page by manually selecting it.
Single-click to open an item (point to select)	Activation of this feature permits the one-click and no-click options.
Underline icon titles consistent with my browser settings	With this setting enabled, Windows 98 will underline all the icon titles.
Underline icon titles only when I point at them	This feature will only activate text underlining when you point at an icon.
Double-click to open an item (single-click to select)	You would activate this option to use "legacy" mouse techniques for launching and selecting icons.

Overview of Custom Settings

FrontPage Express

As mentioned earlier, one of the features that has undergone the most change in the Windows 98 product is the addition of Web Integration tools. One of the most interesting Web tools is the FrontPage Express. Today's Internet surfer is no longer satisfied with just being a passive participant on the World Wide Web. Now people want to produce and publish their own Internet content. In the past, those people with information to share just did not have the opportunity to do so. This, however, is no longer the case. Microsoft programmers have included an easy to use Web Page creation tool (FrontPage Express) in Windows 98. It is now easier than ever to create your own personal Home Page and display it to the world.

Microsoft Windows 98 includes two tools to help you share your personal information on the Web. The first, FrontPage Express, helps you create Web pages using basically the same commands as it takes to publish a memo or business letter. The other tool, Web Publishing Wizard, helps you get that completed page actually published out on the World Wide Web.

A Web page is really nothing more than just a plain text file with instructions that inform the Web browser how and where to display various pieces of information. Now here is the catch those text files are created using a special language called Hypertext Markup Language (HTML). HTML uses instruction sets called tags that control placement and display characteristics of the information placed within the page. Like any type of programming language HTML can get a wee bit fussy about syntax. A misplaced character could cause that graphic of your favorite dog to disappear.

Now, instead of playing around with all the intricacies of HTML syntax, you can use Windows 98 FrontPage Express to create your pages. FrontPage eliminates the messy HTML syntax and lets you create Web pages using simple menu commands with predefined templates. The graphic below shows some of the FrontPage templates:

The Web pages created by the templates provide a fast and easy way to get a jump on creating your own Web page. However if you already have a feel for Web page creation FrontPage will also let you start with a blank page and allow you to create everything from scratch.

If you really feel like spicing up your Web page you can start with a predefined template and then enhance it by adding graphics, background sound or even video clips. The Windows FrontPage program is more than up to the task.

Now once you have your Web page created and honed, it is time to publish your new creation on the World Wide Web for all to see. Once again Windows 98 has included the tools to accomplish this as well. Typically to transfer your page to some server on the Web you had to use some type of FTP program. These programs tend to be a bit scary, especially if you are not familiar with the syntax and terminology. Well, the solution is the Web Publishing Wizard included with Windows 98. This tool makes transferring your files to a Web server a whole lot easier by using menu driven dialog boxes and user friendly help screens.

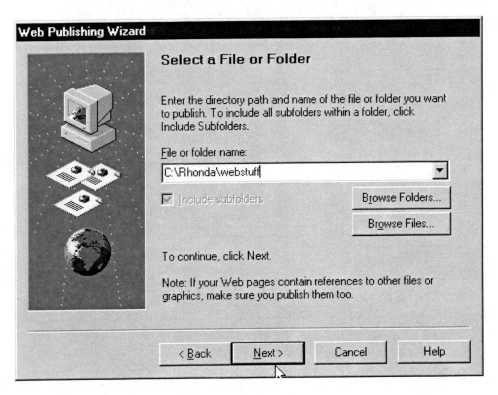

Exercise 13.2 Creating a Web Page

OBJECTIVES

Use Microsoft Windows 98 FrontPage Express to create a Web Page.

PREPARATION

This exercise assumes that you are currently running Windows 98 on your classroom computer.

Step 1 **Launch FrontPage Express**

- Click **Start > Programs >Internet Explorer >FrontPage Express.**
- Click on **File > New.**
- Select **Personal Home Page Wizard**, then click **OK.**
- Select **Biographical, Personal and Contact Information.**
- Click **Next** to continue.

Step 2 **Name your Web Page**

- At the **Page URL** box, enter your last name. **(lastname.htm)**
- At the **Page Title** box, enter the following: **YourName Home Page** i.e. (Lisa's Home Page)
- Click **Next** to continue.

Step 3 **Choose a Biography format**

- Select **Personal.**
- Click **Next** to continue.

Step 4 **Enter Personal Interest Information**
- In the boxed area, enter personal interest i.e. golf, hiking etc.

  Note: Make sure that you include the word **Hiking.** *We will need it later in the exercise.*
- Click **Next** to continue.

Step 5 **Supply contact information**
- Fill in what ever information you want.
- Click **Next** to continue.

Step 6 **Display order screen**
- View information, change if you desire.
- Click **Next** to continue.

Step 7 **Finish and close template**
- Click **Finish**.

Step 8 **Enter Biographical information**
- Scroll down to **Biographical Information.**
- Enter some personal information i.e. **Completed My A+ Certification** and today's date.

Step 9 **Set Home Page background color**
- Right-click on any open area of the page.
- Select **Page Properties**.
- Click on the **Background** tab.
- Select a color from the background dialog box.
- Click **OK**.

Step 10　　**Close and Save template**

·　Close the document by clicking the **X** in the upper right-hand corner of the window.

·　Click **Yes** when prompted to save.

·　Click **Save as a File**.

·　Accept the default name and write down the name and path to its location

　　C:_____

·　Click **Save** to continue.

Step 11　　**Exit completely from FrontPage**

Step 12　　**View your Home Page**

·　Right-click the **Start** button.

·　Click **Explore**.

·　Locate the file saved in Step 10.

·　Open the file saved in Step 10 (double-click it).

·　View your Home Page .

Step 14　　**View the HTML source code**

·　Right-click on any open area on your Web Page.

·　Choose **View Source**. *Note: You should now notice that Notepad opens your Web page and displays the actual HTML code and tags used to create the page.*

·　Now while still in the Notepad window, scroll down and change the letter **H** in hiking to the letter **B**.

·　Click **File**.

·　Click Save.

·　Exit **Notepad**, saying **Yes** to changes.

·　Close Internet Explorer.

·　Locate the file saved in Step 10.

·　Open the file saved in Step 10 (double-click it).

·　View your Home Page.

Note: The change from hiking to biking!

WINDOWS 98

Troubleshooting Windows 98

No matter how refined and robust a system, there will always be those times that you will have to fix some problem area. Windows 98 offers a couple of nice troubleshooting features that will help you isolate and ultimately correct the problems.

The first of these, and probably the most overlooked, is the Windows 98 Help system. Other useful troubleshooting aids include The Registry Checker, and the Dr. Watson utility. When used correctly, these tools can be a valuable aid in troubleshooting common Windows problems.

The Windows 98 Help system includes a very detailed troubleshooting aid that covers most of the common problem areas. The graphic below shows help information for troubleshooting a sound card problem:

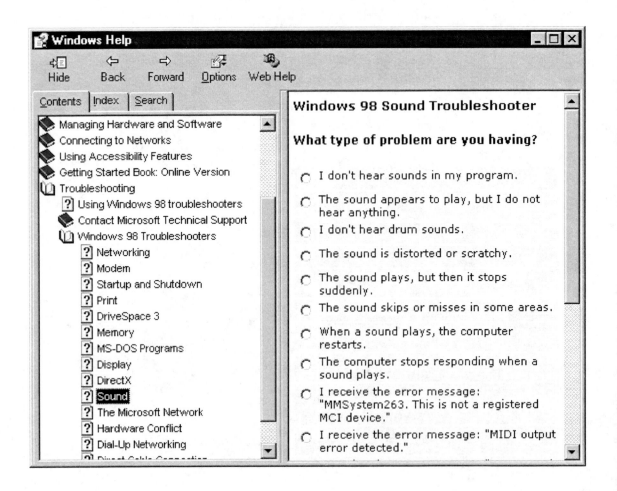

The Registry Checker

The Registry Checker is really more of a maintenance tool than a troubleshooting tool. However, it will find and resolve some registry problems. The Checker will also make regular backups of your registry for you.

The Windows 98 Registry Checker will automatically backup the registry following each and every successful system startup. If any serious problems occur the Registry Checker will restore the most recent good registry from the backup files.

Windows 98 is packaged with two flavors of the Registry Checker program. There is a Windows-based program called **ScanRegW** and a DOS-based version called **ScanReg**

Dr. Watson Utility

The Dr. Watson Utility (**drwatson.exe**) is very useful in collecting information about the state of your computer at the time and just before a fault occurs. Dr. Watson traps software faults, identifying the failed piece of software and offering a detailed description of the possible cause.

You can enable and configure Dr. Watson to load automatically when Windows 98 boots by creating a shortcut to the Drwatson.exe in the startup folder. Once enabled Dr. Watson will automatically log information to a file located in the **Windows\Drwatson** folder. Dr. Watson runs minimized, the icon will appear on the task bar. By double-clicking the icon on the task bar the following summary screen will appear:

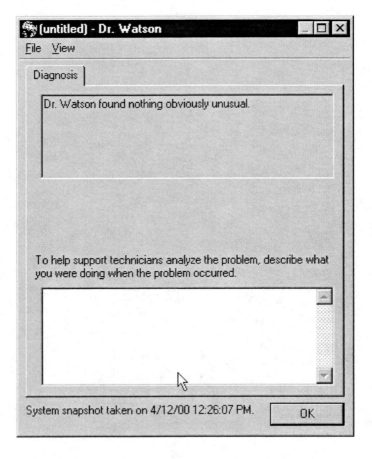

Summary

As you have seen Windows 98 is loaded full of new changes, many of which are internal tweaks that enable Windows 98 to run smoother, faster and more reliable than previous Windows platforms.

Some of the most visible Windows 98 changes can found in the Web Integration tools. Features like the active desktop and the ability to browse your local computer folders and icons in a WEB style format.

WINDOWS 98

Review Questions

1. Which of the following files are created if you select **Yes** to the **Save System Files** option during setup? (Choose two)

13-12

    A. **autoexec.bat**

    B. **config.sys**

    ✳ C. **winundo.dat**

    D. **user.dat**

    ✳ E. **winundo.ini**

2. Which of the following setup options would be best for a computer with limited disk space?

    A. Portable

    ✳ B. Compact

    C. Typical

    D. Custom

3. What tool allows you to create a Personal Web Page?

    A. Web Publisher Wizard

    ✳ B. FrontPage Express

    C. Notepad

    D. Internet Explorer

4. What is name of the language used to create Web Pages?

    A. Basic

    B. TCP

    C. HTP

    ✳ D. HTML

5. Which of the following tools help you transfer your Web Page information to a Web server?

    * A. Web Publishing Wizard
    B. FrontPage Express
    C. Internet Explorer
    D. Windows Explorer

6. Which type of install would be best suited for a traveling user with a laptop computer?

    A. Custom
    * B. Portable
    C. Express
    D. Compact

7. Before starting any install, you should first disable any _____.

    A. HTML
    * B. TSRs
    C. Windows
    D. System files

8. Windows 98 installation files are called _____ files.

    A. INT
    B. CAV
    * C. CAB
    D. WIN

9. There are _____ major steps to the Windows 98 installation process.

    A. 10

 * B. 5

    C. 25

    D. 2

10. Which of the following troubleshooting tools can be used to create a daily backup of the registry files?

    A. Dr. Watson

 * B. Registry Checker

    C. Device Manager

    D. Windows Report Tool

Section 14

Windows NT 4.0

Section 14 - Windows NT 4.0

Introduction

You have two computers sitting in front you. At first glance they both look pretty much the same. They are both running a Microsoft operating system. It is only when you click the start button that you begin to notice a difference. One computer displays the Windows 95 text while the other computer displays Windows NT 4.0.

Yes, Windows NT looks like Windows 95 but that is about where the similarities stop. The Windows NT system was optimized to provide network services to client-side computers. Windows NT ships in two different flavors Windows NT Server and Windows NT workstation. In this section we will compare features of both the server and workstation versions.

Objectives:

- NT Workstation Overview

- NT Server Overview

- Describe the System Hardware requirements for NT Workstation

- Describe the System Hardware requirements for NT Server

- Compare NT Workstation and NT Server Services

- Discuss NT Server Types

- Discuss the NTFS file system

WIN NT 4.0

NT Workstation Overview

The programming team at Microsoft designed Windows NT Workstation to be a powerful end user desktop solution. To minimize the learning curve, Microsoft designed the Windows NT desktop around the already familiar Windows 95 desktop environment. However, Windows NT is not just another release of the Windows 95 product. It offers far better performance and reliability than previous versions of Windows. It also includes many enhanced security features like mandatory logon and a much more robust local file system security through the implementation of the NTFS file system.

The overall performance of Windows NT Workstation was optimized by providing support for multiple processors. The Workstation edition of NT provides support for up to (two) processors creating an optimal multiple tasking platform. Windows NT also is hardware independent, providing support for Intel or Alpha based processors.

Windows NT Workstation security model is more extensive than ever before, it requires that all users be authenticated by the system before they can have access to its resources. After a successful logon, local access to hard disk information can be enhanced by enabling the NTFS file system on selected partitions. The NTFS file system allows for more stringent security on the local hard disk than the FAT file system used by Windows 95.

Windows NT Workstation also facilitates support for Microsoft RAS (Remote Access Service). This provides support for one (1) incoming remote access session. This feature also allows for out-going dial-up networking as well.

System Hardware Requirements for NT Workstation

The following is a list of the official Microsoft minimum requirements for the installation of Windows NT workstation:

Processor

Minimum 486/33 (Pentium or higher strongly recommended). NT also supports MIPS, Power PC and Digital Alpha processing platforms

Hard Disk

A minimum of 125 MB of free hard disk space

Memory

16 MB of RAM recommended

Video

VGA or higher resolution

Mouse

Microsoft approved pointing device

CD-ROM

Compatible CD-ROM

It should be noted that these are the minimum standards just to get the operating system installed. As you add other software options and components these minimums may have to be increased.

WIN NT 4.0

NT Server Overview

Microsoft NT Server was designed to a provide powerful solution for the network server environment. NT Server can provide file and print services as well as acting as an Internet host or providing robust back office functions such as database services. Just like the Windows NT Workstation, the server edition also includes the familiar Windows 95 desktop.

NT Server also supports multiple processors improving multi-tasking capabilities. By default Windows NT allows support for four (4) processors. Optional OEM support will allow for up to 32 processors. As with the workstation edition the NT server version is also hardware independent and supports both Intel and Alpha processors.

The Windows NT Server security model also requires that all users be authenticated by the system before they can have access to its resources. Local access to hard disk information can be enhanced by enabling the NTFS file system. The NTFS file system allows for more security on the local hard disk than the FAT file system used by Windows 95. Windows NT Server also provides and controls security for the network domain environment as well.

Internet Information Server (IIS) is packaged with the NT Server software. When implemented, IIS allows the NT Server to function as an Internet Web Server providing HTTP and FTP services.

Remote Access Services (RAS) and connections are also included with NT Server. Unlike the workstation edition that only provides (1) connection, NT Server provides support for 256 in-coming RAS sessions. NT Server also provides for outgoing dial-up connection as well.

System Hardware Requirements for NT Server

The following is a list of the official Microsoft minimum requirements for the installation of Windows NT Server:

Processor

Intel 486/33 or higher (Pentium PRO or higher recommended). Digital Alpha platform also recommended

Hard Disk

125 MB of free hard disk space (Just for the Installation)

Memory

32 MB of system RAM (64 MB or more strongly recommended)

Mouse

Microsoft approved pointing device

Video

VGA (Super VGA or better recommended)

CD-ROM

Compatible CD-ROM

WIN NT 4.0

Compare NT Workstation and NT Server Services

Windows NT Workstation was designed and optimized to be a desktop computing platform. It was intended to be deployed as a front-end desktop solution for applications like the Microsoft Office Suite running Microsoft Word, Excel and Access.

Windows NT Server was designed and optimized to be used a network server providing file and print services. NT Server design also is optimized to run back-office applications like SQL (Structured Query Language) server, SNA server and Microsoft Exchange.

The following list compares Windows NT Workstation and Server features:

· NT Workstation supports one (1) in-coming RAS connection, while the Server edition allows for 256 in-coming RAS sessions.

· Windows NT server provides support for Windows IIS for Web server support while Windows Workstation uses Peer Web Service (PWS).

· Windows NT Workstation permits support for up to two processors by default, while the server edition supports four processors by default and up to 32 processors with its OEM versions.

· NT Workstation typically requires less system RAM for optimal performance.

· Windows NT Server can run enhanced TCP/IP services like DHCP (Dynamic Host Configuration Protocol) while Workstation can be a DHCP client it can **not** become a DHCP server.

NT Server Types

Windows NT Server can be installed in three different classifications:

- PDC (Primary Domain Controller)

- BDC (Backup Domain Controller)

- Member Server

Primary Domain Controller (PDC)

The PDC is the first server that is installed into a domain. The domain is a logical grouping of servers, client computers and other resources that share the same user and group account database. The concept of "domains" provides for a single entry point to network resources as well as providing centralized control. Each domain on the network is assigned a unique name. The PDC is responsible for maintaining this common user account database referred to as the SAM (Security Account Manager). Any changes made in the SAM are then distributed to any Backup domain controllers.

Note: There can be only one PDC server in each domain.

WIN NT 4.0

Backup Domain Controller (BDC)

Unlike the PDC, there can be multiple Backup Domain Controllers in a domain environment. A BDC provides the network with two primary functions. The first and perhaps most important is to provide a degree of fault tolerance in the event that the PDC should fail. By default the Primary Domain Controller sends up-dates to the BDC about every five minutes. If the PDC should fail for any reason the BDC can be "promoted" to a PDC.

The other role a BDC plays in the domain environment is to enhance the PDC's performance by off loading the logon responsibilities from the PDC. The BDC then performs the logon authentication process for the domain.

Its important to mention that the BDC stores a READ-ONLY version of the database. Any changes are actually made at the PDC and replicated to any BDCs in the domain.

It is recommended that you have at least one BDC in every domain and possibly more depending on the size and geographic layout of your network.

Member Server

Unlike the PDC and BDC the member server does **not** store a copy of the account database. This permits member servers to offer things like file and print services without suffering performance hits due to the overhead of holding and maintaining the account database (SAM).

The NTFS File System

The New Technology File System (NTFS) is the preferred file system when implementing an NT environment. Windows NT is the only system that can use the NTFS file system. If your machine is configured in a dual boot mode, you will need to choose a file system that is compatible with both operating systems.

The following is a list of NTFS primary features:

Enhanced Security

Windows NT directories and partitions that have been converted to NTFS maintain special permissions (rights) that control access to any files created or copied there. NTFS also includes an auditing feature used by the NT security system.

Fault Tolerant

The NTFS file system maintains a log of all changes within the file system. This means that any modifications can be duplicated or removed to compensate for any inconsistencies due to disk failures or power loss. NTFS also includes a "Hot Fix" feature, which means that every time it writes data to the disk, it then reads that information to verify the write. If the data is corrupt the NTFS system will mark that area of the disk as bad and then rewrite the data to a clean area on the disk.

Wɪɴ **NT 4.0**

File Compression

NTFS includes real time file compression. NTFS incorporates file-by-file compression, which means if there is something that goes wrong only that file will be affected.

Increased File and Partition Size

The NTFS file system can store files up to 16 exabytes in length. That's big: it is actually 2^{64th} power.

Increased Performance

NTFS utilizes a directory structure similar to what the OS/2 operating system uses called B-Tree directory structure. This system allows for faster file searches. NTFS will also always attempt to save files in contiguous blocks when possible to reduce fragmentation.

Macintosh File Support

NTFS supports optional MAC file support on NTFS servers. This allows Macintosh files to be stored on the server running Macintosh services.

Converting to NTFS

The NTFS file system can be enabled during the initial install or at a later time from the command prompt. It is typically recommended that you do not to convert during the installation process. That way if anything fails during the install you can still return to original file system i.e. the FAT or whatever file system you started with.

Windows NT includes a utility called **CONVERT.EXE** which can be used to convert existing FAT volumes to NTFS. This process is non-destructive and will not erase or delete any files. However having a good known backup before you start is always a prudent idea.

This utility **CONVERT.EXE** is a command line utility that can be run from the DOS prompt or the **Run** option from the start menu. The following syntax would be used to convert the "C" drive from FAT to NTFS:

Type **convert C: /FS:NTFS**

WIN NT 4.0

NTFS Permissions (rights)

The following is a list of permissions that can be assigned to partitions and drives that have been converted to NTFS:

NO Access

The **no access** permission means just that: you have no access or rights to that folder or directory. This permission will override any other permissions that you may have inherited from a group assignment.

List

This permission allows the user to view directory (folder) and file names but not to view the contents of the file. It is typically used to allow for navigation of folders.

Read

Like the **list** permission, however this permission will allow you to view as well as execute files. It also permits you to copy files.

Add

This permission allows you to add folders and files within that location.

Change

The **change** permission combines the features of the **list**, **read** and **add** permissions. It will also let you delete files and folders.

Full Control

The **Full Control** permission is actually a combination of the **List, Read, Add** and **Change** permissions.

Summary

The Microsoft Windows NT 4.0 release was unique in that it of-fered both a Workstation platform and a robust server environment. The success of Windows NT was due in part to the Microsoft design team that gave us a new operating system but with a familiar Windows 95 style desktop. This lessened the learning curve and made the acceptance of the new system more palatable.

WIN NT 4.0

Review Questions

1. The Windows NTFS file system is compatible with most other operating systems?

   True

   ✗ False

2. How many PDCs can be installed in a single domain?

   ✗ A. 1
   B. 2
   C. 3
   D. unlimited

3. A Backup Domain controller performs which of the following functions (Choose all that apply.):

   ✗ A. Authentication Services
   B. Mail Services
   ✗ C. Fault Tolerance
   D. Print Services

4. Which of the following is a type of NT server installation? (Choose all that apply.)

   ✗ A. BDC
   ✗ B. PDC
   C. IIS
   ✗ D. Member

5. NT Workstation supports _____ RAS
    session(s)?

    Remote access
    service

    ✳ A. 1

    B. 2

    C. 256

    D. unlimited

6. By default Windows NT Server provides support for
    _____ processors.   *14-6*

    A. 2

    B. 3

    ✳ C. 4

    D. 22

7. The syntax to convert an existing DOS drive labeled
    as "D" to an NTFS drive would be:

    A. Convert d: /NTFS

    B. Convert d: /NEW /NTFS

    ✳ C. Convert d: /FS:NTFS

    D. Can not be done at the command line

8. The Windows IIS product permits support for which
    of the following:

    ✳ A. An Internet Server

    B. A Database server

    C. Fault Tolerant Server

    D. International ISO server

9. Both NT Workstation and NT Server can support Windows IIS:

    True

    ✳ False

10. Advanced TCP/IP support is supplied by installing which of the following on the NT server:

    A. RAS
    ✳ B. DHCP
    C. IIS
    D. SOP

Section 15

Windows 2000 Professional

Section 15: Windows 2000 Professional

Introduction

Windows 2000 is a multipurpose operating system that supports file and print, application, web, and communication server functions. Windows 2000 Professional continues the trend towards greater manageability, reliability, security and performance as a replacement for Windows NT Workstation that also includes the best features of Windows 98.

Windows 2000 builds on the potency of Windows NT 4.0 by offering a platform that is faster, more stable, and easier to manage. Windows 2000 further develops the Windows NT 4.0 domain structure and management tools into a fully extensible, scalable directory service called Active Directory. This flexible directory service is scalable, built from the ground up using Internet-standard technologies and is fully integrated at the operating system level. The combination of Active Directory and an enhanced security model allows clients to decrease the number of domains needed in the organization.

Objectives:

- · Windows 2000 Installation Overview

- · Perform Windows 2000 Professional Install

- · Understand the Microsoft Management Console

- · Monitor Access to files and folders

- · Discuss Access to files and folders with Permissions

- · Discuss Web Server Resources

- · Describe Printer objects

- · Configuring the Desktop

- · Discuss the Windows Installer

Installation Requirements

Here is a list of the hardware installation requirements of Window 2000 Professional:

- The recommended processor for Windows 2000 Professional is a Pentium 166 or higher.

- At least one hard disk is needed for installing Windows 2000. The boot drive must have the necessary free hard disk space. At least 500 – 1000 MB are recommended for install.

- The memory needed for Windows 2000 Professional is 32 MB on a x86-based or 48 MB on a Compaq Alpha. However, at least 64 MB is highly recommended.

- The standard VGA is the display needed for Windows 2000 Server and Professional. A keyboard is necessary for installing Windows 2000 and a mouse or other pointing device is recommended but not essential. A single network adapter card is also desirable for Windows 2000 Professional though not essential.

The Hardware Compatibility List (HCL) supplied with Windows 2000 lists each hardware component that has passed the Hardware Compatibility Tests (HCT) when Windows 2000 Professional was released. It also indicates which devices Windows 2000 officially supports.

Important Files to Review

Once the target system meets the hardware requirements for an installation of Windows 2000 Professional, there are at least two important files that one should review prior to the actual installation. These files are **Read1st.txt** and **Readme.doc**. Both should be located in the root directory of the installation CD-ROM.

The **Read1st.txt** file contains critical pre-installation notes vital to the success of the installation and the **Readme.doc**. file contains important usage information about hardware, networking, applications and printing.

Upgrade from a previous version of Windows to Windows 2000 Professional

Prior to the actual installation, you must also decide whether to perform an upgrade of an existing Operating System on the target system(s), or to perform a "clean" installation. This decision will affect the choices made during the setup process – for example, whether or not to format the destination partition!

Performing a "clean" installation has the distinct advantage of not inheriting any system problems from the previous Operating System. In fact, most professionals agree that a "clean" installation will provide a much more stable system than will a flawless upgrade.

Performing an upgrade of a previous Operating System does offer its benefits, including simpler configuration and retention of existing users, settings, groups, rights, and permissions. Files and applications will also not need to be reinstalled. Windows NT Workstation versions 3.51 and 4.0 upgrade directly to Windows 2000 Server or Windows 2000 Professional. All releases of Windows 3.x, Windows 95 and Windows 98 will upgrade to Windows 2000 Professional only.

Many of the same pre-installation tasks must be performed prior to an upgrade of Windows NT 4.0. For example, the hardware requirements, important files to review, and licensing modes all must be checked prior to the upgrade. Review carefully the Performing an Attended Installation section, since almost all of the information applies directly to an upgrade.

Upgrading allows many of the settings from the previous Operating System to be retained and can be very advantageous for the administrator. When a previous Operating System is upgraded, Windows 2000 is installed into the same directory as the previous OS. The upgrade process is actually quite simple. The Setup wizard detects and installs the appropriate drivers, or it creates a report on devices that couldn't be upgraded so you can be sure that the hardware and software are compatible with Windows 2000. Remember to uncompress any DriveSpace or DoubleSpace volumes before upgrading to Windows 2000.

To upgrade Windows 95, Windows 98, or Windows NT 4.0 from the CD follow these steps:

· Start your computer by running your current operating system, and then insert the Windows 2000 Professional CD into your CD-ROM drive.

· If Windows automatically detects the CD and asks if you would like to upgrade your computer to Windows 2000 Professional, click **Yes**.

· Otherwise, click **Start**, and then click **Run**.

At the prompt, type the following command, replacing **d** with the letter assigned to your CD-ROM drive: **d:\i386\winnt32.exe**

· Press **Enter** and follow the instructions.

To upgrade from a network connection:

· Using your current operating system, establish a connection to the shared network folder that contains the Setup files. If you have an MS-DOS or network installation disk that contains network client software, you can use that disk to connect to the shared folder.

· If your computer is currently running Windows 95, Windows 98, or a previous version of Windows NT, at the command prompt, type the path to the file **winnt32.exe**.

\upgrade
winnt.exe = standard installation

· Press **Enter**.

· When you're asked if you would like to upgrade your computer to Windows 2000 Professional, click **Yes** and follow the instructions.

Dual-booting Windows 2000 Professional

Although it is rarely a recommended configuration, Windows 2000 Professional does have limited dual boot capabilities with other Operating Systems. If you decide to dual boot Windows 2000 Professional, please keep the following points in mind:

- Using NTFS as the only file system on a computer that contains both Windows 2000 and Windows NT is not recommended. This is due to updates in the new version of NTFS used by Windows 2000.

Better To place them in separate partitions

- Create a FAT partition containing the Windows NT 4.0 Operating System so that the computer will have access to needed files when the system boots NT. Also, make sure that Windows NT 4.0 has been updated with the latest released Service Pack before implementing dual-boot scenarios.

- Install each operating system on a separate drive or disk partition.

- If the computer is on a Windows NT or Windows 2000

domain, each installation of Windows NT 4.0 Server or Windows 2000 Server on that computer must have a different computer name.

- To set up a computer with Windows 95 or DOS and Windows 2000, install Windows 2000 last. Otherwise, important files needed for starting Windows 2000 could be overwritten.

- On a computer that will contain Windows 2000 and Windows 95 or DOS, the primary partition must be formatted as FAT. On a computer that will contain Windows 2000 and Windows 95 OSR2 or Windows 98, the primary partition must be formatted as FAT or FAT32, not NTFS.

Windows 2000 Compatible File Systems

A file system is the structure in which files are labeled, stored, and distributed. Windows 2000 supports the FAT, FAT32, and NTFS file systems. You will be forced to choose a file system during the installation process, during the formatting of an existing volume, or when installing a new hard disk. Changing a volume's existing file system can be cumbersome and even problematic, so you should choose a file system very carefully and based on long-term factors.

Before making this decision it is imperative to review the benefits and limitations of each file system. If you decide on a different file system then you must back up your data and reformat the volume using the new system.

Windows 2000 Professional supports the Windows NT file system (NTFS version 5), which is the recommended file system for use with Windows 2000. NTFS has all the basic capabilities of FAT including some new and advanced features.

Windows NT and Windows 2000 are the only systems that can read from local NTFS volumes and NTFS is available only in Windows NT/2000. Any operating system, however, can read from NTFS volumes over a network connection as the file system is transparent to the client. Windows NT 3.51 and 4.0 use NTFS version 4 whereas Windows 2000 uses NTFS version 5.

Choosing a File System

Once the partition has been selected for the install of Windows 2000 Professional, the file system to be used on the partition must be selected. NTFS, FAT, and FAT32 are all supported by Windows 2000. While all these file systems are supported, there are so many clear advantages to the NTFS file system that it is almost always chosen. One exception is for the dual boot systems (systems running Windows 2000 and an earlier Windows OS) mentioned previously and this should be rare.

With this being said, it is important to understand the Operating System compatibility of these file systems. The following table will assist with this:

NTFS	FAT	FAT32
Windows 2000, Windows NT 4.0 with SP 4 or later (not recommended)	MS-DOS All versions of Windows OS/2	Windows 95 OSR2 Windows 98 Windows 2000

This table presents some important features that demonstrate the advantages of the NTFS file system on a Windows 2000 system. *Ver.5*

Ver.5 ?

Version 5

NTFS	FAT	FAT32
No practical limit to volume/file size - minimum volume size 10 MB	Volume size from floppy to 4 GB - maximum file size 2 GB	Volumes from 512 MB to 2 TB - maximum file size 4 GB
Features file and folder level security	Domains not supported *Cannot Install*	Domains not supported *Active Directory*
Built-in disk compression	Supports dual boot configurations	Supports dual boot configurations
Built-in disk quotas	No file and folder level security	No file and folder level security
Built-in file encryption		
Remote storage supported		
Dynamic volumes		
Mounting of volumes to folders		

Win 2000 Advanced Server
1) Install
⟶ Stand alone server
   ⟶ Promoted to a Domain Controller   — *must have NTFS*
       Join a member Domain

DCpromo promotes a win 2000 Adv. Server to a
   Domain Controller
       ⟶ Installs active directory

1st domain controllers establishes a domain
   After this each domain controller on = level w/ all
   other Dom. Controllers

Joining a Domain or a Workgroup

To take full advantage of the administrative capabilities of Windows 2000 Professional, most networks organize into domains. A domain is a logical grouping of computers organized for the purposes of administration and security. If the workstation that is being setup is to join a Windows 2000 domain, the following must be provided/exist during installation:

· The name of the domain

· The name of the computer account created for the Windows 2000 Professional in the domain

· An available DNS server and Domain Controller

· In order to join a workgroup (a peer to peer grouping of computers), the workgroup name must be provided.

Perform an attended installation of Windows 2000 Professional

Windows 2000 can be installed using setup boot disks, a CD-ROM or over the network. You can also install Windows 2000 remotely and you can perform an unattended setup. Windows 2000 Professional is distributed on a CD-ROM and includes three setup floppy disks. These setup boot disks can be used if you are installing Windows 2000 for the first time on an x86-based computer that does not support the bootable CD-ROM format. You install Windows 2000 from a CD-ROM if your Windows 2000 installation files are on a compact disk and your computer's BIOS supports the bootable CD-ROM format. You begin this installation method by simply inserting the CD-ROM and restarting your system.

Another method of installing Windows 2000 is over a network. The files needed to install Windows 2000 reside in a shared location on a network file server. It is typically more efficient to install Windows 2000 over the network. At the very least, one does not have to worry about the location of the CD-ROM in order to install the Operating System. In order to carry out the installation over the network, the I386 or ALPHA directory must be copied to a network server and shared with the appropriate permissions. The target system must have appropriate network client software in order to connect to this network share. Often a boot disk is used to provide this connectivity. Once the connection to the distribution server is made, **WINNT.EXE or WINNT32.EXE** is executed to begin the installation. **WINNT32.EXE** is used to upgrade existing installations of Windows 2000 or Windows NT. Both of these setup programs can utilize switches in order to modify the installation in some way.

Many of these switches deal with unattended installation options.

SWITCH	USAGE
/a	Enables accessibility options
/e[:command]	Executes a command before the final phase of setup
/i[:inf_file]	Specifies the file name of the setup information file used in unattended installations.
/r[:folder]	Specifies an optional folder to be installed
/rx[:folder]	Specifies an optional folder to be copied
/s[:source_path]	Specifies the location of the Windows 2000 installation files
/t[:temp_drive]	Specifies a drive for the temporary files and subsequent installation
/u[:script_file]	Specifies the answer file for an unattended installation; requires the /s switch

WINNT.EXE Switches

SWITCH	USAGE
/copydir:folder	Creates an additional folder within the systemroot folder
/cmd:command	Executes a command before the final phase of setup
/copysource:folder	Creates an additional folder within the systemroot folder; setup deletes this folder after installation complete
/cmdcons	Copies the files necessary for the Recovery Console
/debug[level][:file_name]	Creates a debug file at the specified level
/s[:source_path]	Specifies the location of the Windows 2000 installation files
/syspart:drive_letter	Copies Setup files to drive and marks it as active - the drive can then be installed in another system for installation; requires /tempdrive
/tempdrive:drive_letter	Specifies a drive for the temporary files and subsequent installation
/unattend[number][:answer_file]	Specifies the answer file for an unattended installation; also the number of seconds before reboot during Windows 2000 upgrade
/udf:id[,udf_file]	Install via the use of a Uniqueness Database File (UDF)

Here is a quick laundry list of other considerations to make prior to an install of Windows 2000 Professional:

·   Networking information, specifically TCP/IP configuration information must be provided during installation. At the very least, an IP address and subnet mask must be provided, either dynamically via a DHCP server on the network, or manually during the install.

·   Backup any files on the target system that may be needed following the installation.

·   Uncompress the target drive if any compression software was used other than NTFS file compression.

·   Disconnect any uninterruptible power supply (UPS) connected via a serial port to the target system during installation. This could interfere with plug and play processes.

Exercise 15.1 Performing an attended installation

OBJECTIVES:

To successfully perform a Windows 2000 Professional Installation

PREPARATION:

Ask your Instructor for the Windows 2000 CD and product key code number and record it here _____.

Step 1

Start the installation by booting from the CD-ROM (this is accomplished on most systems by choosing to boot from the CD-ROM drive in the system BIOS) or by connecting to the i386 directory on the CD and typing **winnt** at the command line.

You can also use the Windows 2000 Professional Setup Disks or connect to an installation directory stored on the network. If the Setup Disks are not available, they can be created by executing **MAKEBOOT.EXE**. This program is located in the **BOOTDISK** folder on the setup CD-ROM. This Exercise assumes the Setup Disks are used.

Step 2

Use one of the several methods mentioned to access the i386 folder and run **winnt** or **winnt32**.

Step 3

At the Setup Notification screen, press **Enter** to continue as Windows 2000 performs the real-mode portion of copying the files to the hard disk.

Step 4

Take out the disk before restart #1.

Step 5

Windows 2000 loads files and starts Windows. Hit **Enter** to begin, **R** to repair, or **F3** to quit

Step 6

Select **F8** at the Windows 2000 Licensing Agreement screen.

Step 7

Select a partition for the installation of Windows 2000 Professional and press **Enter**. In order to setup Windows 2000 Professional on the selected partition, press **C** to convert to NTFS.

Step 8

Select **Format the partition using the NTFS file system** and press **Enter**, then **F**.

Step 9

To format the partition, press **F**. Setup then copies files to the W2K installation folders.

Step 10

Remove any floppy disk from your system and reboot when prompted. Setup does the file system and disk check then performs the actual conversion to NTFS.

Step 11

This GUI mode Setup Wizard then performs a hardware detection and installation checks for Regional Settings and takes name and organization input.

Step 12

Complete the product key boxes.

Step 13

Complete the **Computer name** field at the **Computer Name and Administrator Password** window. Also, choose an administrator password and confirm this password. Choose **Next** when finished.

Step 14

Select the **Date** and **Time** settings.

Step 15

From the **Networking Settings** window, choose **Typical** or **Custom** then select **Next**.

Step 16

Configure the networking settings and install software typical or custom settings.

Step 17

Next choose between a Workgroup or Domain and select a computer name or accept the default that Windows 2000 gives you.

Step 18

Windows installs components and performs Final tasks.

Step 19

Remove the CD and restart.

Step 20

In the Network Identification Wizard, configure the user names and passwords of the users that will logon to this machine.

Step 21

Windows 2000 Professional runs for the first time.

Deploying Service Packs

A Service Pack deployment can actually be thought of as a mini-upgrade of the Operating System. During a Service Pack deployment, bugs and known issues with the Windows 2000 Operating System are repaired and upgraded. Because a Service Pack deployment is very similar to an upgrade, the steps to prepare for and carry out this deployment are also similar. Be sure to take the following steps prior to/during the deployment:

- **Important files to review** – Be sure to read any "readme" files distributed with the Service Pack and any documentation accompanying the Service Pack.

- **Backup the system** – In order to quickly recover the system in the event the Service Pack actually causes major problems on the system instead of fixing them, be sure to do a full backup of the system that is to be "upgraded".

- **Test the system** – Following the deployment of the Service Pack, test the system thoroughly to ensure a stable upgrade has taken place.

Each Service Pack will provide the mechanisms necessary to perform unattended, network-based deployments to ease administrative burdens associated with the deployment of Service Packs. Check with the Service Pack documentation for unattended installation instructions.

Troubleshoot failed installations

There are several reasons that an installation of Windows 2000 Professional may fail. It is important to be familiar with the most common reasons in order to facilitate successful trouble-shooting methodologies.

The most common installation problems are listed here with the appropriate solutions:

PROBLEM	SOLUTION
Media errors	Contact Microsoft about replacement of the compact disc.
Non-supported CD-ROM drives	Replace drive or use network installation method.
Insufficient disk space	Use the Setup program to create a partition of free space that is large enough for installation.
Failure of dependency service to start	Use the Setup Wizard to navigate back to the Network Settings screen. Ensure the proper network configuration.
Inability to connect to a domain controller	Ensure you have the correct domain name. Ensure domain controller and DNS server are available. Verify network adapter settings.
Failure of Windows 2000 to install or start	Ensure hardware was detected successfully and that all hardware is supported (HCL).

Microsoft Management Console

Microsoft has taken great strides to make computing full-featured for the Windows administrator and power user while still providing an intuitive interface for the newcomer to Windows 2000. The Microsoft Management Console is a powerful and flexible tool supporting a myriad of snap-in programs to manage resources in the Windows environment.

The Microsoft Management Console (MMC) is the chief administrative component that is used to manage resources in Windows 2000 Professional. The MMC itself does not actually carry out the administrative functions but is simply a shell that is used to create, save and open the administrative consoles which are used to manage hardware, software and network components of the system. These components are called "snap-ins". By providing a common interface for many management tools, the MMC can unify and greatly simplify system management.

MMC snap-ins can operate remotely on other computers as well as the local system. The various tools and configurations can be saved in the MMC console to be used at a later time on the same or other computers.

The MMC interface looks a lot like the Microsoft Windows Explorer. It has a parent window and a child window. The left pane is called the console tree, which displays the hierarchical organization of tools contained within MMC. The right pane is called the details pane. The contents of the details pane will depend on the purpose and design of each snap-in as well as the item selected in the console tree.

Monitor Access to Files and Folders

Almost all Windows 2000 tasks will involve working with files and folders. You can perform the basic tasks, such as creating, deleting, copying, and moving files and folders as well as advanced tasks like changing file and folder properties and managing shared folders. You can create a folder from almost anywhere in Windows 2000 by simply right-clicking in a container. Windows 2000 places the new folder in your current location but you can move the folder to any location at a later time.

You configure the auditing feature to monitor and record security-related events like unauthorized attempts to access a particular file or folder. When you audit an object, an entry is written to the Windows 2000 security log whenever the object is accessed in a certain way. Once you set up auditing, you can keep track of users who access certain objects as well as analyze security issues on your machine. The audit trail can show who performed the actions and who attempted to do things that you deem impermissible.

Once auditing is setup in your Group Policy, you can look at the security log in Event Viewer to review successful or failed attempts to access the audited files and folders. Remember that the security log has a limited size. Therefore, you should carefully pick the files and folders you want to audit. You should also consider carefully how much disk space you are willing to allocate to the security log. The maximum size is defined in the Event Viewer.

Controlling access to files and folders by using permissions

You set up file and folder permissions by viewing the security properties of files, folders, shared folders, printers, and Active Directory objects. This can be done by right-clicking the object and choosing "Properties" and then selecting the Security tab. NTFS permissions specify which users and groups can gain access to files and folders and what they can do with the contents of these files and folders. File permissions include Full Control, Modify, Read & Execute, Read, and Write and each of these permissions consists of a group of what are called "special permissions". When you configure the permissions, you specify the level of access for groups and users. For example, you can let one user read the contents of a file, let another group make changes to the file, and then keep all other users from accessing the file.

The following table lists the individual file permissions and specifies which special permissions are associated with that permission:

Do Not Memorize for exam

Special Permissions	Full Control	Modify	Read & Execute	Read	Write
Traverse Folder/Execute File	X	X	X		
List Folder/Read Data	X	X	X	X	
Read Attributes	X	X	X	X	
Read Extended Attributes	X	X	X	X	
Create Files/Write Data	X	X			X
Create Folders/Append Data	X	X			X
Write Attributes	X	X			X
Write Extended Attributes	X	X			X
Delete Subfolders and Files	X				
Delete	X	X			
Read Permissions	X	X	X	X	X
Change Permissions	X				
Take Ownership	X				
Synchronize	X	X	X	X	X

Web Server Resources

When you save a Web document to a given folder from Internet Explorer, IE creates a new folder that contains all of the embedded Web files and images that the document requires. This folder will have the same name as the Web document, with the addition of the word "files" and will contain the embedded Web files. Web documents are saved by default to the My Documents folder. The links from the Web document to the embedded Web files are also retained so that when you re-open the document you will see all of the images that originally appeared on the page. When you move or copy a Web document the accompanying Web files folder containing the embedded files is also moved or copied. Now the images show up on the page when you open your document in the new location.

Shortcuts to Web servers are known as Web folders. Web Folders provide an easy way for you to view resources on Web servers. If you have read and write access to the server, the shortcuts will be automatically created in My Network Places whenever you access resources on the servers. You can also use the Add Network Place wizard to create shortcuts to Web servers and other remote computers. You can manipulate the files and folders on a Web server just as you would in the Windows Explorer. In addition, when you view the contents of a Web folder you see a list of files and folders and their associated HTTP Internet addresses.

Printer Objects

When you create a document you may want to see what your work looks like in print. You must first install a printer to make this possible. In Windows 2000 a "printer" is actually a print object representing a varied collection of properties. A print device is the actual box with the toner and paper in it. The print driver is the software interface between the printer object and the physical device. Installing printers like many other components in Windows 2000 Professional is wizard-driven. Once installed, the printer will be listed in the Printers folder and in the Print dialog box of the application that you are using. There are two different types of printer objects that one can create: a network printer object and a local printer object (attached to your computer).

Configuring the Desktop

The end-users desktop or graphical interface is usually unique to that individual user. Windows 2000 gives us the ability to save these unique configurations as profiles.

A User Profile under Windows 2000 consists of the "look and feel" of the user experience. A profile can provide a tailor-made desktop environment that includes things like display settings and printer or network connections. You can create your own profile or your system administrator may be given that task. There are three flavors of user profiles that include:

· Local Profile - This is created the first time you log on to a Windows 2000 system and it is stored on a the local hard disk. Changes made to the local user profile are machine specific.

· Roaming Profile – This type of profile is created by a system administrator and is stored in a central location on a server. Roaming profiles are available at logon from any computer on the network. Changes made to your roaming user profile are uploaded to the server when you log off. If you access a roaming profile from multiple computers simultaneously, the profile will ultimately consist of the settings of the last computer that logs off.

· Mandatory Profile – This is a special roaming profile used by system administrators to force specific settings on individuals or groups of users on a network.

Exercise 15-2 Configuring your desktop settings.

OBJECTIVES:

To gain experience modifying the user desktop.

Step 1

· Set or change the look of individual desktop items by navigating to the Control Panel and opening Display.

Step 2

· On the Appearance tab, in the Item list, choose the thing that you want to change (like Window, Menu, or Scrollbar), then adjust a setting like color or font.

Step 3

· Select a predefined color and font scheme, click an option in the Scheme list.

Step 4

· Create a customized scheme, choose your settings in the Item list, click Save As, and type a name for the scheme so it can be added to the list.

WINDOWS 2000 PRO

Step 5

· Customize a desktop pattern by opening Display in the Control Panel and on the Background tab, clicking Pattern.

Step 6

· In the Pattern list choose the desktop pattern you want to modify and click Edit Pattern.

Step 7

· Show pop-up descriptions for folder and desktop items by opening Folder Options in Control Panel and click the View tab. Select the "Show pop-up description for folder and desktop items" check box.

Step 8

· Remove the My Documents folder from the desktop by clearing the "Show My Documents on the Desktop" check box.

Install applications by using Windows Installer packages

The Windows 2000 Professional operating system provides a component called the Windows Installer that simplifies the installation of programs. Windows Installer utilizes a set of functions during the install process that controls adding and removal of applications. Also, you can use Windows Installer to modify, repair, and remove programs, monitor file stability, and perform basic disaster recovery through a "rollback" process. Windows Installer uses the .msi package file format to make installation and removal more reliable and flexible with the following tasks:

· Windows Installer can revert back to the original configuration when an install fails by tracking all of the changes to the system during the application installation process.

· The Installer prevents certain types of conflicts between applications and enforces rules that help to prevent conflicts with shared resources. Sometimes conflicts happen when an install procedure makes updates or deletes to shared.dll that is used by an existing program.

· This powerful Intellimirror feature can also reliably remove any existing program that it previously installed by cleaning out all of the associated registry entries and application files, except for the ones shared by other installed software.

· You can uninstall an application at any time after a successful installation.

"group policy" - package to deploy an app to multiple stations.

- WI diagnoses and repairs corrupted programs by allowing applications to query it to determine if the program has missing or corrupted files. If so, the Installer repairs the program by recopying only the missing or corrupted files.

- Windows Installer can be set up to initially install only a minimal piece of an application, for example Word. Then, an additional component (like Mail Merge or Spell Checker) can be automatically installed the first time the user accesses a features that requires that component. (Microsoft calls this feature "Advertising"). Windows Installer could also be configured to remove the component if it goes unused for a certain number of days.

- Unattended application installation is supported with the Windows Installer. Packages can be profiled to require no interaction from the user during install. Windows will query the computer for the needed desktop attributes to finish the installation, including determining whether or not any applications were previously installed by the Windows Installer.

Summary

Windows 2000 is a multipurpose operating system that supports file and print, application, web, and communication server functions. Windows 2000 Professional continues the trend towards greater manageability, reliability, security and performance as a replacement for Windows NT Workstation that also includes the best features of Windows 98.

In this section, we completed a Windows 2000 installation, discussed the Windows file systems and configured the Windows 2000 desktop.

Review Questions

1. Which of the following is not a valid type of User Profile under Windows 2000?

   A. Roaming user profile
   ✳ B. Shared user profile
   C. Local user profile
   D. Mandatory user profile

2. You would like to install Windows 2000 Professional on a system that will have only a single hard disk partition. What file system should you choose for this hard disk partition?

   A. FAT   *if used w/ win 95 or 98*
   B. FAT32
   C. HPFS
   ✳ D. NTFS

3. You would like to install Windows 2000 Professional on a computer in your department. This computer is a Pentium class system of 60 MhZ. It is equipped with 128 MB of RAM, a 2 GB hard drive, and a 12X speed CD-ROM. What should be your main concern with this system regarding a successful install of Windows 2000 Professional?

   ✳ A. The 60 MhZ processor
   B. The 128 MB of RAM
   C. The 2 GB hard drive
   D. The 12X speed CD-ROM

4. A domain is a _____ grouping of computers.

*   A. Complete
*   B. Logical
     C. Divisional
     D. Numeric

5. The Windows 2000 Professional product can be installed in a dual boot configuration?

*   True
    False

6. You are installing a new sound card and are not sure if it is Windows 2000 compatible, which of the following could be of help?

*   A. HCL   *Hdwe compatibility list*
     B. HDL
     C. SOP
     D. POC

7. Windows 2000 supports the following file systems: (Choose all that apply).

*   A. NTFS
*   B. FAT
*   C. FAT32
     D. LIN32

8. An NTFS volume size is limited to:

    A. 2 TB
    B. 32 TB
    C. 512 MB
    D. No practical limit

9. A service pack could best be described as a
   _____ of the operating system.

    A. Mini-upgrade
    B. Backup
    C. Replacement
    D. Deployment

10. The special permission delete implies which of the
    following:

    A. Modify
    B. Full Control
    C. Execute & Read
    D. Full Control & Modify

or *Best →*

Section 16

Linux Overview

Section 16: Linux Overview

Introduction

The Linux operating system was nurtured by individuals that held to a mindset of free exchange of software and innovation. The rallying goal of these developers was an open exchange of information that would foster the growth and flexibility of the "source code". The source code in this case was Linux. If you have heard that Linux is just a free stripped down version of UNIX, you would be partially correct. Actually most of the Linux software code was created from scratch, using the UNIX operating system specifically the (POSIX) Portable Operating System Interface for UNIX as a model.

The Linux operating system was original developed by Linus Torvalds at the University of Helsinki in Finland. Torvalds made the source code freely available and encouraged others to add their own refinements and enhancements.

Objectives:

· Discuss the Advantages of the Linux Operating System

· Discuss the System Hardware Requirements

· Discuss Linux Applications

· Describe the Linux X-Window Interface

· Discuss the Superuser Admin account (root)

· Discuss Linux Administration files

The Linux Advantage

Why would anyone choose Linux over the more established UNIX? Well, for starters, it's FREE! Yes, free. You can download a working version from the Internet for free or you can purchase a boxed version with CD and documentation (books) for a nominal fee about $39.00 US dollars for the very popular RED HAT version.

Another very good reason to choose Linux over its big brother is that Linux is fairly compact in size as compared to UNIX. When you are talking about the PC environment, this can be a concern. A typical UNIX installation can require upwards of 500 MB of free disk space, whereas Linux can be installed and run on as little as 150 MB of hard disk space.

The list below includes some of the major advantages and benefits of the Linux operating system:

Full Multitasking Capabilities

Multiple tasks can be completed concurrently.

X-Windows

Linux supports and runs the X-Window interface, the standard for UNIX based machines. This Desktop interface supports many applications and closely resembles the Microsoft Windows 95 desktop.

Networking Support

Linux has built in networking support and uses standard TCP/IP protocols.

IEEE POSIX.1

Linux is IEEE POSIX.1 compliant, which means it supports many of the same standards as UNIX based systems.

Nonproprietary source code

The Linux source code does not use any proprietary routines or code, making it a very open development platform.

System Hardware Requirements

Another feature that makes Linus a very attractive choice is its relatively low hardware requirements. The following list summarizes the system hardware requirements for the RED HAT edition of Linux:

- Intel 80386 processor (Pentium or higher recommended)

- 300 - 500 MB of free hard disk space recommended

- 8 MB of System RAM (16 MB or more recommended)

- CD-ROM

- Video card (most cards are supported, VGA or better recommended)

- SCSI or IDE drives

- 3.5" Floppy disk drive

As with any operating system the above list is a moving target and subject to change. For the most up to date hardware list you can access the RED HAT supported list at the following URL: **www.redhat.com/support/docs/hardware.html**

LINUX

Linux Applications

Unfortunately, unlike DOS based applications, you will not be able to just walk into any computer store and find a large assortment of Linux-based apps. This is not to say they do not exist, it is just that you have to know where to look. The best place to find UNIX and Linux apps is on the Web. Many of these applications are shareware, freeware and commercial packages. Most can be downloaded from the Web or ordered from various Linux web sites specializing in this software.

The following is a list of some of the more popular places to find Linux Applications on the web:

The Linux Mall

The Web site offers a large selection and description of various Linux software applications. **www.linuxmall.com**

Linux Apps and Utilities Site

This site has many links pointing you to a wide variety of freeware, shareware and commercial applications. **www.xnet.com/~blatura/linapps.shtml**

Linux Applications Web Site:

This is a great site if you are just browsing to see what is available. It lists software by category as well as descriptions and links to the apps homepages. **www.linuxapps.com**

X-Windows

Linux can be completely administrated and run from the command prompt; that cold, black, unintuitive screen. Or, you can install and use the X-Window interface, sometimes referred to as the X11 or just the X interface. And then, almost as if by magic, you have icons representing your programs and files. You can launch a program with just a click of the mouse. If you are a current Microsoft Window's user, then you will have no problems here.

When you initially install Linux, it will not, by default, install the graphical interface (GUI) for you. The installation program by default will take the less risky path and start up in the text-mode first.

The X-Window interface can be started in a number of different ways including the following:

· During the boot process

· After logging into the computer

· During the login process

The Boot Process

You can configure your system to use the **xdm** command during startup, which will then automatically launch the graphical desktop when you login. The Linux graphical desktop is typically referred to as the GNOME environment.

After Logging into the Computer

Once you have logged into the computer in the text mode, you can then start the GUI at any time by using the **startx** command.

During the Login Process

To start with a text-based interface and to have the GUI launch only when you login, you can include the **startx** command in one of your user profiles (startup configuration file) such as the **bash_profile** located in the users home directory.

The Superuser Account

No matter the operating system, each has a special superuser (God-like) login. The Linux operating system is no exception. Linux, like the UNIX systems before, uses a special login name called the "root" user account. This root user has complete control of the operating system. This user account is used to install software, add new user accounts, set security rights and administrate password policy on the network. The root user also has to the ability to open any file or launch any program.

To gain access to the system as the root user, you simply login from the initial login prompt using the name root as your user name. After entering the user name "root" you will be prompted for the password associated with this user. Once logged in as the root user you now have complete control over all the files, directories and user accounts.

Administration Files

Linux, perhaps more than any other operating system, depends on various configuration files to control network resources. These files contain information on just about anything that you can define on a particular computer. The users desktop environment, user accounts, network information are all stored in plain text files.

There are advantages and disadvantages with using text files for all your configuration settings. A distinct advantage is that you can use just about any text editor to modify these files. However, there is no error checking for syntax. It isn't until you try to run one of these files that you will notice a problem. A misplaced comma or space could cause an entire interface to fail.

These configuration files are stored in several locations within the Linux file system. Many of the more common configuration files are stored in the **\etc** directory. The following is a list of some of the basic configuration files found in the **\etc** location:

passwd

This file stores account information for all users on the system. Other than password information it also stores information such as a users home directory.

shadow

The shadow file contains encrypted passwords and is more secure than the standard passwd file. This file can only be viewed logged in as the root user.

profile

This file is used to set global (system-wide) environment settings and is read when the user logs into the system.

lilo.conf

This file is used by he Linux bootstrap loader, used to specify various boot options.

hosts

This file defines the location of domain names on a TCP/IP network.

These are actually only a few of the total Linux configuration files. For a complete listing, consult the Linux installation guide for location and use.

Summary

The Linux operating system was created by Linux Torvalds in 1991 and is distributed free throughout the world. The UNIX operating system provided the framework that was used to create Linux. Linux philosophy is based on the free exchange of software and information.

LINUX

Review Questions

1. Which of the following GUI (Graphical User Interfaces) is incorporated into the Linux operating system?

   A. Y-Windows
   B. Windows 95
   C. X-Windows
   D. Windows 98

2. The Linux operating system is based upon a proprietary kernal.

   TRUE
   FALSE

3. The command to start the Linux GUI interface is:

   A. **setup**
   B. **GO**
   C. **startx**
   D. **xwindow**

4. Which of the following user login names would be used to access the Linux superuser account?

   A. Admin
   B. Administrator
   C. Supervisor
   D. Root

5. Which of the following configuration files contains information about a users password?

A. shadow
B. passwd
C. password
D. hosts

6. The recommended free hard disk space required to install Linux is:

A. 100-250 MB
B. 300-500 MB
C. 1GB
D. 28 GB

7. The Linux operating system can be administrated from both the command line or from the GUI interface.

TRUE
FALSE

8. What is the minimum **recommended** system RAM requirement for a Linux based PC?

A. 15 MB
B. 12 MB
C. 16 MB
D. 64 MB

Section 17

The Internet

Section 17: The Internet

Introduction

The Internet. So what is it? To some it is the "information super highway," yet to others it is the "information super parking lot."

In reality, the Internet and all of its tools as we know them today are many different things to many different people. The Internet has come a long way from its early beginnings as a communication link for the Department of Defense. The Internet and its subsets, like the World Wide Web (WWW), are used for everything from serious government research projects, to a teenager playing interactive games with someone across the world.

Objectives

When you've completed this section, you will be able to identify the following:

- The definition of the Internet.
- The history of the Internet.
- Who's responsible for the Internet.
- Capabilities of the Internet.
- How to get connected to the Internet.
- Security on the Internet.

INTERNET

What is the Internet?

Understanding what the Internet is, without first knowing a bit about computer networks in general, would be something akin to an astronomer trying to understand the universe without having a clue about our own planet. In a nutshell, a computer network is two or more computers that are linked together for the purpose of sharing information and services.

The Internet is actually made up of thousands of individual computer networks of various sizes. With this conglomeration of resources, the Internet could then be viewed as one large "super computer network."

The ability to share the information and resources on a network depends upon the computers' abilities to communicate with each other. A computer generally has no problem communicating with you. It accomplishes this by outputting information via a printer or displaying information on your screen. We, on the other hand, communicate with the computer by inputting information through a keyboard, mouse, and in some cases, via a speaker or microphone.

Unfortunately, computers can't communicate with each other in quite the same way as people communicate with each other. Hence, the "computer network" allows different computers to talk and communicate with each other. Networking multiple computers together is no easy task. Many things must be in place in order for the computers on the network to communicate.

Every computer on the network must have special hardware to connect to and communicate with the network. On many computers this is a built-in feature of the machine, but for the majority of computers, this hardware suite must be added later. This usually consists of a *Network Interface Card* (NIC) or a modem.

Every computer on the network must also have specialized pieces of software installed and running. Usually the software must be added, although some computers are shipped with the software in place by the manufacturer. However, even the computers that come with networking software pre-installed still usually require a fair amount of configurations before being operable.

All the computers on the network must share a common link. This is usually accomplished with a cable. This cable could be a wire that is isolated, local to a building, or a telephone line connection linking multiple buildings or sites.

Some networks called "**wireless networks**" have eliminated the need for a physical wire connection by using infrared or radio waves as the communication link.

There are two broad categories of computer networks: Local-Area Networks (LANs), and Wide-Area Networks (WANs).

The *Local-Area Network* (LAN) is usually a group of computers connected together in the same office or building for the purpose of sharing resources and information within the company. In the corporate workplace today, local-area networks are common fare.

The *Wide-Area Network* (WAN) is a network of geographically smaller networks linked together, typically through telephone lines or, in some cases, via satellite connections. The WAN is one way for a business to join together all of its various facilities. The WAN is usually controlled by the main or corporate headquarters.

The Internet is much like a WAN in that both are a collection of multiple computer networks linked together. The internal structure and makeup of the Internet is much different than that of a Wide-Area Network. The WAN is usually maintained and administrated by a single organization, usually the corporate headquarters of a particular company. They maintain the network, dictate how to access it,. They also control who can access the WAN and they assume the financial cost of the network.

The Internet, on the other hand, consists of thousands of networks, with no single group responsible for it. It could be stated the Internet is a "network of networks." While somewhat hard to believe, it is this very lack of a single governing body that makes the Internet so useful.

One unifying component of the Internet is that each LAN or WAN connected to the Internet is independent of the other. Every LAN or WAN is responsible for its own network. There is however a common point of agreement, that both parties agree to a common protocol "language" to speak while communicating across the Internet.

History of the Internet

The Internet today is very dynamic and still in its formative stages. The basic look and feel of the Internet today is a far cry from what it was just a few years ago, and will probably look different a few years into the future. To really have an idea of what the Internet is all about today, it is useful to know something about how it all got started.

Contrary to many popular ideas, the Internet was *not* created so that businesses could sell their wares or so we could discuss the existence of UFOs or why Madonna named her child "Lourdes." The modern Internet was first designed in the late sixties, but its early roots actually go back to the fifties during the Cold War Era.

The need for our government to have access to information in the event of a nuclear war spawned the Advanced Research Projects Agency (ARPA). ARPANET was funded by the military and developed by universities across the country. The goal was to share information and resources between military and research facilities around the country. It was designed in such a way as to make it a very open platform to promote and exchange information. The project was a success from the very beginning.

Access to the Internet, while open to all, was limited at first to mainly military personnel and academic researchers. Today, however, the Internet is used by millions of people around the world for almost as many reasons.

INTERNET

Responsibility for the Internet

Even though no one individual or organization owns or controls the Internet, many people from different organizations have volunteered their time and energy to ensure that the concept of free information flow would survive and thrive.

The Internet Society (ISOC) is the main watchdog who oversees the development of the Internet. While ISOC has no governmental power to speak of, it is the center for people who desire to help maintain and manage the Internet. ISOC also has the responsibility to oversee many other volunteer organizations and groups. Of these groups, the IETF (Internet Engineering Task Force) is one of the most important since it sets the technical guidelines for how the network is to operate.

As you might guess, it is no easy job to get thousands of different networks to communicate with each other. Membership is open to all and meetings are held about three times a year. Improvements or suggestions for the Internet can also be proposed by users of the net in the form of an RFC (Request for Comments).

Capabilities of the Internet

Trying to list all the features and uses of the Internet could take volumes and, because it is so dynamic, would probably never be up to date. The following is a list of some of the most popular Internet services:

- E-mail
- WWW
- Newsgroups
- Download services
- Search engines

E-mail

Perhaps one of the most widely-used services of the Internet is electronic mail. E-mail is a basic feature of the Internet. It probably won't replace the U.S. Post Office in the near future, it has become the staple for businesses and colleges around the world. Don't think it's just useful for the business world. For anyone with an Internet address, it provides a fast and economical way to communicate with friends and relatives anywhere in the world for the price of a local call.

E-mail offers many advantages over standard paper mail, including almost instant delivery. Sending mail to other countries can actually happen in just minutes. Organization is also a distinct advantage of e-mail. The ability to store messages in multiple locations and later perform key word searches to find an old message is one of the many conveniences.

E-mail also provides the ability to type a message once and forward it to many people or groups without retyping the message. Perhaps one of the most-used features of e-mail is the added ability to attach other documents to your mail, including text, video and audio files.

INTERNET

WWW

The World Wide Web *("The Web")* has been getting the most attention in recent months It lends itself to graphical interfaces, like *Microsoft*'s Windows environment and the *Macintosh* World. It is for this reason that people find it much easier to use and navigate than other services on the Internet.

Using and accessing the Web is quite easy. Users point and click on the information they need. The Web is a way to organize various pieces of information in the form of hypertext documents. The hypertext document is made up of text or pictures that are linked to other documents. Users can then click on a piece of text that will move them to a different location, perhaps just another place within the document or, in some cases, to a different document located on another computer. The Web is an excellent entry point and collection place for all the resources on the Internet.

Exam

Newsgroups

If your intent is to communicate with just one other person or perhaps a small group of people, e-mail is a good choice. However, when you have the need to talk with many people about a given subject a different form is required.

About ten years ago, that need was addressed by creating a channel where news about a particular subject could be passed from one computer to another. This system was referred to as *Usenet,* which eventually became part of the Internet. The Usenet is a collection of different newsgroups, and these groups are based on a hierarchy structure. This serves as a open forum for discussions that center around a particular topic.

The group name matches their hierarchy and is usually descriptive to the subject area.

> *For example,* **rec.woodworking** (The **rec.** would represent the hierarchy which discusses recreation, and in this case, special attention to a group that has an interest in woodworking).

Listed below are some of the major newsgroups:

- **alt.** - almost anything you can think of—*very open and uncontrolled.*
- **rec.** - recreation
- **comp.** - computer related topics
- **news.**
- The **Usenet** itself
- **misc.** - a catch-all for hard to categorize topics
- **sci.** - health & science-related
- **soc.** - society/cultures
- **talk.** - a place to chat, usually politically heavy dialogue.
- **k12.** - education

It should be noted that each hierarchy can contain many subsets or levels.

Like most other things on the Internet, these newsgroups are loosely controlled. Most anyone can participate by reading and posting responses. These **Usenet** groups cover everything from the very serious to the very bizarre.

Download Services

One of the more popular services on the Internet is the ability to download files. Some of the large and fast computer systems search through the Internet daily to collect information from computers around the world. These files of information are then made available for people to download. Much of the public domain software is collected and distributed in this manner.

There are many computer sites on the Internet that have downloadable files, however some are considered the ultimate host for these services. Not all the files and software from these sites are free. Much of it is called *shareware*. This is a common method of distributing new programs. Shareware lets you freely copy it and try it. The idea is if you like it, you will register and pay for the product.

Search Engines

As you have already seen, there is a abundance of information out there. So how can you find something you need? The answer comes in the form of *search engines*, or Web sites that are dedicated to responding to request for information. (Examples of popular search engines today include Yahoo, Excite, Infoseek, Lycos & Altavista.) These Web sites use programs sometimes referred to as *web crawlers*. Using one of these programs allows you to do word or phrase searches and the program will return all the relevant links.

Tools and Terms

- **Browser**- Any application that enables you to view web pages. Two popular browsers are Netscape and Internet Explorer.

- **URL** - The Uniform Resource Locator is a unique address for a web site or other resource on the Internet. Mindworks Professional Education Group's web site URL is **http:// www.mindwork.com**

- **UNC:** The UNC (Universal Naming Convention) allows a user to specify a path (location) to a shared network resource, printer, computer, folder, etc. The syntax for the UNC is **\\computername\share_name**. The following is an example of an UNC for a shared folder called DATA on a computer called ACCT: **\\ACCT\DATA.**

- **FTP** - The File Transfer Protocol utility allows a user on one computer to transfer files to and from another computer over a TCP/IP network. (It was installed when you set up the Windows operating system.) To access an FTP site, type in the URL (Uniform Resource Locator) address bar in your browser (e.g., Internet Explorer).

- **HTML**- Hypertext Markup Language is the language used for all documents created for the World Wide Web.

- **DNS** - Domain Name System translates text-based Internet network addresses **http://www.mindwork.com** = numerical Internet network address 206.165.12.60.

- **IP address** - Every computer in a network (such as the Internet) requires an IP address. An IP address is four numbers (between 0 and 255, inclusive) separated by periods. 128.190.123.45 is a valid IP address.

Getting Connected to the Internet

You want to start using and accessing the Internet—so where do you start? Perhaps the first step in establishing an Internet connection is to figure out if you are already part of an organization that is on the Internet. This could be the company you are working for or a school or University you're attending. If you do not currently have access to the Internet, your next step should be to find a local *ISP* (*Internet Service Provider*). These are companies that provide a standard telephone line (dial-up) connection to the Internet.

There are many companies which provide this service, however choosing one can sometimes be confusing. Most of the providers will all have different pricing structures. Some will have a very low monthly fee and charges based on connection time. Many others will have a little higher monthly rate but no connection charges. These flat rate providers are probably the best choice if you plan to be spending a lot of time on the net.

The location of your ISP service is called its **POP** (*Point-of-Presence*). Many of the large providers have locations throughout the country. When choosing an ISP, it's very important to select a provider that has a local phone number. This eliminates the accumulation of large long distance telephone bills. The beauty of the Internet is that you can communicate with people around the world for the price of a local telephone call.

Next step is deciding what type of connection to use. Your provider will help you with this, however, there are two basic connection types: *PPP (point-to-point protocol)* and *SLIP (serial line internet protocol)*. Today the most widely-used connection type is PPPwhich allows your personal computer to connect directly to the Internet over serial lines, such as the telephone wire.

SLIP - older, cleartext, less secure protocol.

Security on the Internet

The Internet today is not small town America— you have to keep those doors locked. In the early days of the Internet, security was not a big issue. The idea was to make it very easy for people doing research to exchange information. If a person was worried about some sensitive issue, they didn't post it on the Internet. Today, however with all the people and businesses on the Internet, security has become a primary concern, especially with regards to future growth.

The basic rule is that you or your company are responsible for security in what you do. Your password is your first line of security. Remember not to tell anyone and change it often. Some corporations use a *firewall* to protect their local networks and computers from connections by deceitful sources. A firewall is basically a computer that is attached to both the Internet and a local network. It blocks the connections by filtering Internet addresses or protocols.

Summary

The Internet has come a long way from its original beginnings as a tool for government and academic research. The "information-super highway," as it is referred to today, has become a communication channel for everyone from students, to business people, to the average recreational computer user from their home.

Internet access has become much easier because of the vast numbers of ISPs (Internet service providers) around the world. The rapid growth of the Internet has created many unforeseen security problems, which, if left unsolved, could be a large stumbling block to the future growth of the network.

Review Questions

1. The Internet was started in the late 1980s.

    A. True

   ✱ B. False

2. Suggestions for improvement for the Internet can be proposed by submitting the following document.

    A. DOC
    B. RFD
   ✱ C. RFC *request for Comments*
    D. CFR

3. The location of your Internet provider service is called the POP. What does this abbreviation stand for?

    ● A. Place of Presence
   ✱ B. Point of Presence
    C. Point of Provider
    D. Provider on Premises

4. Which of the following will help protect your local network from unauthorized access?

    A. Breakwall
    B. Remote bridge
   ✱ C. Firewall
    D. Firestarter

5. The World Wide Web (WWW) is the Internet.

   ✱ A. True
    B. False

INTERNET

6. Which of the following are two types of networks?

    A. Big and small

    B. SWAN and LAN

    C. Long and short

✳ D. LAN and WAN

7. Which of the following is an Internet connection protocol? Select two.

    A. PCP

✳ B. PPP

✳ C. SLIP

    D. CLIP

8. E-mail is a basic service of the Internet.

✳ A. True

    B. False

9. Which newsgroup extensions are a catch-all for multiple topics? Select two.

    A. **sci.**

    B. **rec.**

✳ C. **alt.**

✳ D. **misc.**

p. 17-11

10. Hypertext documents are usually associated with which of the following? Select one.

    A. E-mail

    B. Newsgroups

✳ C. WWW

    D. Down services

Section 18

Diagnosing and Troubleshooting

Section 18: Diagnosing & Troubleshooting

Introduction

Diagnosing and repairing a computer problem can seem overwhelming until you learn to trust your instincts and approach the problem systematically.... and above all, Don't Panic! In this chapter, you'll learn how to approach computer hardware and software troubleshooting in a clear, logical fashion. A deliberate approach is necessary to avoid overlooking an obvious, simple solution to a problem.

Objectives

When you've completed this chapter, you'll understand:

· The seven steps of PC troubleshooting

· The common problems that occur in the various parts of the PC and peripheral devices.

· How to recognize common error codes and start-up messages and use them to diagnose problems.

· How to find solutions to common Windows problems

· How to detect, prevent and protect against viruses.

Seven Steps of PC Troubleshooting

Step 1 Check for User Error.

Users are the primary cause of most PC problems. Your communication skills may be the most valuable tool in your repair kit. Learn to ask simple questions in a kind, non-threatening manner and then remember to LISTEN carefully. Don't assume the user has your level of technical knowledge and expertise.

Step 2 Is Everything Plugged In?

Check power strips, the PC power cord connected to the computer, every cable connection, the wall switch and the wall outlet.

Step 3 Check the Software

For keyboard, screen, disk and timer conflicts with TSR programs, software may be the source of the problem. Applications and driver programs may have "bugs." Software may generate errors when it looks for hardware that isn't connected or activated such as: trying to print to a nonexistent printer or a printer that is offline; trying to display graphics on a monochrome monitor; or trying to run a program that requires more memory than is available.

Step 4 If the PC was once working properly, what was done differently? What is new?

Ask if a board was recently added to a system or perhaps a software program was added which was contaminated with a virus.

Step 5   Be observant and write down external signs on the PC.

What do the indicator lights show? Are all the modem lights on? Is the printer's "ready" light on? Is the monitor's image distorted? Are the hard drives grinding or making unusual sounds?

Step 6   Run a Diagnostic Program

While not entirely useful for most problems (the system has to be running to run the program!), a diagnostic disk may buy you some repair time. Each time the PC boots, the system is tested by the POST for memory, conflicts, controllers, video, adapters, monitor, keyboard, drives, parallel ports, etc. Record what the POST displays on the screen for helpful clues to the problem.

Step 7   Take PC Apart, Clean, Check Connections & Reassemble.

Open the PC, clean the connectors carefully with a cleaning compound or a clean white eraser and push all chips into their sockets. Are boards securely installed on the motherboard? A good investment for your repair toolbox would be a pocket version of IBM POST error codes and POST audio messages.

When all else fails, call for help from a professional computer repair facility.

Common Problems

Processor/Memory Symptoms

To discover if your system has a memory problem you could:

· Receive a memory error message 201 during POST.

· Run a memory test periodically.

· Get a **PARITY CHECK** error in the middle of an application. **PARITY CHECK 1** indicates a problem on the motherboard; **PARITY CHECK 2** indicates a problem on an expansion board.

Each time you power up your computer, the POST runs a memory test. The error message will contain the type of error as well as the location of the bad memory chip (its "address").

Memory is very power-dependent and needs a clean power source to function properly. Even a slight power surge can generate a memory error when, in fact, the memory is not bad. The problem is power-related. Likewise, ESD or a failing power supply can also result in false memory errors.

How do you determine between a true memory problem and a false memory error? Check the memory address in the error message. The same address will appear repeatedly if the chip has indeed failed. If the errors report different locations, the problem is most likely caused by power – either an interruption or insufficient power

Keyboard

Before spending time repairing a keyboard, keep in mind that new keyboards have come down in price in the past several years. A new enhanced keyboard can be purchased for as little as $25 in many markets.

To determine if the keyboard has failed, first check...

- Is the keyboard plugged into the correct port? The keyboard port and the mouse port look identical on many PCs.

- Are several keys malfunctioning or only one key? If only one key, then you can replace the key spring easily.

Mouse

When troubleshooting a mechanical mouse...

· Check to see that the mouse driver is set up correctly.

· Clean the mouse. On the bottom of the mouse, remove the retaining ring by turning it in the direction of the arrows. The ball will drop out. Clean off any dust and debris that may be on the ball. The ball moves against small white wheels on either side. These tend to accumulate a black buildup of dirt, which can be easily cleaned with a Q-tip and a bit of alcohol.

· Check to be sure the mouse is plugged into the mouse port, not the keyboard port.

· On an optical mouse, polish the sensors with a soft cloth and keep the mouse pad clean so the grid lines are visible to the mouse.

Floppy Drive

When a floppy drive fails, you may receive one of these error messages when you attempt to read a disk.

Data error reading Drive A: or General error reading Drive A:

· Retry the procedure at the prompt.

· Remove the diskette, then reinsert it again. Sometimes it's a hub-centering problem.

· Try the diskette in another drive. Is the floppy the right size for the drive? You may be trying to read a 5.25" high-density diskette in a double-density drive, or a 3.5" 2.88MB diskette in a 1.44MB drive.

· Does the drive read other diskettes? The diskette may have been written by a drive with a misaligned head.

Drive won't operate

· Check for a **Drive A: 601** error message during POST. This would indicate the system is not configured properly to see the drive; the controller failed; Drive A failed; or the cable failed.

· Try to format another diskette. If the newly formatted diskette is unreadable by other drives, then the head of your floppy drive is misaligned.

· Remove the case and check to see that the controller is seated snugly and that all cables are secure and nick-free.

· Swap out the controller, cable and drive one at a time. If the problem doesn't go away after each swap, put the component back.

During POST, the Drive A light stays on...

· The floppy drive cable is most likely backwards if the floppy drive light comes on and stays on during POST. The error could also mean there is insufficient memory if you are trying to load a program from a floppy.

Parallel Ports

Once parallel ports are installed and configured they seldom fail. If a problem occurs, the POST may report an **Error Code 423: Parallel Port Failed**. First, troubleshoot the particular device attached to that port. Printers – most often attached to LPT ports – are often the source of the problem. Also look for a device conflict. Check to see that two devices are not configured for the same LPT port and reconfigure the boards if necessary.

When a PC boots up, BIOS checks the LPT ports. If it doesn't find LPT 1, it looks for LPT 2, then LPT 3. If you've configured your PC for a LPT 2 port but not LPT 1 port, the BIOS will convert the LPT 2 to LPT 1 and a device conflict might occur.

Scanner

Some scanners work off a SCSI host adapter and others work off a proprietary interface card. To troubleshoot a scanner;

· Check for a device conflict with another device configured for the same LPT or COM port.

· Is the scanner cable securely inserted into the board and is the cable connector tight?

· Was the scanner recently moved? If the scanner is a flat-bed type, check to be sure the movable head is not locked.

· Is the scanner software installed correctly?

Tape Drive

If you plan to backup your PC's data regularly, a tape drive is a wise investment. When purchasing a tape drive, consider an external drive rather than an internal drive so you can use the device to backup more than one PC. Some tape drives use the floppy controller which limits their speed to that of your floppy drive, which may be too slow to be efficient. Higher capacity drives usually run off the SCSI interface but some drives require their own interface card.

When buying tapes, purchase the pre-formatted variety because formatting can take up to an hour.

To troubleshoot a tape drive, first look for a device conflict, then check the manufacturer's documentation for procedures to diagnose or repair problems with your particular tape drive.

Hard Drive

There are two types of hard disk drive errors:

- *Hard Errors* - The disk surface itself cannot record data. Hard errors are usually caused by a manufacturing defect in the disk or abuse of the disk. A low-level format will record hard errors, marking them in the bad track table so data is not recorded there. If the drive just stops working, it may be a physical problem with the drive. The coating on the disk that stores data may have rubbed off or the drive arm may wobble and not reach a particular part of the disk.

- *Soft Errors* - Data has faded on the hard disk to the extent it cannot be read. Soft errors are intermittent – a bad sector may be recorded once and then skipped on subsequent tests of the sectors. A recovery effort is needed to restore lost data (regular backup is strongly recommended).

When a sector has lost its ID, you'll receive a **Sector Not Found** error. When the data in a sector is unreadable or otherwise unreliable, you'll receive a **Data Error Reading Drive** error. To troubleshoot these problems:

- Try to low-level format the disk to restore the IDs if possible.

- If you don't have a current backup of the data on the hard disk, you'll want to recover as much data as possible.

Hard Drive Crash Procedure

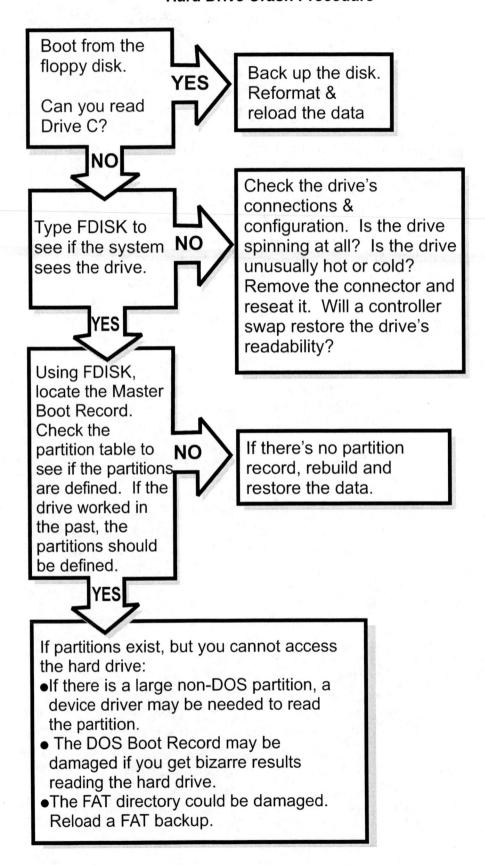

Boot from the floppy disk.

Can you read Drive C?

YES → Back up the disk. Reformat & reload the data

NO

Type FDISK to see if the system sees the drive.

NO → Check the drive's connections & configuration. Is the drive spinning at all? Is the drive unusually hot or cold? Remove the connector and reseat it. Will a controller swap restore the drive's readability?

YES

Using FDISK, locate the Master Boot Record. Check the partition table to see if the partitions are defined. If the drive worked in the past, the partitions should be defined.

NO → If there's no partition record, rebuild and restore the data.

YES

If partitions exist, but you cannot access the hard drive:
- If there is a large non-DOS partition, a device driver may be needed to read the partition.
- The DOS Boot Record may be damaged if you get bizarre results reading the hard drive.
- The FAT directory could be damaged. Reload a FAT backup.

Sound Card (Audio)

If you are having difficulty with receiving sound (audio) from your PC, check the obvious first. Are the speakers plugged into the correct outlets at the back of the PC? Are they connected to a power source? If you suspect the problem is your sound card, check the card's configuration. Most sound cards require three I/O addresses, two DMA channels and an IRQ.

NOTE: Get in the habit of writing down all the jumper and switch settings whenever you install any type of new card.

DIAGNOSING AND TROUBLESHOOTING

Monitor (Video)

Before you attempt to take apart a monitor - STOP. If you were to open a monitor while the computer was plugged in (even if the power was OFF), you could receive a charge of the full 120 volts. Even if the PC is OFF, the capacitors store power and can shock you.

If the monitor is malfunctioning, follow these troubleshooting steps.

· Check the simplest things first. Is the monitor turned ON? Check to see that the brightness or contrast controls are not turned way down. Is the monitor plugged correctly into the PC, as well as into the power source?

· Check the DIP switch and jumper settings on a multiple display board. Also check the DIP switches on the motherboard to see if your display adapter is configured correctly.

· If you heard a POST audio error code of one long and two short beeps, it could mean a problem with the video card.

· If you determine the problem lies with the video card, check the card's seating, clean the edge connector and the video connector and then retry the monitor.

When troubleshooting a monitor, it's best to use the VGA mode. Load the VGA drivers and see if the problem disappears. If so, then you had a driver problem. Make sure you have the most up-to-date drivers and a board that matches your monitor.

If you suspect the Graphics acceleration setting is causing problems with your PC, check the **Advanced Graphic** settings in **System Properties**. This area tells Windows how to interact with your graphics hardware. It can be very useful when troubleshooting display related problems.

Modem

The most common problem with communication devices is software. Both ends of the communication channel – the sender and the receiver – must have the same communication settings, parity, number of data bits, number of stop bits, and local echo ON or OFF.

- If you cannot connect to another computer's modem or if you get garbage letters when you do, most likely the speed or data bits are set incorrectly.

- If you connect and are able to receive a response from the receiving modem but cannot see what you've typed, the **Local Echo** setting is incorrect. Set **Local Echo** to ON to display the characters you type. If you get double characters as you type, set the **Local Echo** to OFF.

- If you suspect the problem is hardware-related, check the phone jack connection both at the PC and at the wall outlet. Make sure the modem's cable is connected securely. Check the phone line. Do you get a dial tone on other phones on that line? If you use an electronic phone system, check the required dial-out procedures. Also check the quality of the line for exceptional "noise." The problem may be with your phone wiring or the call-waiting feature may be interrupting the session.

BIOS

The BIOS tests your system whenever you power-up the PC. The BIOS start-up procedure consists of these steps.

Step 1	Low Memory Test	If this test fails, it means the lowest bank of RAM has failed.
Step 2	Scan for other BIOS	Some installed boards may contain their own ROM BIOS. The system BIOS searches for any additional BIOS.
Step 3	Yield to other BIOS	The system BIOS yields to other BIOS it may find before it checks the main system.
Step 4	Inventory the system	Reads the CMOS and checks all hardware (drives, memory, etc) that it will control. This may take several minutes, so be patient.
Step 5	Test the system	This is the diagnostic part of the BIOS. Any failed device will generate an error message at this point.
Step 6	Load DOS	Before the BIOS loads the operating system, it first loads DOS. The system looks for a drive that's ready. (It looks in the boot-up sequence you've chosen in CMOS...first Drive A, then Drive C, for example.)
Step 7	DOS loads Master Boot Record (MBR), then DOS Boot Record (DBR)	The DBR contains the hidden files IO.SYS and MSDOS.SYS.
Step 8	IO.SYS loads MS DOS.SYS, CONFIG.SYS, then COMMAND.COM	CONFIG.SYS loads device drivers which can shut down a system if they have a bug. If the COMMAND.COM has been corrupted somehow (wrong version, contaminated by a virus for example), you'll get a Bad or Missing Command.Com error message and your system will not boot.
Step 9	COMMAND.COM loads AUTOEXEC.BAT	TSRs such as anti-virus programs, network shells, protocol stacks, disk cache programs and disk compression programs are loaded by the AUTOEXEC.BAT. Problems with any of these programs will cause your system not to boot.

POST Audio Messages

POST Audio Signal	Probable Cause
No beep, nothing happens	Bad power supply or power supply not plugged in.
Continuous beep	Bad power supply or keyboard stuck.
Repeating short beep	Bad power supply.
1 long beep, 1 short beep	System board has failed.
1 long beep, 2 short beeps	Display adapter or cable is missing or has failed.
1 short beep, no boot	Floppy drive adapter has failed.
2 short beeps (PS/2)	Configuration error.

DIAGNOSING AND TROUBLESHOOTING

Motherboard

Double-check all cable connections, BIOS settings, and jumpers if you suspect a motherboard problem. Often, what appears to be a faulty motherboard, may be simply a hardware configuration problem.

All system components meet and connect at the motherboard, so a motherboard problem can affect any part of the computer. However, motherboard failures are rare. Usually the problem is the motherboard has been configured incorrectly or there is a failure with a component connecting to it. Try to avoid swapping out the motherboard. Exhaust all other possibilities before you take that drastic step.

- If the system isn't booting at all, make sure all components are inserted correctly into the motherboard. Partially inserted memory modules can often cause bizarre behavior.

- Remove all optional devices (expansion cards, external peripherals) to see if the problem is corrected.

- Double-check all jumper settings. Check the processor type, Bus speed, clock multiplier and voltage jumpers. Make sure the CMOS is clear and flash BIOS jumpers are in the normal default position. Reset all BIOS settings to default. Set all cache, memory and hard disk timing as slow as possible. Turn off BIOS shadowing and then see if the problem goes away

- Check the inside of the case to see if any components may be overheating.

- Inspect the motherboard for cracks, broken pins or broken components on the board. Check for any socketed components that may be loose in their sockets.

- Is the keyboard inserted correctly into the motherboard?

· A failed cache module or the wrong type of cache module may cause a motherboard problem. Trouble-shoot the secondary cache.

· Troubleshoot the processor.

· Memory problems are often mistaken for motherboard problems. Troubleshoot the memory.

· Troubleshoot the video card or replace it with a simple, straight VGA card that you know works correctly.

· Replace a weak power supply (less than 200W) especially if you've added new drives to the system.

· Check your BIOS manufacturer's technical support to see if there are any known bugs with your motherboard.

· Check your motherboard's manufacturer's hotline for additional troubleshooting hints.

· Last resort, swap out the motherboard with another board to see if the problem is resolved. If it is, then the original motherboard may have indeed been faulty or it could have been misconfigured or incorrectly installed.

CMOS

Record the current CMOS settings *before* you change any hardware in a system. If, after adding a piece of hardware, your CMOS has cleared, follow these steps to restore settings:

· Reboot the system and start the CMOS setup (consult the BIOS manufacturere for the specific way to enter the CMOS setup for your particular BIOS).

· Select **Load Bios Default Values.**

· Set the system date and time, floppy drives, keyboard and display type. These settings will be on the first CMOS setup screen or they may be listed under **Standard CMOS Setup.**

· Set up your hard drive parameters. If your CMOS setup provides an auto-detect function for the hard drive, use it. If it doesn't, enter the hard-disk settings manually: cylinders, heads and sectors. (See your hard drive documentation for this data.).

· Select **Save** and exit.

· Let the system reboot with the new BIOS settings.

Getting Troubleshooting Information From Customers

Most of the work in fixing a computer for a customer is diagnosing the problem. When you're working to solve a computer malfunction, Rule No. 1 is L.I.S.T.E.N. The user has firsthand knowledge that may help you unearth the problem.

· Watch for verbal cues - Ask the customer if the device was working prior to the problem? What was the customer doing just before the computer malfunctioned? Collect as much information as possible. *Warning:* Be careful not to make users feel stupid or they will react defensively and may withhold vital information that could help you solve the problem. If you're working over the phone with the user attempting to solve the problem, have the user perform the steps necessary to rectify the problem if at all possible.

· Respond sympathetically to the customer's situation. Empathize with the customer's frustration, but don't be afraid to say "I don't know what the problem is, I need more information."

· Users learn from their errors, especially if they can fix the problem themselves, with your coaching of course. Speak slowly when giving instructions and anticipate the user's technical level when explaining the repair procedure. You may have to break down the information into less technical terms so the user can fully understand the process.

Common Error Codes & Startup Messages

Incorrect DOS Version

This message will appear when the system boots up if you attempt to run the wrong version of DOS with a particular program. The file that contains the command you just entered is from a different version of DOS such as trying to use **DEFRAG** while running Windows.

> *For example*, some versions of **MSCDEX.EXE** for a CD-ROM drive may require an earlier or later version of DOS than is currently on your system. Many programs designed to run with a previous version of MS-DOS will run correctly with Windows 3.1 or 95.

The version table indicates to the program that it is running with the MS-DOS version for which it was designed, even though it is running in the MS-DOS subsystem.

SETVER can be used to modify the version table. By interpreting MS-DOS version 6.0, for example, as the earlier version, the program will probably run correctly; however, using **SETVER** will not solve the problem if the program is not compatible with Windows.

Adding the following line to your **CONFIG.SYS** file will load the version table into memory.

> **DEVICE=C:\DOS\SETVER.EXE** (if the DOS commands are located in the \DOS subdirectory)

To view the version table, at the **DOS** prompt, type:

> **SETVER C:\DOS\SETVER** (or indicate the drive and path where you indicated in the **CONFIG.SYS** line)

After you've added or deleted entries, you must restart the system before the changes will take effect. As you update existing entries, when you specify a filename that is already in the version table, the new entry replaces the existing entry.

Bad or missing COMMAND.COM

If the boot record on the hard drive is corrupted or has been deleted, you will get this error message when you boot up the system. Use the **SYS** command or reload DOS to restore the boot record to the hard drive, then restart the system to see if the problem is solved. Also, make sure the hard drive is identified correctly in CMOS.

HIMEM.SYS not loaded

The file **HIMEM.SYS** did not load properly so it cannot make extended memory or high memory area (HMA) available to your system. Without this file, Windows 3.x is unable to use extended memory and DOS will not be able to load into the HMA. This problem often occurs because **HIMEM.SYS** did not correctly identify your type of PC, or if the /**CPUCLOCK** or /**MACHINE** switches need to be added to the **DEVICE=** line in your **CONFIG.SYS** file.

DIAGNOSING AND TROUBLESHOOTING

Swapfile corrupt

This error message means that your swap file has been damaged and you've lost your virtual memory. You don't have enough memory left to run a particular program.

Information is moved in blocks from memory to a swap file that Windows creates on the hard disk. This swap file can either be permanent or temporary. When all of the virtual memory (RAM) is in use, idle programs and data will be loaded into the swap file to make more actual RAM available.

When Windows creates a permanent swap file, it actually creates two hidden files. These hidden files are **386SPART.PAR** (located in the root directory) and **SPART.PAR** (located in the Windows directory). To fix the problem, you'll need to delete the old swap file:

· Click on the **Control Panel** icon.

· Click on the **386 Enhanced** icon.

· Click the **Virtual Memory** button.

· Set the swap file type to **None**.

· Click **OK**.

· Click **Yes** in the confirmation dialog box, but DO NOT let **Control Panel** restart Windows.

· Click the **Continue** button.

· Exit Windows.

To be sure the file has been deleted, at the DOS prompt, switch to the root directory on the drive that held the swap file and type the following command: **ATTRIB -r -s -h 386SPART.PAR**

If you receive a **File Not Found** error message, you successfully deleted the file. If somehow the file wasn't deleted, delete it by typing the following command: **DEL 386SPART.PAR**

Next, you must delete the **SPART.PAR** hidden file if it also didn't get deleted earlier. Switch to the Windows subdirectory and type **DEL SPART.PAR**

To ensure that you don't receive this error message again, defragment your hard disk by running the DOS **DEFRAG** program. Defragmenting frees up contiguous space that is needed by the permanent swap file.

DIAGNOSING AND TROUBLESHOOTING

A device referenced in SYSTEM.INI could not be found.

The computer is looking for a device that is listed in your System Initialization file. Perhaps the device driver isn't finding its hardware, an icon was deleted or a device was physically removed from the PC and the line wasn't removed from the initialization file. When Windows asks the drive to locate its hardware, the hardware must be there and be operational or Windows will generate an error message.

Missing or corrupt HIMEM.SYS

If you get this error message, check your **CONFIG.SYS** file. Using a text editor such as Notepad, open the **CONFIG.SYS** file. If the **HIMEM.SYS** line is missing, add the following line:

DEVICE=HIMEM.SYS

Save and close the **CONFIG.SYS** file. Restart the PC.

No operating system found.

This error means that the battery on the motherboard may have died which would prevent CMOS from running. Replace the battery and restart the PC.

Safe Mode

Sometimes after a system crash, the PC will boot into **Safe Mode**. If you don't want your system to automatically boot into **Safe Mode** after a crash, disable this option in the system BIOS CMOS.

Common Problems in Windows

General Protection Faults (GPFs)

Most GPFs occur because of depletion of memory resources. A GPF signals that something unexpected has happened in the Windows environments. Another common problem is range name violations. Naming a file with restricted characters, like numbers, dates and times will often cause a GPF. If a GPF occurs while you're working in a file, the problem may be caused by fonts. In Windows 3.1, the message provides specific information about which applications and Windows components were running at the time of the error and where the error occurred. If the GPF is not too serious, the application may continue to run allowing you to save your work before the application closes.

First troubleshooting step is to close all programs that are not needed. Disable any screensavers and close all open folders. If the computer is running on a network, disable the network software to determine if the software is causing the problem.

When you get the GPF message, you are given the option to return to Windows and wait for the system to recover before you need to restart the system.

System Lock-Up

A system lock-up means that the system boots up but the boot process stops. As the operating system software comes up, the system locks up, or a system could lock up in the middle of an application. There are several potential causes for a system lock-up:

· Do you have the most current BIOS for your motherboard? If not, call the motherboard manufacturer to obtain a copy of the latest BIOS.

· Are the BIOS settings correct? After booting your computer, enter the BIOS setup by pressing the **Delete** key. Try loading the BIOS defaults. Save the changes and exit. Reboot your computer to see if the system still locks.

· The problem may be with a fragmented hard disk. Run **DEFRAG** and/or **SCANDISK** to see if the problem corrects itself.

· Does your processor have the correct CPU fan and heat sink installed and working properly? A small fan should be on top of a heatsink that covers the entire surface of the processor.

· Are all the adapter cards seated properly? Remove the cards and reinstall them.

· Is the processor seated properly? The processor should be firmly and evenly down into the socket.

· Is the voltage setting correct for the motherboard?

· Is the motherboard set to the right speed? If a processor is running faster than its megahertz rating, the computer may not boot up.

· Are all peripheral devices on and functioning properly? The application you're working in may try to write to a peripheral that is offline, not initialized or not functioning.

· Has the operating system been reinstalled? Sometimes the Registry will become corrupted and only reinstalling Windows will fix the problem.

After you've worked through this checklist and the system still locks up, try swapping out the components one by one. Older and slower devices can cause the system to lock up.

Illegal Operation

DOS halted the system because it ran out of space to hold the necessary data to process hardware interrupts. The default amount of stack space being reserved is too low. To increase the amount of DOS stack space, add the following line to your **CONFIG.SYS** file:

STACKS=X,YYY   (X is the new number of stacks, and YYY is the size of each one in bytes -- Recommended values are: **STACKS=12,256.)**

If the problem recurs, increase the values. A particular application may have a bug that is causing the problem. Contact the application's technical support for help.

Invalid Working Directory

In Windows 3.1, you cannot specify a universal naming convention (UNC) name as the working directory for an application in the **Program Item Properties** dialog box. This limitation also applies to the startup directory specified in program information files (PIFs) for MS-DOS-based applications.

If a working or startup directory must point to a network share, associate a drive letter with the connection and then use the associated drive letter rather than the UNC as the working or startup directory. When a network drive is used as the working directory, Windows may generate this warning message indicating that the application may not always be available (because the network is unavailable, the network drive letter is changed or deleted, and so forth).

Application Will Not Start or Load

In troubleshooting an application problem, first try to isolate the problem. Did the application *ever* load correctly? What has changed? Was a new driver or peripheral added that may have triggered the problem?

If the application works directly with hardware on your system, you may have a resource conflict, configuration problem or hardware fault. If the software may have been contaminated by a virus, run a virus scanning program to see if that's the problem.

DIAGNOSING AND TROUBLESHOOTING

Cannot Log Onto Network

A workstation and a server cannot recognize each other unless the adapter and its network connection are functioning and the workstation's network configuration is correct.

- Run the diagnostic utility that came with the adapter. If the adapter fails, look for resource conflicts or, as a last resort, replace the adapter. If the adapter passes its internal tests and can transmit and receive data on the network, then the problem is most likely with the workstation's configuration.

If you suspect the problem is at the workstation:

- Is the user connected to the correct server? The workstation might specify a preferred server, but if that server is down, the user's workstation may be trying to log on to the wrong server.

- Is the user entering a valid user ID and password? See if they can log in from another workstation that is functioning. See if another user can log in from the problem workstation.

Connecting to a Windows 95 Dial-Up Server:

- Make sure the workstation protocol selected is the same as the protocol used by the server.

- In the **Dial-Up Networking** utility, add another connection with the appropriate phone number.

- Select **PPP, Windows 95** as a **Server Type**

- Check the **Logon to Network** box.

- Check either **NetBEUI** or **IPS** for Allowed Network Protocols. In order for any two computers to communicate with each other, they must be speaking the same language (protocol). In Windows 95, you can configure the protocol that your machine will use. Windows 95 supports three major protocols: TCP/IP, IPX/SPX and NetBEUI. Support for other protocols, such as NETBIOS, is also available.

Windows-Specific Troubleshooting Tools

Device Manager

Device Manager is a useful tool to get troubleshooting information about devices connected to your system and your system's configuration settings. If you're having a hardware problem, check **Device Manager** first.

- Click **Start** menu.
- Click **Settings**.
- Click **Control Panel**.
- Click **System**.
- Click **Device Manager** button.

You can also open **Device Manager** by right-clicking on **My Computer** and choosing **Properties**, then **Device Manager.**

In the list shown, find the device that's giving you problems and click the **+** sign for that device to see what's installed. If Windows 95 has detected a configuration problem or conflict, you'll see an exclamation point in a yellow circle over the name of the device. Double-click the device's icon and look at the **General** tab. If the wrong driver was installed or if it's not working properly, you'll see it here.

A handy resource guide is the **System Resource Report** feature of **Device Manager**. This comprehensive summary of your hardware is available in printed form or in a **.prn** file for later printing. It's a good idea to keep a hard copy of this report for later reference in an emergency. It lists IRQ assignments, I/O addresses, hard disk parameters and other resources. To print the report:

- Click **Print** button at the bottom of the **Device Manager** screen.
- Select **All Devices**
- Select **System Summary** under **Report Type**.

Conflict Troubleshooter

To check for device conflicts, use Windows built-in **Help** and **Troubleshooting**:

- Click **Start**, then **Help** on the **Start** menu

- In the **Help Topics** dialog box, click **Troubleshooting**.

- Select a **Help** topic from the list by double-clicking it. The **Troubleshooting** for that topic is displayed.

Viruses

What is a Virus?

Viruses are intentionally destructive computer programs. Some viruses attach themselves to other programs and spread when the program is executed. Some infect the boot sector of the floppy or hard disk destroying the files the system needs to boot up. They are loaded into memory when the PC is booted from an infected drive.

Sources

Viruses can be transmitted by e-mail, from a floppy diskette, from a network, or downloaded from an online service. On a PC, viruses can only be spread by program files not data files. When searching for a potential source of a virus, look at new program files you've added, such as:

· Games

· Pirated software

· Networks

· Files loaded from a home PC where users may unknowingly have picked up a virus elsewhere.

· Public domain software

· Bulletin boards

DIAGNOSING AND TROUBLESHOOTING

How to Determine Presence

A virus may do something as innocent as flashing a message on the screen *"You've been stoned."* or it may damage or erase your entire hard disk. You may not be able to boot up, or the system may crash unexpectedly. Programs may be erased, characters on the screen may drop randomly to the bottom of the screen, or the PC may reboot in the middle of an operation. Watch for unexpected increases in file size.

Removal

To enable a virus scanner program to look for boot sector viruses, cold boot from a virus-checker write-protected floppy diskette.

A memory-resident virus scanning program, such as *McAfee's* **VirusScan**, will constantly monitor your system for viruses and give you options such as cleaning or deleting the infected file. Whichever third-party virus scanning program you purchase, be sure to update the program regularly for new viruses.

Prevention

- The best prevention: *Back up your hard drive on a regular basis.* If you do become infected and you lose important files, you can only restore them after you've reformatted your hard drive.

- Write-protect any floppy you put in your floppy drive, if possible, and leave the floppy drive door open so the computer won't try to boot from the floppy drive.

- Don't use pirated software.

- Run virus-scanning programs regularly. The DOS program **MSAVE.EXE** can be used to check DOS sessions and **MWAV.EXE** can be used to check Windows sessions. Be sure to check for a virus *before* you run a program.

- Set an office policy that anyone using your system must run the virus scan program on any diskette that is put into your machine.

- Create one or more emergency diskettes: one with boot sectors, partition table and CMOS information; one with DOS commands and one with a low-level format and setup program.

- Protect your **COMMAND.COM** file by putting it in the DOS subdirectory and giving it hidden or read-only attributes with the **ATTRIB** command. At the DOS prompt, type:
  ATTRIB +r +h COMMAND.COM.

  If you move **COMMAND.COM** to the DOS subdirectory, be sure to modify your **CONFIG.SYS** file: type
  SHELL=C:\DOS\COMMAND.COM C:\DOS

- Keep a damage control procedures list.

DIAGNOSING AND TROUBLESHOOTING

Summary

Repairing a computer hardware or software problem is not an exact science. Software manufacturers have provided many helpful tools, codes and error messages that will help point you in the right direction. Learn to trust your instincts and follow the systematic approach outlined in this chapter and you'll have a good start at solving computer problems.

Review Questions

1. A customer attached an external drive to his notebook computer but the computer is not recognizing it. What should be considered? Select all that apply.

   A. The cables are attached firmly.

   B. The external drive has been pre-loaded with the appropriate software.

   C. The external drive was attached before the computer was turned on.

   D. The external drive is turned on.

   ✷ E. All of the above.

2. After displaying the directory of a floppy disk, a different floppy is inserted in the drive. The contents of the original floppy continue to display regardless of the directory requests on the other floppies placed in the drive. You remove the drive in question and install it into your test system, and it does not exhibit the problem. What is your next step?

   A. Replace the system's floppy drive device driver.

   B. Replace the original IDE controller.

   ✷ C. Replace the floppy drive ribbon cable.

   D. Replace the system's power supply.

3. What questions could be asked to determine if a problem is software or hardware related? (Select all that apply.)

   ✷ A. Does the computer BEEP during the boot phase?

   ✷ B. Did peripheral devices initialize, i.e. printers?

   ✷ C. Will hardware components pass diagnostics?

   D. Determine how many serial ports are installed in the system.

4. What is the first step to diagnose a software problem?

    A. Call the software vendor.

    B. Reboot the computer.

    C. Examine any error messages on the screen.

    D. Check the **AUTOEXEC.BAT** file.

5. Which of the following would be a logical first step in troubleshooting a PC?

    A. Check the computer CMOS.

    B. Define the circumstances of the problem.

    C. Call the vendor.

    D. Define what applications are being used.

Review Answers

Review Answers

Section 1
Computer Safety

1. B
2. B
3. B
4. B
5. A
6. A

Section 2
PC Hardware, Components & Tools

1. A
2. D
3. A
4. B
5. Low-level formatting, partitioning, and high level formatting.
6. Twist
7. B
8. A
9. C
10. B

Section 3
PC Configuration

1. B
2. B
3. B
4. C
5. C
6. A

Exercise 3.1

Available IRQs = 5, 10, 11, 12

Available I/O = 320, 340

Section 4
Peripheral Hardware Devices

1. C
2. C
3. D
4. B
5. B
6. B
7. A

Section 5
Disassembly and Reassembly

1. C
2. C
3. B
4. B
5. B
6. B
7. B
8. C

Section 6
DOS

1. A
2. C
3. B
4. B
5. C
6. B
7. A
8. B

Sction 7
DOS Memory Optimization

1. D
2. 0K-640K
3. C
4. B
5. A
6. B
7. C
8. 1024K to 16MB, 1024K to 4GB
9. B
10. B

Section 8
Printers

1. C
2. D
3. D
4. A
5. C
6. C
7. B
8. C
9. B
10. A,B,C

Section 9
Local-Area Networks

1. B
2. C
3. A,C,D
4. C
5. C
6. C
7. D
8. D
9. D

Section 10
Preventive Maintenance
1. C
2. B
3. B
4. B
5. A

Section 11
Windows 3.x
1. B
2. C
3. B
4. B
5. C
6. B
7. B
8. D
9. C
10. A
11. A,B,C,D

Section 12
Windows 95
1. C
2. A
3. D
4. A
5. B
6. C
7. B
8. C
9. A
10. A

Section 13
Windows 98
1. C, E
2. B
3. B
4. D
5. A
6. B
7. B
8. C
9. B
10. B

Section 14
Windows NT 4.0
1. False
2. A
3. A, C
4. C
5. A
6. C
7. C
8. A
9. False
10. B

Section 15
Windows 2000 Professional
1. B
2. D
3. A
4. B
5. True
6. A
7. A, B, & C
8. D
9. A
10. D

Section 16
Linux
1. C
2. TRUE
3. C
4. D
5. B
6. B
7. TRUE
8. C

Section 17
The Internet
1. B
2. C
3. B
4. C
5. B
6. D
7. B, C

Section 18
Diagnosing & Troubleshooting
1. E
2. C
3. A, B, C
4. C
5. B

Glossary

GLOSSARY

A

Abend

Contraction of Abnormal END. A message issued by an operating system when it detects a serious problem.

ACK

Abbreviation for acknowledgment. In communications, ACK is a control code.

ADB

Apple Desktop Bus.

Address

An identifying number that specifies the location of a computer resource such as a node, a process, or a memory allocation.

Advertising

The process by which services on a network inform other devices on the network of their availability.

AFP

AppleTalk Filing Protocol.

Amplitude

The size or magnitude of a voltage or a waveform.

Amplitude modulation

Changing the voltage or level or amplitude of a carrier frequency to transmit digital or analog signal.

Analog data

Data that varies continuously on some interval.

Analog signal

A continuously varying electromagnetic wave.

ANSI

American National Standards Institute, responsible for the ASCII code set (American Standard Code for Information Interchange).

Architecture

A logical structure for network communications. It is constructed of protocols, formats and operation sequence.

ARPANET

Acronym for Advanced Research Projects Agency Network. A research network funded by the defense Advanced Research Projects Agency.

ASCII
American Standard Code for Information Interchange.

Asynchronous
When used to define a code set, character codes that contain start and stop bits. When used to define data transmission, a signal that does not need a separate clock synchronization signal for data reception. Asynchronous transmission is also called start-stop transmission because one character is sent at a time.

Attenuation
Loss of signal energy characterized by a weakening signal.

AUTOEXEC.BAT
A DOS batch file that, if present, is automatically executed during boot-up.

B

Backbone
A portion of a network that manages the bulk of the traffic. The backbone may connect several different locations or buildings, and other, smaller networks may be attached to it.

Balun
A contraction of BALanced Unbalanced. A small device used to connect a balanced line I.E. twisted pair cable to an unbalanced line (coaxial cable). The balun matches the impedance between the two media.

Bandwidth
The size of the transmission channel (width). The difference expressed in hertz (frequency) between the highest and lowest frequencies of a band. In modern usage, bandwidth defines the maximum specified throughput of a communication channel.

Baseband
A signal transmitted at its original frequency. In modern usage, baseband refers to a transmission system where the original signal uses up all the channel's available bandwidth.

Baud
The number of signal level changes per second. Each signal level contains one (or more) bit of information.

Beaconing
In a Token Ring network, the process of informing other nodes that token passing has been suspended due to a very severe error condition, such as a broken cable.

Binary
A method of representing information. It relies on two states: an "on" or "off" state.

Binary Synchronous Communication

Developed by IBM in the 1960s, Binary Synchronous Communication is a data link control procedure for use with synchronous transmission.

BIOS

Basic Input Output System.

Bisync

Binary Synchronous Communications.

Bit

Binary Digit. The smallest unit of information. All digital information is composed of bits.

Bit-oriented protocol

Data transmission protocol that moves one bit of information at a time without regard for the bit's meaning.

Block

Set of continuous bits and /or bytes that contain definable information.

Bootable Diskette

A disk that contains the boot files of an operating system and is used to "boot" the computer.

Bottleneck

The weakest or slowest link in a communications chain; commonly the cause of a slowdown in a network environment.

bps

Bits per Second. Measure of the number of bits of information transmitted per second.

Bridge

Hardware and software used to connect networks. It is normally used in connecting LANs of identical communication methods, mediums, and topologies.

Broadband

A transmission channel able to simultaneously carry multiple signals.

Buffer

Temporary data storage area located in a computer's memory.

Bus

A common set of communication channels connecting parts of a system.

Byte

Generally, a set of eight continuous bits making up the smallest addressable item of information in a computer system.

C

Carrier
An analog signal whose frequency, amplitude, or phase which has been altered to allow it to represent data.

CSMA/CD
Carrier-Sense Multiple Access/Collision Detection. A technique of transmitting over a local access network where only one transmitter may use the line at a time.

CCITT
Consultative Committee on International Telegraphy and Telephony. An international standards group.

Channel
A path used for data communications.

Character
A single element from a particular character set.

Checksum
A block check character or block check sequence computed by adding the bits of the block by simple binary addition.

Chip
An integrated circuit, sometimes called an IC, containing many electronic circuits, transistors, switches, etc. in a single silicon wafer.

Chooser
An Apple menu utility which allows you to select printers.

Circuit
An electronic path allowing communications between two devices.

Circuit switching
Data transmission technique that directly connects a sender and receiver in an unbroken path.

Clock
A device which generates a high-speed synchronizing signal.

Cluster
The smallest unit of disk space for data storage, typically 512 bytes in size.

Coaxial cable
Transmission media (cable) composed of two shielded conductors that share the same axis and are separated by a non-conducting element.

Code

A set of rules specifying the representation of characters. A code set is formally known as an alphabet.

Cold Boot

Restarting a computer's operating system by turning the computer off and then back on.

Common carrier

A transmission facility available to the public that must abide by public utility regulations.

Communication

The transfer of information between devices.

Communication medium

A physical entity that hosts communications. It may be bounded, such as coaxial wire or twisted pair cable, or unbounded, such as air waves.

Config.sys

A DOS user-created text file that contains parameters read during start-up, located in the root directory.

Connectivity

The logical or physical linking of network workstations or devices.

CPS

Characters per second. The number of characters transmitted per second.

CPU

Central Processing Unit. The part of the computer where the data is processed.

CRC

Cyclic Redundancy Check. An error checking procedure using a predefined mathematical divisor to check the integrity of a transmitted block of data.

CSU

Channel Service Unit. A device that functions as a certified safe electrical circuit, acting as a buffer between the customer's equipment and a public carrier's wide area network equipment.

D

Data communications
The transmission of data between network devices.

Data packet
A logical group of data.

Decibel
A numerical expression of the relative loudness of sound.

Dedicated line
Medium used solely for data transmission between two locations. It is sometimes referred to as a "leased line"or a "private line."

De Facto
Commonly accepted, as in *"de facto* standard."

De Jure
As specified by law, as in a *"de jure* standard."

Demodulator
The section of a modem that converts analog signal to digital signal.

Digital data
Data consisting of a sequence of discrete elements.

Digital signal
A signal composed of two energy states (on and off or positive and negative current). Digital signals are used by computers to transmit data. The pattern of the current state represents individual bits of information.

Directory
A logical portion of disk space identified by a name.

DNA
Digital Network Architecture. A network designed by Digital Equipment Corporation.

Distributed processing
The ability of network nodes to execute shared network applications, or parts of network applications, independently of other nodes.

DRAM
Dynamic Random-Access Memory

DTE
Data Circuit-Terminating Equipment. Equipment at the source and the destination allowing communications to take place. It establishes, maintains, and terminates connections and performs signal conversion and coding between the transmission medium and the DTE.

E

EBCDIC
Extended Binary Coded Decimal Interchange Code. An eight-bit code set developed by IBM.

Echoplexing
A crude form of error checking where the receiver repeats all signals it receives from the sender. The sender then checks for accuracy.

EIA
Electronics Industries Association. A standards organization comprised of electronic manufacturers in the United States.

Emulation
The ability of one device to mimic the operations of another. A common use involves running software on a microcomputer that allows it to operate as a terminal attached to a mainframe computer.

Encryption
Modifications of a bit stream so it appears to be random. Encryption is used for security reasons. The sender and the receiver agree on a encryption method prior to data transmission.

Enterprise network
A network (usually very large) that connects all sites of a particular organization.

Ethernet
A popular network protocol and cabling scheme with a transfer rate of 10 mega bits per second, originally developed by the Xerox Corporation in 1976.

F

FAT
File Allocation Table

FCS
Frame Check Sequence. An error detection mechanism used in bit-oriented protocols.

FDM
Frequency Division Multiplexing. A technique used by a multiplexer to allow shared use of a single channel based on differences in frequency.

Fiber optics
Glass fibers that can carry information as light signals.

File server
A device providing shared access to files and data.

Finder
The finder is what Macintosh users run in lieu of an operating system.

Flag
A bit field or character used to delimit data on either side of it. The term "flag" is sometimes used to reference a single bit indicating the presence or absence of a condition.

Footprint
The amount of space a computer takes up on the desktop.

Format
The structure of a message or data that allows it to be recognized.

Frame
A data block in a bit-oriented protocol.

Frequency
The number of cycles of a signal per second.

Frequency modulation
Changing the frequency of a carrier frequency to transmit digital or analog information.

FTAM
File Transfer, Access and Management. The Open Systems Interconnection (OSI) protocol for transferring and remotely accessing files on different makes and models of computers also using FTAM.

FTP
File Transfer Protocol. The TCP/IP protocol used to log-in to a network, list files and directories, and transfer files.

Full-duplex transmission
A channel allowing simultaneous transmission in both directions.

G

Gateway
A hardware/software combination that allows communications between dissimilar systems.

Global network
A computer network extending over a very large geographic area, often to various countries and continents.

GOSIP
Government Open Systems Interconnection Profile. A suite of standards based on the OSI reference model. Intended for use in government projects. Both the United States and United Kingdom GOSIP exists.

H

Half-duplex transmission
A channel allowing transmission in only one direction at a time.

Handshaking
Synchronization message sent between devices.

HDLC
High-Level Data Link Control. Standard bit-oriented communication line protocol developed by the ISO.

Hertz
International unit of frequency. The number of cycles per second. It is abbreviated "Hz."

HFS
Hierarchical File System.

Hop count
In routing, the number of links that must be crossed to get from any given source device to any given destination device.

Host
A computer system on a network.

Hub
A central point to and from which communications flow.

I

IEEE
Institute of Electronic and Electrical Engineers. A standards organization dealing with electronics.

Impedence
An electrical property of a cable that combines capacitance, inductance, and resistance, measured in OHMs.

Internetwork
A series of network segments connected by bridges, routers, or gateways.

ISDN
Integrated Services Digital Network. CCITT project for standardization of networks to allow mixed digital and transmission services.

ISA
Industry Standard Architecture.

ISO
International Standards Organization. A standards organization recognized for its development of the OSI protocols and the OSI Reference Model.

J

Jabber
A continuous and meaningless transmission generated by a network device, usually the result of an error or a hardware malfunction.

Jitter
A type of distortion found on analog communication lines that result in datSG-transmission errors.

Jumper
A small plastic and metal connector that completes a circuit, usually to select one option from a set of user-definable options. Sometimes referred to as a "shunt."

K

Kermit
A file transfer protocol developed at Columbia University and placed in the public domain, used to transfer files between PCs and mainframe computers over standard telephone lines.

L

LAN
Local-Area Network. A collection of connected computers allowing users to share data and peripherals.

LCD
Liquid crystal display, used in flat-top monitors.

Line
A communications circuit.

Line protocol
Consisting of both handshaking and line-control functions, line protocols perform data communications over network lines.

LocalTalk
The Macintosh built-in networking protocol.

Leased line
A communications circuit or telephone line reserved for the permanent use of a specific customer.

M

Mark
Condition of the digital signal sending a binary "1."

MAN
Metropolitan-Area Network. A communication network that serves an urban area.

MCA
Micro Channel Architecture. (IBM proprietary 32-bit design)

Message
Information communicated from one location to another. It is usually composed of a header, the body of the information, and the trailer.

Message switching
Data transmission in which there is no need to establish a dedicated physical path between the sender and receiver. Sometimes referred to as a "store and forward" network.

MHz
Megahertz; unit of measurement. (Millions of cycles per second.)

Microwaves
Very short radio waves used for unbounded transmission.

Modem
MOdulator/DEModulator. A device that converts digital signal to analog for transmission and then converts it back to digital after the reception.

Multiplexer
(MUX) An electronic device that accepts several signals and combines them into one high-speed data stream.

N

NDIS
Network Driver Interface Specification. A device driver specification developed by Microsoft and 3COM in 1990.

NetBEUI
Net BIOS Extended User Interface. A network device driver for the transport layer supplied with *Microsoft* Windows and Windows NT suite.

Network
A collection of devices that can communicate with one another.

NIC
Network Interface Card. A printed circuit board installed into a network device. When the card is connected to a common cabling system, the NIC allows the device to communicate with the other devices on the network.

Node
Any device on the network.

Noise
Unwanted signals on a channel.

Nondedicated
A term used to describe a file server that can be used simultaneously as a workstation.

Nonproprietary
A specification or implementation that was not created by a single private organization.

O

Open System Interconnection
A term used to refer to a set of protocols as well as a communication reference model created and promulgated by the ISO.

P, Q

Packet
See data packet

Packet switching
Data transmission where packets are divided into packets, each with a destination address.

Parity bit
A bit added to character bits to make the total number of bits odd or even. It is used in error checking schemes.

PDS
Processor Direct Slots.

Peripheral device
A device attached to a computer to perform a task such as printing or data storage.

Peer-to-peer communications
Communications between similarly capable network devices.

Phase modulation

Modifying the phase of a signal to transmit digital data.

Point-to-point

Physically, a channel that runs from one point to another point without passing through intermediate devices. Logically, communication between two devices.

Polling

Sequentially contacting several network devices to see if they wish to transmit or communicate.

Proprietary

A specification or implementation created by a single organization.

Protocol

A formal set of rules that governs message exchange and communication.

PSTN

Public Switched Telephone Network.

R

RAM

Random Access Memory. Storage area that is initialized after a reboot or power cycling.

Repeater

A device that amplifies and improves the quality of signals on a network.

ROM

Read Only Memory. A type of memory that can only be written to with a special device.

RS-232

Communications interface developed by the EIA. It is commonly used between electronic devices such as computers, modems, and printers.

Router

A device capable of sending information along various paths through an internetwork.

S

SCSI

(Pronounced "scuzzy.") Stands for Small Computer System Interface.

SDLC

Synchronous Data Link Control. A bit-synchronous data communication protocol developed by IBM.

Session
A logical connection between network addressable units.

Shielded twisted pair
Twisted pair cable surrounded by a metallic or foil shield.

Signal splitting device
A device used in a network to distribute signals from node to node. An example is an active hub.

Simplex transmission
Channel that allows communication in only one direction.

SNA
System Network Architecture. A network blueprint developed by IBM.

Start bit
A bit added in synchronous transmission that indicates the beginning of a character.

Station
An individual device on the network.

Stop bit
Bit added in synchronous transmission to indicate the end of a character.

Synchronous transmission
Method of transmission where the messages are sent as continuous bit streams. Each block of data is preceded by a synchronous character or character sequence and is followed by an end-of-message sequence.

T, U

T-connector
Hardware used to connect coaxial cable to a computer's network interface card.

TCP/IP
Transmission Control Protocol/Internet Protocol. Two protocols developed by the Department of Defense.

Terminator
A device needed to terminate a linear bus; It marks the beginning and end of the cable segment.

Throughput
A measure of the productivity of a computer, network or device.

Topology

The physical arrangement of the network nodes and links. Examples are ring, star, and bus.

Trunk

A multiple line-circuit connecting switching or distribution centers.

Twisted pair

A cable consisting of four or more pairs of copper wires, twisted together in pairs. Telephone wire is an example of twisted pair cable.

V

Virtual Memory

A method of emulating physical memory on the hard disk.

Voice grade

Media suitable for voice or analog data.

Volt

A standard unit of electrical potential.

W

WAN

Wide-Area Network. Large network formed by connecting LANs or MANs.

Warm Boot

Reloading a computer's operating system through the use of reset keys on the keyboard.

Watt

A standard unit of power.

WYSIWYG

(Wiz-ee-wig) What you see is what you get.

Workstation

An individual personal computer attached to the network with a network interface card. Sometimes referred to as a node on the network.

X, Y, Z

X.25

Transmission protocol standardized by the CCITT for packet switching networks.

Index

Index

C

INDEX

INDEX

INDEX

INDEX

INDEX

INDEX